RORSCHACHIANA XXX

Rorschachiana

Journal of the International Society for the Rorschach

Volume 30, Issues 1 & 2, 2009

Editor-in-Chief:
Sadegh Nashat, Tavistock Clinic, London, UK

Rorschachiana

Editorial Board Members

Publication

Rorschachiana is available as a book and as a journal (consisting of two online issues
per year, an annual print compendium, and online access to back issues):

ISBN 978-0-88937-366-2 (Rorschachiana, Vol. 30)
ISSN 1192-5604 (journal)

Copyright Information

Rorschachiana, Volume 30, 2009 (book)

PUBLISHING OFFICES
USA: Hogrefe Publishing, 875 Massachusetts Avenue, 7th Floor, Cambridge, MA 02139,
Tel. (866) 823-4726, Fax (617) 354-6875, E-mail customerservice@hogrefe-publishing.com,
Web http://www.hogrefe.com
Europe: Hogrefe Publishing, Rohnsweg 25, 37085 Göttingen, Germany, Tel. +49 551 49609-0,
Fax +49 551 49609-88, E-mail publishing@hogrefe.com, Web http://www.hogrefe.com

SALES AND DISTRIBUTION
USA: Hogrefe Publishing, Customer Service Department, 30 Amberwood Parkway, Ashland,
OH 44805, Tel. (800) 228-3749, Fax (419) 281-6883, E-mail customerservice@hogrefe.com
Europe: Hogrefe Publishing, Rohnsweg 25 37085 Göttingen, Germany Tel. +49 551 49609-0,
Fax +49 551 49609-88, E-mail publishing@hogrefe.com

OTHER OFFICES
Canada: Hogrefe Publishing, 1543 Bayview Avenue, Suite 514, Toronto, Ontario, M4G 3B5
Switzerland: Hogrefe Publishing, Länggass-Strasse 76, CH-3000 Bern 9

Hogrefe Publishing
Incorporated and registered in the Commonwealth of Massachusetts, USA, and in Göttingen,
Lower Saxony, Germany

Printed and bound in Germany

ISBN: 978-0-88937-366-2

Rorschachiana: Journal of the International Society for the Rorschach

Publisher: Hogrefe Publishing, Rohnsweg 25, D-37085 Göttingen, Germany, Tel. +49 551 999
500, Fax +49 551 999 50 425, E-mail publishing@hogrefe.com, Web http://www.hogrefe.com

Production: Anne-Lisa Löck, Hogrefe Publishing, Rohnsweg 25, D-37085 Göttingen, Germany,
Tel. +49 551 999 500, Fax +49 551 999 50 425, E-mail loeck@hogrefe.com

Subscriptions: Hogrefe Publishing, Robert-Bosch-Breite 25, D-37079 Göttingen, Germany,
Tel. +49 551 50 68 80, Fax +49 551 50 68 824

Advertising/Inserts: Gundula von Fintel, Hogrefe Publishing, Rohnsweg 25, D-37085 Göttingen,
Germany, Tel. +49 551 999 500, Fax +49 551 999 50 425, E-mail marketing@hogrefe.com

Publication: Published in two online issues and a print compendium per annual volume.

Subscription Prices: Annual subscription (2010): Individuals: US $112.00 / € 80.00 /
CHF 135.00; Institutions: US $168.00 / € 120.00 / CHF 202.00 (postage & handling:
US $8.00 / € 6.00 / CHF 10.00). Single issue (online): US $112 / € 80.00.

Payment: Payment may be made by check, international money order, or credit card to Hogrefe
Publishing, Rohnsweg 25, D-37085 Göttingen, Germany, or, for customers in North America, to
Hogrefe Publishing, Inc., Journals Department, 875 Massachusetts Avenue, 7th Floor, Cam-
bridge, MA 02139, USA.

Electronic Full Text: The full text of *Rorschachiana* is available online at
http://www.psycontent.com/content/1192-5604 and also in PsycARTICLES®.

Abstracting/Indexing Services: *Rorschachiana* is abstracted/indexed in PsycINFO and PSYNDEX.

ISSN: 1192-5604

Contents

Rorschachiana 30, 1–2
© 2009 Hogrefe & Huber Publishers

DOI: 10.1027/1192-5604.30.1.1

Editorial

Sadegh Nashat

Following the XIXth International Congress of Rorschach and Projective Methods that took place in Leuven (Belgium) in July 2008, I had the opportunity to reflect on what it is about *Rorschachiana* that is important to us as members of the International Society of the Rorschach and Projective Methods in the context of our day to day work and the wider scientific community.

Clearly, a significant development for the Society was the decision of both the Executive Board of the International Society of the Rorschach and Projective Methods and the Assembly of delegates to support the move toward an electronic version of the Society's journal when they met in Leuven. This has had the effect of raising the profile of *Rorschachiana* (The Journal for the International Society for the Rorschach and Projective Methods) within the International scientific community. *Rorschachiana* is now available online and is cataloged as a journal by databases such as PsychInfo. In addition, *Rorschachiana* articles can be found on PsycArticles, the APA full-text database to which many academic institutions have access. This development is of particular benefit to all the ISR members who now have a state-of-the-art publication to represent their ideas and findings, and make their views known to the international psychological community.

The range and variety of presentations at the XIXth International Congress clearly illustrate the diversity of the many uses of the Rorschach (and projective methods in general) within different settings and adopting various theoretical approaches. This enables practitioners and researchers to engage in rich debates, simultaneously creating the risk of polarized positions, which in turn may be less productive. It is, therefore, important to offer a containing space for these debates that can help to avoid a damaging splitting process. *Rorschachiana* aims to be that forum. It is important to emphasize that *Rorschachiana* will continue to reflect this diversity, by providing a forum for practitioners and re-

1

searchers, from all theoretical approaches and methods, to disseminate their ideas and findings, while also respecting the methodological and editorial rigor necessary for an international publication.

The content of *Rorschachiana* will, to some extent, be determined by contextual factors. Many articles result from papers presented at national and international conferences demonstrating the innovations and current practice in the field of projective methods. An active role of the Editorial Board has been to encourage those authors to turn their presentations into manuscripts for *Rorschachiana*.

This second volume of *Rorschachiana* well illustrates the diversity of ideas and the many possibilities that projective methods can offer to researchers. The general section includes a blend of research papers, innovative methods, and complex theoretical ideas; the special section is dedicated to the use of the Rorschach and projective methods in psychotherapy research and outcome studies.

Finally, the Editorial Board would like to encourage readers who may have manuscripts buried in their drawers to dig them out and submit them to *Rorschachiana*!

Rorschachiana 30, 3–25
© 2009 Hogrefe & Huber Publishers

DOI: 10.1027/1192-5604.30.1.3

The Rorschach and the Body

The Study of Self-Esteem in Enuretic Children Through the Rorschach Method

Norma Lottenberg Semer[1] and Latife Yazigi[2]

[1]*Universidade Federal de São Paulo,* [2]*Universidade Federal de São Paulo, both Brazil*

Abstract. *Introduction:* The Rorschach has proved to be of value in studies addressing the mind-body relationship since it enhances the understanding of this complex relation and its repercussions. *Objective:* To use some aspects of the Rorschach to explore the mental representation of the body through the study of self-esteem in children with enuresis. *Method:* The Rorschach Comprehensive System was administrated to 26 children with enuresis and 26 children without enuresis (children of the same age and social class) and 10 selected variables were tested; the Concept of the Object Scale for assessing object representations (ORS) was also used. *Results:* There is a significant difference in the *X+%* and *EGO*, so the children with enuresis show low self-esteem and difficulties perceiving reality. As for ORS, the children without enuresis showed greater freedom to fantasize, to use their imagination, and to identify their emotions and anxieties. The children with enuresis exhibited a greater tendency toward fragmentation in the perception of the self and of others, thus, a partial object relation. *Conclusions:* The Concept of the Object Scale for assessing object representations proved to be a useful instrument to grasp the level of the child's psychological development. The study of the psychosomatic aspects permits an identification of relations between the body and self-esteem.

Keywords: self-esteem, Rorschach in children, enuresis, body and mind issues, Object Representation Scale

Introduction

Very few authors have concerned themselves with the body-mind relation in children. The child's body sensations, in their interactions with the environment, result in the constitution of a body, or body-scheme,

3

representation. Schilder (1950) pointed out that the body's emotional unity can only be maintained when all the relations are developed. For other authors, mainly the psychoanalytical ones, however, the mental configuration of the body occurs very early in the baby's mind through the representation of its relation with the mother. Freud (1915/1974) defined instinct as a concept situated between mind and body, as the psychic representation of stimuli that originate from the body and reach the mind. Furthermore, Freud (1923/1974) held that all psychic development is based on the body experience: "The ego is first and foremost a bodily ego" [...] and added in 1927: "the ego is ultimately derived from bodily sensations, chiefly those springing from the surface of the body." (p. 26). In the vicissitudes of the instincts, the erogenous zones play a special role in the psychological development of the child – the "support" on a biological basis is always present.

Klein (1946/1952), when referring to the baby's mind, emphasizes fantasy more than body experience. This body experience is charged with meanings and emotional investments. In her writing, Klein expresses the primitive fantasies through "an organ language" (Cintra, 2004, p. 107). However, Anzieu (1985) stresses that the body surface is absent from Klein's theory. Winnicott (1949), referring to mind and body relationship, says:

> "There is a body, and the psyche and the soma are not to be distinguished except according to the direction from which one is looking [...] I suppose the word psyche here means the imaginative elaboration of somatic parts, feelings, and functions, that is, of physical aliveness. Gradually the psychic and the somatic aspects of the growing person become involved in a process of mutual interrelation. This interrelating of the psyche with the soma constitutes an early phase of individual development. At a later stage the live body, with its limits, and with an inside and an outside, is felt by the individual to form the core for the imaginative self" (p. 243).

According to Anzieu (1985), the psychic functioning, although looking for its independence, is dependent on the biological body or the organism that is its support; on the social body or its stimuli; and the beliefs, norms, and values of the group to which it belongs. However, there is also a mutual support, as the organic life and the social life need a psyche. To Sandler and Rosenblat (1962), the notion of body representation can be extended to self-representation, which will be the self, the precursor of self-esteem. Self-esteem is a development condition of the self, which involves self-perception, attention to one's own needs, perception of one's own individuality, autonomy, and separation from others.

What does the Rorschach have to do with the body?

Schachtel (1967) drew attention to the spatial organization of the Rorschach's blots, mainly the most compact ones, and how their symmetry around a central axis favors identification with the body image. Schachtel pointed out that:

> "the symmetry very often leads to an unconscious identification with the inkblot. This is a result of the fact that the approximately, but never exactly, symmetrical arrangement of the two sides of the blots in conjunction with the presence of a central axis creates a semblance of organic forms and especially of the anatomy of the vertebrates" (p. 28).

Husain (2005), in her study about symmetry, recalls that regarding the phenomenological approach of symmetry in the Rorschach, authors such as Rausch de Traubenberg and Sanglade (1984) and Chabert (1983) developed the notion of self-representation, comparing the structural dimension of Rorschach inkblots to body image. Fisher and Cleveland (1958) introduced the concepts of barrier (firmness and solidity) and penetration (fragility, vulnerability) related to the external boundaries of the blots. Each subject's body image reflects the kind of object relation they can establish. People with high scores in the barrier index will have strong images of their bodies and will relate to others through a solid and well-integrated self-image. People with high scores in the penetration index will have a vulnerable self-image and will relate to others through a weak attitude. Therefore, these notions imply not only a theory about the body but mainly a personality conception. The body is important to the extent that it reflects experiences of development. The body boundaries are equivalent to the ego boundaries, and the body image is equivalent to the self-concept.

The studies of Fisher and Cleveland (1958) with somatic-disorders patients led them to establish a relation between body image and type of psychosomatic symptoms; the mental representation of the body coming prior to the arousal of the symptoms.

In a literature review of Rorschach in patients with somatization disorders, Acklin and Alexander (1988), Semer and Yazigi (1990), Yazigi, Silva, Semer, Dias, & Catropa (1995), and Porcelli and Meyer (2002) show impoverished and restricted psychic functioning, difficulties in abstraction and symbolization, lack of emotional resonance, and affective discharges. These characteristics confirm the hypothesis of alexithymia to the point that Porcelli and Meyer (2002) were able to build an alexithymia index in the Rorschach Comprehensive System.

Self-Esteem and Enuresis

Since 1550 BC, enuresis has been identified as an infantile symptom that can be treated. Enuresis is important nowadays probably more because of its inconvenience than for its gravity. It is a symptom referred to by various different cultures, being considered a malady by the Navaho Indians as well as by some African tribes (Glicklich, 1951).

Enuresis is considered a daytime or nighttime lack of control in the voluntary emission of urine that remains after physiological maturity, usually at the age of five, in the absence of any physical or organic abnormality (Garfinkel, Carlson, & Weller, 1990). Enuresis is considered either primary, when urinary continence was never achieved, or secondary, when the trouble develops after a period of already established urinary continence; the primary version being the most frequent (85% of the cases). The enuresis can be diurnal, nocturnal, or mixed. The prevalence of enuresis at the age of five is around 7% for boys and 3% for girls; at the age of 18 the prevalence is of 1% for males and less than 1% for females (DSM-IV; APA, 1995).

As for the predisposing factors, there are a variety of theories that can be divided into two main groups: Those which stress the troubles of urination, for example, those related to DSM-IV(APA, 1995) or theories related to genetic factors (Hjälmas, 1997), and other theories that stress the difficulties in gaining control, related to psychological aspects such as the child's affective development and sphincter organization, such as Ajuriaguerra (1976), Senn and Solnit (1971), Kaffman and Elizur (1977), and Brazelton (1989). Until 1980, there was an emphasis on the psychological aspects responsible for eliciting the symptom. From 1985 onward the psychological features stopped being regarded as triggers but rather as an emotional effect of the symptom. More recently, there have been some psychological studies with enuretic children, which emphasize the self-esteem aspect considered as a result of the symptom. Hinde, Hjertonsson, and Broberg (1995), using self-reports, found lower self-esteem in enuretic children when compared with children with chronic diseases. Hagglof, Andrén, Bergstron, Marklend, and Wende-

6

lius (1996), using the same instrument and methodology, found that the relief of the symptom from drug treatment increased self-esteem.

Self-esteem building begins with the first interactions between the baby and its mother. Gradually, through daily and constant experiences with its mother, the child learns to "digest" both internal and external stimuli. This very close contact establishes the rudiments of tolerance and continence for sensations and emotions in the baby. As time goes by, these experiences will constitute a nucleus inside the baby endowed with hope, confidence, and competence to get on with life and to cope with problems and difficulties. Of course, this development will depend on the child's own biological constitution as well as the established relations between the child and its family and environment. Difficulties in the process of establishing satisfactory psychological development open the door to regressions and somatic manifestations. The possibility to perceive, to hold inside, and to endure emotions as well as internal and external stimuli will depend on the course of psychological development, and on the objects and object relations capable of "digesting" these stimuli.

For Bion (1962), it is the thinking process that transforms the sensorial and emotional experiences into a more elaborated and symbolized expression. If this does not happen, the growth of emotional experiences will generate turbulence that must be eliminated. This elimination may occur through hallucinations or psychosomatic disturbances. Therefore, the enuresis can be regarded as the child's failure in its capacity for continence, and consequently the emotions leak without control, without being processed or thought out. The difficulties in symbolization pave the way for the body's manifestations of the psychic conflicts.

Objectives

The rationale for this study on self-esteem in enuretic children was: Children with enuresis have difficulties in building their self-esteem and developing their identity; this factor, together with its biological vulnerability, facilitates the arousal of enuretic symptoms.

Therefore, the purpose of this paper is to study, in children with enuresis, the psychological aspect related to the constitution or building of self-esteem. Self-esteem is considered a construct related to the development of the inner world, of self-cohesion through self-representation and self-continence. We intended to verify: (1) Whether children with enuresis have low self-esteem; (2) If children with enuresis do indeed have low self-esteem, we want to discuss, according to the theories of personality, if this low self-esteem is a consequence of the symptom of enuresis or if it is related to some failure in the psychological development of the self.

Method

The research design is a case-control study using the Rorschach Method Comprehensive System (Exner, 1993). The case group consisted of 26 children with enuresis, 15 females (57.7%) and 11 males, from 5 years and 6 months to 11 years and 6 months (average of 8.08 years), referred by the pediatric outpatient service of the Hospital Israelita Albert Einstein, São Paulo, Brazil. All the patients were examined by a pediatrician from the hospital; the patients with enuresis from an organic cause were excluded. Of the 26 subjects, 22 (84.6%) had primary enuresis, that is, when urinary continence was never achieved.

Twenty-six children were matched for age, sex, and socioeconomic level to serve as controls; that is, 16 (61.5%) girls and 10 boys, from 5 years and 7 months to 11 years and 11 months (average of 8.60 years). These children attended the same pediatric outpatient service with different simple complaints, such as sore throat, fever, cold, or even for vaccination programs, but without enuretic symptoms. This choice of another clinical group as control follows Exner's suggestions (1995) to use the homogeneity of children attending a health service.

All the children underwent two sessions, one for the psychological interview in which socioeconomic data were collected, and one for the Rorschach test. They were all assessed at the hospital, in the outpatient unit.

In the present study nine variables of the Rorschach Comprehensive System were selected for analysis: *EGO; X+%; X-%; WSumC; SumC':WSumC; M; DQ+; MOR; and Anatomy,* as described in Table 1.

- *EGO* is the egocentricity index that is related to self-esteem. It represents the proportion of reflection and pair responses in the total record, with each reflection determinant weighed as being equal to three pair responses (Exner, 2001, p. 99).
- *X+%* is the conventional extended form use. This variable concerns the extent to which the appropriate use of form features has included common object definitions (Exner, 2001, p. 97).

Table 1. Selected variables of the Rorschach method

Variables	Code	Observed aspect	Relation with enuresis
Egocentricity Index	*3(Fr + rF) + (2)/R*	Self-esteem, self-perception	Low
Conventional perception	*X+%*	Reality perception	Low – Immaturity
Distorted perception	*X–%*	Distorted perception	High
Weighted color responses	*WSumC*	Affective expression	Tendency to discharges, low reflection
Proportion of affective constriction	*SumC': WSumC*	Affective-emotional modulation	High – Internalized affects facilitates the somatic expression
Movement responses	*M*	Thinking, fantasy	Low – Greater difficulty in abstraction, symbolization, and thinking.
Developmental Quality	*DQ+*	Capacity to establish relations between different aspects	Low – Greater difficulty to/with integration
Morbid responses	*MOR*	Negative self-image	High – Difficulties in self-image and self-esteem
Anatomy responses	*Anatomy*	Worry with the body, psychosomatic aspects	High – Body complaints, archaic representation of itself/oneself

- *X–%* is the distorted extended form use. This variable concerns the proportion of answers in which the form use is not commensurate with the features (Exner, 2001, p. 97).
- *WSumC* is the weighted sum of chromatic color responses (Exner, 2001, p. 96).
- *Sum C': WSum C*. This ratio relates to excessive internalization of affect. It is entered with the total number of achromatic color responses (*C'*) on the left and the weighted sum of chromatic color (*WSumC*) on the right (Exner, 2001, p. 96).
- *M* is the number of human movement responses (Exner, 2001, p. 35).
- *DQ+* refers to developmental quality; the synthesis responses: More than one object must be involved and they must be reported in a meaningful relationship to each other (Exner, 2001, p. 28).
- *MOR* is the morbid content, used for any response in which an object is identified either as dead, destroyed, ruined, spoiled, damaged, injured, broken, or there is an attribution of a clearly dysphoric feeling or characteristic to an object (Exner, 2001, p. 76).
- *Anatomy* is the content used for responses in which the content is skeletal, muscular, or of internal anatomy (Exner, 2001, p. 54).

9

A reliability scoring analysis was performed with the selected Rorschach variables. The interscorer agreement was based on rescoring 20 of the 52 protocols, 10 of the case group and 10 of the control group, by two external Rorschachers not involved in the study (Exner, 1995; McDowell & Acklin, 1996). Table 2 displays the obtained kappa of the two groups.

Blatt, Brenneis, Schimek, and Glick (1976) developed a scale applied to the Rorschach, which allows an evaluation of the person's object representation through the human figures analysis. The human figures are assessed in their dimensions of (a) differentiation – *H, (H), Hd* and *(Hd)*; (b) articulation (attributes such as age, sex, occupation), and (c) integration – possibilities of interactions.

Table 2. Analysis of the reliability among Rorschachers in the ten selected variables

Variables	Case group			Control group		
	PA	κ	BR	PA	κ	BR
DQ+	0.973	0.818	0.057	0.972	0.884	0.095
M	0.973	0.319	0.014	0.979	0.834	0.045
FC, CF, C	0.993	0.920	0.031	0.966	0.709	0.043
FC', C'F, C'	0.986	–	0.005	0.986	0.743	0.019
FQo	0.856	0.695	0.264	0.917	0.828	0.276
FQ–	0.870	0.726	0.269	0.903	0.791	0.248
Fr, rF	1.000	–	0.000	1.000	–	0.005
Pairs	0.966	0.797	0.064	0.903	0.664	0.119
Anatomy	0.979	0.878	0.064	0.972	0.785	0.048
MOR	0.979	0.393	0.012	0.993	0.885	0.021

PA = proportion of agreement, BR = base rate.

Procedures

All the Rorschach were administered and classified according to the Comprehensive System specifications for children, mainly the inquiry made after the association phase (Exner and Weiner, 1995). After the scoring and indexes calculations, all the human responses of each Rorschach protocol were evaluated and scored according to the categories proposed by the Concept of the Object Scale for assessing Object Representation (ORS), as proposed by Blatt et al. (1976) and Blatt and Lerner (1983).

Results

Comprehensive System Variables

All the children were allocated to one of the four subgroups according to two conditions (a) case (enuresis) or control, and (b) small (up to 7 years and 11 months) or big (more than 8 years of age). The age category was chosen because a 5-year-old child is very different from an 11-year-old. In the first group, small children, functioning more typical of the latent phase predominates whereas the second group will be closer to puberty. Besides, older children, mainly in the case group, could present more personal difficulties because of the length of time of the symptom has manifested and as a consequence of the symptom's persistence.

The reliability scoring analysis showed that reflection responses (*Fr*) were absent in both groups, and the case group had very few achromatic color responses (*WSumC'*), so there is no kappa correlation in these three situations. The high absence of *M* and *MOR* in the case group explains the low kappa in spite of the high proportion of agreement.

The confounding variables *R, Lambda,* and *EB* style are present in equal proportions in both groups (Table 3).

Table 3. Distribution of the confounding variables

Variables	Case group		Control group	
	Number of protocols	%	Number of protocols	%
R < 14	7	26.9	8	30.8
R = 14	19	73.1	18	69.2
Lambda ≤ .99	4	15.4	4	15.4
Lambda > .99	22	84.6	22	84.6
EB introversive	4	15.4	6	23.1
EB extratensive	15	57.7	10	38.5
EB ambitent	7	26.9	8	30.8

The statistical design of the study follows the 2×2 factorial planning or 2×2 MANOVA in both directions.

The variables were divided according to their nature in continuum (*EGO; X+%; X-%; DQ+; WsumC*) and in ordinals (*SumC':WSumC; M; MOR; Anatomy*) following Exner's (1995) orientations. The ordinals received the values 0, 1, and 2 matched to the level of responses (low, medium, or high), respectively.

11

Continuum Variables *EGO, X+%, X-%, DQ+, WSumC*

The means of each of the four subgroups were compared using the "*F*" statistics of a multivariate variance analysis and the results indicated: (a) no significant interaction between the factors Condition (enuresis vs. no enuresis) and Age (small vs. big); (b) no significant effect of the factor Age, that is, small and big children had a similar mean profile in these five variables; and (c) a significant effect ($F = 2.684$, $p = .033$) of the factor Condition, that is, in at least one of the five variables the mean of the children with enuresis could be considered different from the mean of the children without enuresis.

Therefore, the Age factor was dropped, which means that the differences found are not a result of age. However, since a difference was detected in the factor Condition, a Student t test for each of the five variables was conducted, and a difference was found in two of them. The effect sizes for relevant comparisons, Cohen's d, was also calculated (Table 4).

As for the ordinal variables, there were no statistical differences among the four variables. Therefore, *EGO* and *X+%* are the variables that show statistical differences, the control group having higher values. These differences are confirmed by the effect size data (Table 4).

Table 4. Mean t scores and standard deviations for the five Rorschach's continuum variables and effect sizes (Cohen's d)

Variables	Case group		Control group		Statistics		
	Mean	SD	Mean	SD	t	p	d
EGO	.11	.11	.24	.13	−3.58	.008*	−.99
X+%	.37	.15	.47	.19	−2.17	.035*	−.60
X-%	.35	.15	.28	.18	1.38	.17	.38
DQ+	1.62	2.37	2.58	1.94	−1.60	.12	−.44
WSumC	1.44	1.44	2.34	2.21	−1.60	.12	−.44

The Concept of the Object Scale for Object Representation of the Human Responses

The means of the human content responses, *H*, were compared between the case and control groups in a total of 18 categories of object representation in OR+ or accurate *H*, and OR- or distorted *H*. The 36 comparisons were submitted to Student t tests as well as to Cohen's d effect sizes for relevant comparisons (Table 5).

Table 5. Mean *t* scores and standard deviations for Blatt's OR+ and OR– variables and effect sizes (Cohen's *d*)

| | OR+ | | | | | | | OR– | | | | | | |
| | Case | | Control | | Statistics | | | Case | | Control | | Statistics | | |
	Mean	SD	Mean	SD	t	p	d	Mean	SD	Mean	SD	t	p	d
(Hd)	.11	.32	.23	.51	.23	.34	.06	.03	.09	.07	.27	-.59	.56	-.16
Hd	.80	.93	.42	.90	.42	.14	.12	1.26	2.20	.88	1.81	.69	.50	.19
(H)	.46	.70	1.11	1.18	1.11	.01*	.31	.15	.46	.30	.97	-.73	.047	-.20
H	.61	.94	.73	.77	.73	.63	.20	.19	.50	.03	.19	1.78	.08	.49

As for the ORS, the *(H)* variable proved to be higher in the control group, however, its effect size was small.

Conclusions

The lower *EGO* index in the case group indicates that the children with enuresis displayed a tendency to perceive themselves in a negative and damaging way, which can be understood as a signal of low self-esteem. Since no reflection *(Fr)* responses were found in their protocols, we discarded the possibility of narcissistic configurations in these children.

According to Exner (2003), the lower *EGO* index indicates difficulties in adaptation. Weiner (1998) interprets it as an attentional deviation to others at the expense of oneself. Exner and Sendin (1995) mention devaluated self-image and lack of confidence in one's own resources.

It is rare to find the lower *EGO* index in children, since they are usually more centered in themselves. Weiner (1998) states that the *EGO* index is stable during these years, which is in agreement with the development theories and the notion of continuity of self-esteem as a personality trait. It is, therefore, less probable that the lower *EGO* index in the children with enuresis occurred recently or as a reaction to some current inadequate or failure experience. On the contrary, the low *EGO* index should be associated with chronically lower self-esteem since infancy, which usually shows little fluctuation.

Therefore, it seems less probable that the self-esteem of the children with enuresis is a consequence of their symptom and that once the symptom is suppressed the self-esteem problem will be solved by itself. Self-concept and self-esteem are built during psychological development,

13

from the very start of life. Therefore, it looks as though the low self-esteem in these children with enuresis results from their experiences during their life.

The studies of Hinde et al. (1995) and Hägglof et al. (1996) employed self-report instruments, and self-reports and the Rorschach evaluate different areas of personality (Meyer, 1992). Their results, therefore, cannot be correlated to this present study.

As for perceptive acuity $(X+\%)$, the children with enuresis showed more difficulty in perceiving reality in a more accurate and objective way. Halpern (1953) pointed out that the perception and the comprehension of reality are the first prerequisite for self-concept development. Thus, perceptive acuity is an important component in the self-perception process. The self-concept is formed from interrelation experiences, which will occur from birth onward. The child will feel itself in the same way that the environment will feel the child.

Besides, $X+\%$ is also related to the development of other ego functions, mainly the possibility of a psychological functioning according to the secondary process. This involves the capacity for tolerating frustration and postponing more immediate gratifications with the use of thinking and reflection, that is, maturity and control of emotions.

Therefore, the children with enuresis present problems of adaptation, since they can neither observe and understand the data according to common sense nor respond to the demands of the external world, which compromises their communication and their interpersonal exchanges.

As for object representation, in the control group there is a significantly greater number of *(H)* in the good form humans (OR+) category. These children, therefore, show a greater tendency to fantasize, to express their anxieties and their fears. This is a positive aspect since these are adaptive fantasies, according to Donahue and Tuber (1993). Halpern (1953) considers that a child's identification with unreal characters can be a satisfactory compensation for feelings of inadequacy, inefficiency, and frustration that the child experiences. Identification with the supernatural and the fantastic is natural and is part of the developmental process. The themes of *(H)* responses can illustrate feelings of insecurity when facing powerful or destructive figures, and can express anything from phobic tendencies to aspects of helplessness, carelessness, and loneliness. These events are common in all children, who effectively have fewer resources than adults, which make them more vulnerable and fragile.

As for the enuretic group, there is a predominance of human detail responses over the human figure (*Hd* > *H*) indicating a more archaic and precarious process of self-notion development and of object representation, which can be related to their lower self-esteem. It also points to difficulty with self-cohesion, as Gaddini (1977) stated:

> "The 'self' is the outcome of the infant's total bodily experience of the first months of life. These are sensations which, in the course of growing, are gradually elaborated in a process of mentalization [...] The young child lives his physical experiences, while growing, with disintegration anxieties and fears. Mental activity comes just at a point when the child can use it (he is in need of it) to master them. In the child's mind fantasy takes place, to save him from disintegration" (p. 260, 266).

Therefore, the mental activity works as organizational to the anxieties and fears and guarantees nondisintegration, that is, self-cohesion.

In conclusion, the children with enuresis revealed difficulties with the self-image, self-concept, and self-esteem areas of personality, not as a consequence of the symptom, but as a result of a more immature development in which a distorted perception of the self and of others prevails, besides their lack of ability to symbolize and fantasize. In spite of their immaturity, the enuresis symptom is not a means of discharge but a lack of control, which is a result of self-development.

Bick (1968), referring to her concept of "second skin" tells us:

> "In its most primitive forms the parts of the personality are felt to have no binding force among themselves and must, therefore, be held together in a way that is experienced by them passively, by the skin functioning as a boundary. But this internal function of containing the parts of the self is dependent initially on the introjection of an external object, experienced as capable of fulfilling this function" (p. 114).

Therefore, it is possible that the children with enuresis in our study had failed in their construction of the continence function, which would allow them to reunite, to connect the parts of the self in a whole. This condition should be understood as a foundation for the constitution of self-esteem.

Acknowledgments

Acknowledgment is due to Hospital Israelita Albert Einstein where the research was conducted. Acknowledgment is also due to Mr. Antonio Carlos Pacheco e Silva Neto who figured out the Kappa index and Mr. Ricardo Primi with the Cohen's *d* statistics.

References

Acklin, M.W. & Alexander, G. (1988). Alexithymia and somatization. A Rorschach study of four psychosomatic groups. *Journal of Nervous and Mental Disease, 176,* 343–350.

Ajuriaguerra, J. (1976). *Manual de psiquiatria infantil* (3rd ed.) [Manual of child psychiatry]. Barcelona: Toray-Masson.

American Psychiatric Association. (1995). *Manual diagnóstico e estatístico de problemas mentais* [Diagnostic and Statistical Manual of Mental Disorders] (DSM-IV) (4th ed., pp. 106–108). Porto Alegre: Artes Médicas.

Anzieu, D. (1985) *Le moi peau* [The ego skin]. Paris: Dunod.

Bick, E. (1968). The experience of the skin in early object relations. *International Journal of Psychoanalysis, 49,* 484–486.

Bion, W.R. (1962). *Learning from experience.* London: W. Heinemann Medical Books.

Blatt, S.J., Brenneis, C.B., Schimek, J.G., & Glick, M. (1976). Normal development and the psychopathological impairment of the concept of the object on the Rorschach. *Journal of Abnormal Psychology, 85,* 364–373.

Blatt, S.J., & Lerner, P.M. (1983) Assessment of object representation. *Journal of Personality Assessment, 47,* 7–28.

Brazelton, B.T. (1989). *Toddlers and parents: A declaration of independence.* New York: Delta/Seymour Lawrence Book.

Chabert, C. (1983). *Le Rorschach en clinique adulte* [The Rorschach in adult clinic]. Paris: Dunod.

Cintra, E.M.U., & Figueiredo, L.C. (2004). *Melanie Klein. Estilo e pensamento* [Melanie Klein. Style and thought]. São Paulo: Escuta.

Donahue, P.J., & Tuber, S.B. (1993). Rorschach adaptive fantasy images and coping in children under severe environmental stress. *Journal of Personality Assessment, 60,* 421–434.

Exner, J.E. (1993). *The Rorschach: A comprehensive system. Basic foundation.* New York: Wiley.

Exner, J.E. (1995). *Issues and methods in Rorschach research.* New Jersey: Erlbaum.

Exner, J.E. Jr. (2001). *A Rorschach workbook for the comprehensive system* (5th ed.). Asheville, NC: Rorschach Workshops.

Exner, J.E. Jr. (2003). *The Rorschach: A comprehensive system* (4th ed.). New York: Wiley.

Exner, J.E. Jr., & Sendin, C. (1995). *Manual de interpretación del Rorschach para el sistema compreensivo* [Rorschach interpretation workbook for the comprehensive system]. Madrid: Psimática.

Exner, J.E. Jr., & Weiner, I.B. (1995). *The Rorschach: A comprehensive system. Assessment of children and adolescent* (2nd ed.). New York: Wiley.

Fisher, S. & Cleveland, S.E. (1958). *Body image and personality.* Princeton: Van Nostrand.

Freud, S. (1974). *The instincts and their vicissitudes. Standard edition of the complete psychological works of Sigmund Freud* (Vol. 14, p. 111). London: Hogarth. (Original work published in 1915).

Freud, S. (1974). *The Ego and the Id. Standard edition of the complete psychological works of Sigmund Freud* (Vol. 19, pp. 1–59). London: Hogarth. (Original work published in 1923).

Gaddini, R. (1977). The pathology of the self as a basis of psychosomatic disorders. *Psychotherapy and Psychosomatics, 28*, 260–271.

Garfinkel, B.D., Carlson G.A., & Weller, E.B. (1990). *Psychiatric disorders in children and adolescents.* Philadelphia: W.B. Saunders.

Glicklich, L.B. (1951). An historical account of enuresis. *Pediatrics, 8*, 859–76.

Hagglof, B., Andrén, O., Bergstron, E., Marklend, L., & Wendelius, E. (1996, October). *Self-esteem before and after treatment in children with nocturnal enuresis and urinary incontinence.* Proceedings of the 3rd International Workshop: International Enuresis Research Center, Aarhus, Denmark.

Halpern, F. (1953). *A clinical approach to children's Rorschach.* New York: Grune & Stratton.

Hjälmas, K. (1997). Pathophysiology and impact of nocturnal enuresis. *Acta Pediatrica, 86*, 919–922.

Hinde, M., Hjertonsson, M., & Broberg, A. (1995). Low self-esteem of children with enuresis. *Lakartidningen, Sep6, 92*, 3225–3229.

Husain, O. (2005). Propos sur la symétrie au Rorschach: de l'objectif à l'objectal [Regarding the symmetry in the Rorschach: From the objective to the objectal]. In F. Rossel, O. Husain, & C. Merceron, *Les phenoménes particuliers au Rorschach* [The special phenomena in the Rorschach] (Vol. I., p. 68). Lausanne: Éditions Payot.

Kaffman, M., & Elizur, E. (1977). Infants who become enuretics: A longitudinal study of 161 kibutz children. *Monography Society Child Development, 42*, 1–54.

Klein, M. (1952). Notes on some schizoid mechanisms. In *Developments in psychoanalysis.* London: Hogarth Press. (Original work published in 1946).

McDowell, C., & Acklin, M.W. (1996). Standardizing procedures for calculating Rorschach interrater reliability: Conceptual and empirical foundations. *Journal of Personality Assessment, 66*, 308–320.

Meyer, G.J. (1992). The Rorschach's factor structure: A contemporary investigation and historical review. *Journal of Personality Assessment, 59*, 117–136.

Porcelli, P., & Meyer, G.J. (2002). Construct validity of Rorschach variables of alexithymia. *Psychosomatics, 43*, 360–369.

Rausch de Traubenberg, N., & Sanglade, A. (1984). Représentation de soi et rélation d'object au Rorschach. Grille de réprésentation de soi [Self-representation and object relation in the Rorschach. Table of self representation]. *Revue de Psychologie Appliqué, 34*(1), 41–57.

Sandler, J. & Rosenblatt, B. (1962). The concept of the representational world. *Psychoanalytic Study of the Child, 17*, 128–145.

Schachtel, E.G. (1967) *Experiential foundations of Rorschach test.* London: Tavistock Publications.

Schilder, P. (1950). *The image and appearance of the body*. New York: Internationale Universities Press.

Semer, N.L., & Yazigi, L. (1990). Douler chronique, réponses d'anatomie au Rorschach et narcisisme primaire [Chronic pain, responses of anatomy in the Rorschach and primary narcisism]. *Psychologie Médicale, 22,* 697–700.

Senn, M.J., & Solnit, A.J. (1971). *Transtornos de la conduta y del desarollo en el niño* [Conduct and developmental disorders in children]. Barcelona: Ed Pediatrica.

Weiner, I.B. (1998). *Principles of Rorschach interpretation*. New Jersey: Erlbaum.

Winnicott, D.W. (1949). *Mind and its relation to psyche-soma*. In *Through pediatrics to psycho-analysis*. London: Hogarth.

Yazigi, L., Silva J.R., Semer, N.L., Dias, S.B., & Catropa, S. (1995). Rorschach et plaintes somatiques rebelles chez des patients ambulatoires [Rorschach and somatic persistent complaints in patients at a clinic service]. *Bulletin de La Société du Rorschach, Paris, 38,* 143–150.

Norma Lottenberg Semer
Rua Batataes 349 ap 122
01423-010 São Paulo SP
Brasil
E-mail norma.lsemer@terra.com.br

Summary

The aim of this paper is the study of self-esteem in enuretic children through the Rorschach method. The authors seek an integration of empirical research with psychoanalytical concepts about psychological development, mainly the role of the body in early experiences of life, in the first interactions with the environment. Some of the psychoanalytical authors consider that the mental configuration of the body occurs very early in the infant's mind, starting from the relationship with his/her mother and this builds the basis for self representation, the self, which is the precursor of self-esteem.

The authors consider the utilization of the Rorschach method for capturing the psychic functioning in persons with disorders related to body-mind repercussions. Therefore, the purpose of this paper is to study, in children with enuresis, the psychological aspect related to the constitution or the building of self-esteem. Self-esteem is considered as a result of the development of the inner world, of possibilities of self-confidence and self-acceptance.

The research design is a case control study using the Rorschach Method, Comprehensive System, with specifications for children (Exner & Weiner, 1995). The case group consisted of 26 children with enuresis without an organic cause, referred by the pediatric outpatient service of Albert Einstein Hospital. Twenty-six other children were matched for age, sex, and socio-economic level to serve as controls without enuretic symptoms.

The two groups were compared and nine variables were selected: Egocentricity Index, related to self-esteem and self-perception (*EGO*); perceptive acuity (*X*+%); perceptive distortion(*X*-%); affective expression (*WSumC*); proportion of affective constriction (*Sum C':WSumC*); capacity of thinking and symbolization (*M*);capacity of synthesis (*DQ*+); perception of negative aspects of self-image (*MOR*); concern about the body and alteration of self-image (*Anatomy*).

The human content responses of each protocol were also selected and classified according to the categories of the Concept of the Object Scale for Assessing Object Representation (ORS) proposed by Blatt (1976, 1983). This scale allows an empirical evaluation of object representation through the analysis of human content response.

The results showed significant differences in the following variables: *EGO* (p = .008) and *X*+% (p = .35),the control group with higher values. The lower *EGO* index in the case group indicates that the children with enuresis display a tendency to perceive themselves in a negative and damaging way, which can be understood as a signal of low self-esteem.

This index is stable during childhood, which is in agreement with development theories, and children tend to be self-centered. Therefore, it is less probable that the lowering of *EGO* in these children with enuresis occurred recently or as a reaction to some failure experience. On the contrary, the low *EGO* index should be associated with chronically lower self-esteem.

Regarding perceptive acuity (*X*+%), the children with enuresis show more difficulties in perceiving reality in a more accurate and objective way, which compromises the development of self-concept. This index is also related to the development of other ego functions, the possibility of a psychological functioning according to a secondary process, such as the capacity for tolerating frustration with the use of thinking. Therefore, as a consequence, the children with enuresis present problems of adaptation, with less maturity and difficulties in dealing with their emotions.

As for the object representation in the control group, there is a significantly greater number of (*H*) in the good form humans categories (p = .01). These children show more possibilities to fantasize, to express their anxieties and fears in an adaptive way (content of the responses).

19

The children with enuresis reveal difficulties in self-image, self-concept, and self-esteem as a result of a more immature development in which a distorted perception of the self and of others prevails, besides their lack of ability to symbolize and fantasize. Therefore, the enuresis can be regarded as the child's failure in its capacity for continence, and consequently the emotions leak without control, without being processed or thought out. The difficulties in symbolization pave the way for the body's manifestations of the psychic conflicts.

Résumé

Ce travail se propose d'étudier, au moyen de la méthode de Rorschach, l'estime de soi chez les enfants énurétiques. Les auteures cherchent à intégrer recherche empirique et concepts psychanalytiques liés au développement psychologique et particulièrement à ce qui concerne le rôle du corps dans les expériences précoces de vie, les premières interactions avec l'environnement. Pour les auteurs psychanalystes, la configuration mentale du corps surgit précocement dans la psyché du bébé, à partir de sa relation avec sa mère et elle forme la base de la représentation de soi, le *self*, précurseur de l'estime de soi. Les auteures réfléchissent sur l'utilisation de la méthode de Rorschach visant à l'appréhension du fonctionnement psychique de sujets chez lesquels sont présentes des répercussions esprit-corps, comme dans le cas de l'énurésie.Dans ce travail, les auteurs ont étudié les aspects psychologiques liés à la constitution et à la construction de l'estime de soi considérée comme le résultat du développement psychologique, des conditions du monde intérieur, des possibilités d'acceptation de soi et de confiance en soi. Ont été soumis à un test 26 enfants présentant le symptôme de l'énurésie et chez lesquels celle-ci n'avait pas d'explication organique, de l'Ambulatoire de Pédiatrie de l'Hôpital Albert Einstein, ainsi que 26 autres enfants du même âge et de la même catégorie sociale que les premiers, mais ne présentant pas le symptôme en question. Pour ce, on a utilisé la méthode de Rorschach, Système Compréhensif dans ses spécifications pour enfants (Exner and Weiner, 1995). Les deux groupes ont été comparés à partir de neuf variables choisies à cet effet et répondant aux caractéristiques suivantes: aspects se rapportant à: estime et perception de soi-même (*EGO*); adéquation perceptive (*X+%*); distorsion perceptive (*X–%*); expression affective (*WSumC*); proportion de constriction affective (*Sum C':WSumC*); capacité de réflexion et de symbolisation (*M*);

capacité de synthèse (*DQ+*); perception d'aspects négatifs de l'image de soi (*MOR*); préoccupation du corps et altération de l'image de soi (*Anatomie*).

Outre ces variables, les auteurs ont évalué et classé les réponses à contenu humain de chaque protocole, selon les catégories proposées par l'Échelle de Concept de l'Objet pour l'évaluation de Représentation de l'Objet proposée par Blatt (1976). Cet instrument permet d'évaluer empiriquement la représentation de l'objet au moyen de l'analyse des réponses à contenu humain.

Les résultats du Rorschach ont fait apparaître des différences significatives dans les variables: *EGO* (p = .008) e *X+%* (p = .35) et c'est le groupe de contrôle qui a obtenu les valeurs les plus élevées. L'indice *EGO*, plus bas chez les enfants énurétiques, indique que ceux-ci se perçoivent eux-mêmes d'une manière négative, ce qui peut être compris comme un signe de faible estime de soi. Comme cet indice est stable tout au long de l'enfance et que les enfants ont tendance à être centrés sur eux-mêmes, il est possible que cette faible valeur de l'indice soit associée à des problèmes chroniques d'estime de soi et non à une réaction à la présence du symptôme. En ce qui concerne l'activité perceptive (*X+%*), les enfants énurétiques ont montré qu'ils avaient plus de difficulté que d'autres à percevoir la réalité de manière objective, ce qui compromet la formation du concept de soi. Cet indice est en outre associé à d'autres fonctions de la personnalité, tels que fonctionnement selon le principe de la réalité, tolérance à la frustraction, capacité à penser et à contrôler les émotions. Dans ce sens, il est possible que les enfants énurétiques présentent d'une manière générale une plus grande immaturité dans leur développement.

Quant à l'échelle de représentation de l'objet, la variable se rapportant au contenu para-humain (*H*), dans les réponses plus objectives, a obtenu une valeur significativement plus élevée dans le groupe contrôle (*p* = .01). Les enfants du groupe contrôle montrent une plus grande possibilité de fantasmer et d'exprimer leurs anxiétés et leurs peurs, d'une manière adaptative (contenu des réponses).

En résumé, les enfants énurétiques révèlent des difficultés par rapport à l'image que chacun a de soi, au concept et à l'estime de soi, difficultés résultant de problèmes dans leur développement psychologique, avec prédominance de perception déformée de soi-même, ainsi que des déficiences dans la capacité à symboliser et à fantasmer. L'énuresie peut être considerée comme un échec de la capacité de contenance et par conséquent, les émotions échappent sans contrôle, sans élaboration. Les difficultés de symbolisation préparent le chemin pour les manifestations corporelles des conflits psychiques.

Resumen

El objetivo de este trabajo es un estudio de la autoestima en niños enuréticos con el método de Rorschach. Las autoras buscan integrar una investigación empírica con conceptos psicoanalíticos sobre el desarrollo psicológico, sobre todo en lo que se refiere al papel del cuerpo en las experiencias precoces de vida, en las primeras interacciones con el ambiente. Para los autores psicoanalistas, la configuración mental del cuerpo ocurre precozmente en la mente del bebe, a partir de la relación con la madre y forma la base de la representación de si, el *self*, precursor de la autoestima. Las autoras reflexionan sobre la utilización del método de Rorschach para la aprehensión del funcionamiento psíquico de personas en que están presentes repercusiones mente-cuerpo, como en la enuresis. En este trabajo las autoras estudiaron los aspectos psicológicos relacionados a la constitución y a la construcción de la autoestima, considerada como el resultado del desarrollo psicológico, de las condiciones del mundo interno, de las posibilidades de auto aceptación y autoconfianza. El estudio comprende un estudio de caso control, utilizando el Método de Rorschach, Sistema Comprensivo, con las especificaciones para niños (Exner & Weiner, 1995). El grupo caso fue formado por veintiséis niños con síntomas de enuresis, sin compromiso orgánico, provenientes del Ambulatorio de Pediatría del Hospital Albert Einstein. Otros veintiséis niños fueron pareados en edad, sexo y nivel económico para el grupo de control, sin síntoma de enuresis. Ambos grupos fueron comparados y nueve variables fueron seleccionadas: índice de egocentrismo, relacionado con la autoestima y la auto percepción (*EGO*); la acuidad perceptiva (*X+%*); distorsión perceptiva (*X–%*); expresión afectiva (*WSumC*); proporción de la constricción afectiva (*SumC':WSumC*); capacidad de pensamiento y simbolización (*M*); capacidad de síntesis (*DQ+*); percepción de aspectos negativos de la autoimagen (*MOR*); preocupación con cuerpo y alteración de la auto imagen (*Anatomía*).

Además de estas variables, las autoras evaluaron y clasificaron las respuestas de contenido humano de cada protocolo, de acuerdo con las categorías propuestas por la Escala de Concepto de Objeto para evaluación de Representación de Objeto propuesta por Blatt (1976).

Este instrumento posibilita un examen empírico de representación de objeto por medio del análisis de las respuestas de contenido humano.

Los resultados del Rorschach presentan diferencias significativas en las variables: *EGO* (p = .008) e *X+%* (p = .35), siendo que el grupo control obtuvo valores más elevados. El índice EGO mas rebajado en niños enuréticos indica que ellos se perciben de manera negativa, lo que puede ser entendido como señal de baja autoestima. Como este índice es estable a lo largo de la infancia y los niños tienden a ser centrados en sí mismos, es posible que el valor bajo del índice esté asociado a problemas crónicos de autoestima y no a una reacción a la presencia del síntoma. Con relación a la actividad perceptiva (*X+%*), los niños enuréticos indican mayores dificultades en percibir la realidad de una manera objetiva, lo que compromete la formación del auto concepto. Además, éste índice está asociado a otras funciones de la personalidad, tales como funcionamiento por el principio de la realidad, tolerancia a la frustración y capacidad de pensar. En éste sentido, es posible que los niños enuréticos presenten problemas de adaptación, con inmadurez y dificultad para ocuparse con las emociones.

Cuanto a la escala de representación de objeto, la variable relacionada al contenido para-humano (*H*), en las respuestas bien vistas, obtiene valor significativamente más elevado en el grupo de control (p = .01). Los niños del grupo de control presentan mayores condiciones de fantasear y de expresar sus ansiedades y miedos, de una forma adaptativa (contenido de las respuestas).

En suma, los niños con enuresis rebelan dificultades en la auto-imagen, auto concepto y autoestima como resultado de problemas en el desarrollo psicológico, con predominio de percepción deformada de si mismos, además de fallas en la capacidad de simbolizar y fantasear. De esta manera, la enuresis puede ser considerada como una falla en la capacidad de continencia, y consecuentemente las emociones escapan sin control, sin ser procesadas o elaboradas. Las dificultades en la simbolización preparan el camino para las manifestaciones corporales de los conflictos psíquicos.

　本論文のねらいは、ロールシャッハ法によって遺尿症児の自尊心について調査することである。著者らは、心理的発達に関する精神分析的概念を用いて、人生早期の経験における、また環境との最初の相互作用における身体の主な役割について、実証的研究の統合につとめた。精神分析的立場の著者の中には、身体の心的認識は、母親との関係を開始することによってかなり初期の乳児の心にも生じており、それが自尊心の前駆である自己表象や自己の基礎を構築すると考察している者もいる。

　著者らは、心と身体の影響と関連する障害のある人々の心理的機能をとらえるためにロールシャッハ法を活用することを考えている。従って本論文の目的は、遺尿症児における、自尊心の形成や確立に関係する心理的様相を検討することである。自尊心は、内的世界の発達の結果、あるいは自己信頼と自己受容の可能性の成果と考えられている。

　本研究のデザインは、包括システムの児童に対する施行法（Exner & Weiner,1995）によるロールシャッハ法を用いた症例コントロール研究である。症例群は、アルバート・アインシュタイン病院の小児科外来から紹介された、器質的問題の認められない遺尿症児 26 名である。それとは別に、遺尿症状が見られず、年齢、性別、社会的経済的な水準が事例群と一致している 26 名の児童を統制群とした。

　2 群の比較において、9 つの変数が選択された。自尊心や自己知覚と関係する自己中心性指標（**EGO**）、認知的正確さ（**X+%**）、認知的歪曲（**X-%**）、感情表現（**WSumC**）、感情の萎縮の割合（**SumC':WSumC**）、思考と象徴化の能力（**M**）、統合能力（**DQ+**）、自己イメージのネガティブな側面の知覚（**MOR**）、身体と自己イメージの変化への関心（**Anatomy**）である。

　それぞれのプロトコルの人間内容反応も収集され、Blatt（1976，1983）によって提案された対象表象評価のための対象尺度（ORS）の概念のカテゴリーにより分類された。この尺度は、人間内容反応の分析による対象表象の実証的評価を得ている。

　結果として、以下の変数において顕著な差が示された。統制群は EGO（p=.008）と X+%（p=.35）が高い数値を示した。症例群における低い EGO 指標は、遺尿症児が自身を否定的で傷ついたやり方で知覚する傾向があることを示しており、低い自尊心のサインであると理解することが出来る。

　この指標は、これは発達論とも一致しているのであるが、児童期の間安定しており、また児童には自己中心的傾向がある。したがって、遺尿症児の低い EGO 指標は、最近生じたもの、あるいは何らかの失敗体験への反応、ということはあまりありえない。反対に、低い EGO 指標は慢性的に低い自尊心と関連しているに違いない。

　認知的正確さ（X+%）について見ると、遺尿症児は、現実をより正確に客観的なやり方で知覚することに困難を示しているため、自己概念の発達が損なわれる。この指標も、他の自我機能の発達、思考することでフラストレーションに耐える能力といった二次過程に従って心理的に機能できる可能性と関係している。従って結果として、遺尿症児は自身の感情を扱うことの未熟さと困難さによる適応の問題を呈している。

　統制群の対象表象に関しては、良質の形態の人間カテゴリーに含まれる（H）反応が有意に多く見られた（p=.01）。統制群の児童は、適応的なやり方（反応内容）で空想にふけったり、不安や恐れを表現したりすることが出来る可能性を示している。

　遺尿症児は、象徴化や空想する能力の不足に加えて、自身や他者についてのゆがんだ知覚がゆき渡っているによる未熟な発達の結果として、自己イメージ、自己概念、自尊心における困難を示している。従って遺尿は、児童の我慢する能力における失敗であり、その結果コントロールされず、処理されず、よく考えられずに漏洩した感情、と見なすことが可能である。象徴化の困難さは心理的葛藤を身体で表現する下地となっている。

Rorschachiana 30, 26–47
© 2009 Hogrefe & Huber Publishers

DOI: 10.1027/1192-5604.30.1.26

Exploring the Validity of Graphology with the Rorschach Test

Benjamin Thiry

Université catholique de Louvain, Belgium

Abstract. Considered by some as a personality assessment technique, graphology is defended by its partisans but finds little solid scientific base. Our research ($N = 45$) compares the judgment of graphologists ($k = 2$) and 13 graphological variables with 13 variables of the Rorschach test according to the comprehensive system. The average reliability of graphologists' judgments was .43. Their average validity was .05. Sixteen correlations were significant ($p < .05$) between graphological variables and Rorschach variables. Some are compatible with graphological theories. Others are random or difficult to understand. Great caution is essential in the isolated use of graphology as a personality assessment technique.

Keywords: graphology, handwriting, Rorschach, projective test, personality

Graphology is a technique for deducing psychological characteristics of an individual from the observation of his or her handwriting. Handwriting is defined for this purpose as a set of graphic signs that, grouped in syndromes (Peugeot, Lombard, & de Noblens, 1986), leads the graphologist to formulate personality assumptions. Seen as a projective technique (Anzieu, 1991, p. 682), handwriting would be "an expressive movement, which, like drawings, has an excellent rationale for the assumption that personality is projected into the activity" (Crumbaugh & Stockholm, 1977, p. 403). Personality would be projected in one's handwriting according to a rule of expression where "any psychic state tends to express itself in the outside world by analogical correspondences [free translation]" (Delamain, 1949, p. 8). For graphologists, the writer personalizes his/her handwriting according to psychological characteristics. Although previous work had been done in this field, graphology was officially born in 1872 when the French abbot Michon published the first book proposing correspondences between graphic signs and character features. Crépieux-Jamin (1889/1951, 1930) continued Michon's theorization and still remains a major reference for French graphologists. In the United States, graphology is usually taught in correspondence schools (Backman, 2001) and in Europe, mostly in private schools. Associations of professional graphologists organize examinations, deliver diplomas, and militate for the official recognition of their profession. In Europe, graphology is mostly used in France and Belgium (Bruchon-Schweitzer & Lievens, 1991). Graphologists are often seen as consultants in various fields such as employment profiling, educational and vocational orientation, psychological analysis, forensic analysis, etc.

Validity of Graphology

Early in the history of scientific psychology, the validity of graphology was questioned. Binet (1906, p. 252) collaborated with Crépieux-Jamin in several experiments and concluded that there was a "certain truth" but that the graphologists' judgments were "never infallible."

In the United States, Hull and Montgomery (1919) reported a mean correlation between character and handwriting variables equal to –.016, which is far from graphologists' assumptions. Since then, in the history of research, several authors (Castelnuovo-Tedesco, 1948; de Gobineau & Perron, 1954; Lemke & Kirchner, 1971; Lockowandt, 1992; Oinonen cited by Asp, Yalon, & Turk, 2004) have reported significant links between handwriting and personality. Others (Mandeville, Peeples, & Stutler, 1990, 1992; Tett & Palmer, 1997; Furnham, Chamorro-Premuzie, & Callahan, 2003) assume independence between the two. Recently published studies confirm the weak reliability and validity of graphology.

Authors who looked further into this question (Beyerstein & Beyerstein, 1992; Huteau, 2004; Nevo, 1986) have drawn relatively similar conclusions: (a) there are few satisfying studies, (b) graphology postulates are problematic, (c) valid studies indicate low validity, (d) graphology as a recruitment tool should be proscribed, (e) the belief of the general public in graphology rests on irrational phenomena, (f) many studies (with replications) would be necessary to convince the scientific community of the relevance of graphology. Dean's meta-analysis (1992) remains relevant and concludes that graphology would be correlated with intelligence and personality variables but that the average effect size (r = .12) is too low compared to other psychological tools that present significantly higher validity indices and should, consequently, be preferred in psychological assessment.

However, criticisms against graphology are not themselves free from criticisms (Huteau, 2004, pp. 161–162): (a) There are very few serious studies, (b) they are often based on small samples, (c) they are seldom replicated, (d) they are often old (methodology changes over time), (e) they often test graphologists' validity and not graphology itself (Michaux-Granier, Vrignaud, & Ohayon, 1999), and (f) they seldom define graphological variables with precision. For our part, we wished to examine other empirical arguments concerning graphological assumptions while trying to avoid these criticisms. A previous study (Thiry, 2008) aimed at building a sufficiently reliable grid of handwriting analysis and at correlating the graphological variables with facets of a self-report questionnaire in reference to the five-factor model, the NEO PI-R (Costa & McCrae, 1985). There were significant correlations, however, these were probably the result of type I errors. This result did not support graphological assumptions claiming to cover the whole personality. Nevertheless, a major counter-argument to that study could be that projective techniques do not evaluate the same "realities" (Petot, 2004) of personality as questionnaires do. Stein Lewinson (1991), thus, proposed comparing graphological variables with those of other projective tests. We chose to use the Rorschach test because it is currently the most widely used projective technique in the world. Our approach is exploratory.

Graphology and the Rorschach Test

In 1936, Hartoch & Schachtel (quoted by Fluckiger, Tripp, & Weinberg, 1961) independently analyzed handwritings and Rorschach protocols of 32 subjects. They noted particular links between the number of M and the inhibition of the handwriting, the number of W and (hyper-)simplification of the letters, the number of D with handwriting development and plenitude, the number of Dd with the tendency to decorate or complicate the shape of letters or the repetition of pseudo-original eccentricities.

In 1944, Munroe, Lewinson & Waehner (quoted by Anderson & Anderson, 1951, p. 456) compared Rorschach responses with the spontaneous drawings of 11 students. They stated that quantitative studies offer little evidence and recommended an individual qualitative approach.

Castelnuovo-Tedesco (1948) used the Multiple Choice Group Rorschach with 104 students and calculated three quantified indices: *anxiety* (percentage of *F–, CF, C,* and rejection of cards), *compulsivity* (percentage of *FC* and *small D*) and *masculinity* (counting of answers with male, female, or neutral connotation from a psychoanalytical point of view to cards IV, VI, and VII). Six judges (not graphologists) independently evaluated (on a scale from 1 to 5) the 104 handwritings. Without graphological knowledge and on the basis of the spontaneous handwritings, the judges predicted ($p < .01$) the score of *anxiety* ($r = .30$), *compulsivity* ($r = .29$), and *masculinity* ($r = .31$). However Castelnuovo-Tedesco (1948) is critical of the calculation of these three Rorschach indices, especially that of *masculinity*: "It is obvious at first glance that this measure of Masculinity is inadequate in many ways" (p. 186).

Oinonen (1960, 2004) asked six judges to classify the handwritings of 122 children aged from 7 to 9 years into three groups: *poor, average,* or *superior.* Twelve graphic variables were measured. A factor analysis identified only one factor that discriminated *poor* writing from the others. This factor was loaded by the following graphic variables: smudging, correction by retouching, uneven pressure, straying off the straight line, errors in letter-forms, and slant fluctuations. During the Rorschach test, children whose handwriting was *poor* gave significantly more answers (*R*), *Confabulations, M, m, FM, F(C),* and a lowered *F%.* "Poor writers are, therefore, more associated than good writers with: affectivity, lack of control, lack of sense of reality, fluency, lively imagination, introversion and motor inhibition, tension, anxiety, uncertainty, and neurotic traits in general" (Oinonen, 2004).

Demarche (1982) used the Rorschach test with 49 nonpatient adults and measured 22 graphological variables. According to a structural definition of personality (Bergeret, 1974), he classified protocols into three categories: psychotic, borderline, and neurotic. On the whole, he reported 26 results that would indicate or would exclude each personality structure. His results, however, are redundant and not very consistent.

Belin and Aubert (1989) studied rapists' personalities using the Rorschach test and graphological analysis. They present 23 short clinical cases: "graphological analysis can finally be carried out according to the validated succession of the 10 cards of the Rorschach test. We are, therefore, brought to the proof of correlations" [free translation] (p. 75).

Gilbert and Chardon (1989) used the collective Z test of Zulliger (1957) with 100 engineers and compared the variables of that test with 16 graphological variables. They retained 21 significant correlations.

29

For example, (a) the lowered $CF\%$ is accompanied by the left slant of the letters and by the absence of movement of the handwriting, (b) the number of W and the lowered $A\%$ are accompanied by a small middle zone, (c) the low number of K is accompanied by rigid lines and by compactness or excess spacing between words, (d) high $F+\%$ is accompanied by high letter bounding, (e) low number of Dd is linked to the readable shape of the letters, (f) coartation to simplified letters and (f) high $H\%$ to a large right margin.

These seven studies present different methodologies, diverging results, ignore type I errors and only one reports effect sizes. Administration, scoring, and interpretation of Rorschach are not well specified. To our knowledge, no research has compared handwriting variables with Rorschach variables as defined by the comprehensive system (Exner, 1982). That is the goal of this study.

Method

Participants

A total of 45 individuals took part in our study. Fourteen of them answered an invitation letter sent by e-mail. Sessions were organized in Brussels school classrooms that were likely to accommodate a sufficient number of people. A short presentation of the study was made to the voluntary participants.

Thirty-one other participants were imprisoned at the time of study. This particularity will be criticized in the Discussion (below). This sample was composed of 17 women (37.8%) and 28 men (62.2%). The average age was 38.7 years (SD = 12.5). Among the participants who indicated their manual laterality, 9 (81.8%) were right-handed and 2 (18.2%) were left-handed. Concerning the qualifications of participants who answered the question, 6 (23.1%) held a primary education diploma, 4 (15.4%) a secondary education diploma, and 16 (61.5%) a higher education diploma.

Procedure

Each participant was given an A4 white sheet and a picture representing human characters. The writing instrument was left free. We asked participants to write a text based on the presented image. The texts were invented and did not contain personal information. No time limit was set. We did not recorded writing gestures but focused on the produced handwriting, which is the norm for graphology. The Rorschach test was taken individually in another quiet room. Passing and protocol-noting followed Exner's instructions (1996). The protocols were noted by two psychologists trained in the comprehensive system. Problematic scores were discussed. For data analysis we chose only the variables that seemed the most relevant within each cluster of the formal summary: R, EA, L, $FC - (CF + C)$, Afr, Zd, P, $X+\%$, $Wsum6$, Ego, $FD + V$, MOR, and $SumH$.

We chose to keep Rorschach protocols with $10 \leq R < 14$ for three reasons: (a) We postulate that handwriting is a projective technique (defensiveness at the Rorschach test could mean defensiveness in the handwriting), (b) for offenders, R can have psychopathological meaning (Gacono, Meloy & Bridges, 2000), and (c) to keep the power of our sample. In this one, average $R = 22.6$ ($SD = 13.56$) and 9 protocols (20%) had less than 14 responses but more than 9.

The 45 handwritings were scanned (300 dpi) and were sent to two certified graphologists, members of the Belgian Graphology Association. They both received an Excel file in which to encode their ratings. These related to 12 variables (see Appendix B) directly inspired by Exner's comprehensive system (1982) and graded from 0 *absence* to 5 *strongly present*. These two ratings were done independently. Each graphologist subsequently sent a summary of his/her ratings in a separate e-mail.

Moreover, the following variables were measured for each handwriting: (a) average height of the middle zone, (b) average width of the letters, (c) average height of the lower extensions, (d) average height of the higher extensions, (e) spacing between words, (f) spacing between lines, (g) slant of the letters, (h) left margin, (i) right margin, (j) top margin, (k) slope of the lines, (l) continuity of the graphic thread, and (m) motionlessness. See Appendix A for details about the measures. The reliability of these variables was checked previously (Thiry, 2008) and ranges from .72 to 1.

Measures and analysis don't refer to graphological theories. Indeed, we wanted our data analysis to be exploratory. Only the Discussion compares our results to graphology literature.

Statistical processing was carried out with SPSS 12.0.

Results

Reliability of Graphologists' Ratings

Table 1. Interraters reliability (k = 2) for each graphological variables estimated by Spearman's ρ (*N* = 45)

Graphological variable	r_2
Available resources	.21
Tendency to simplify reality	.34*
Emotional control	.28
Interest in emotional stimuli	.58**
Cognitive processing	.62**
Inclination toward banality	.50**
Conventional thought	.32*
Thought disturbance	.59**
Self-concern	.68**
Introspection	.22
Negative self-image	.56**
Interest for others	.29

Note: *p < .05, **p < .01.

Table 1 shows the reliability (Spearman's Rho) of the two graphologists for each evaluated variable. Generally, the graphologists rated the variables following a similar trend. The average r_2 was equal to .43. This result was consistent with Nevo's (1986, p. 259) where reliability of the *graphodiagnostical* scales ranged from .30 to .60. Four reliability indices were not significant (*p* > .05). They related to available resources, introspection, emotional control, and interest for others. The four most agreed on variables (in descending order) were: self-concern, cognitive processing, thought disturbance, and interest in emotional stimuli.

Table 2. Correlations (Spearman's ρ) between Rorschach variables and graphological variables. (*N* = 45)

Graphological variable	Rorschach variable	r_s
Available resources	EA	.46**
Tendency to simplify reality	L	−.02
Emotional control	FC: CF + C	.08
Interest in emotional stimuli	Afr	−.24
Cognitive processing	Zd	.13
Inclination toward banality	P	.26
Conventional thought	X+%	.30*
Thought disturbance	WSum6	−.21
Self-concern	Ego	−.05
Introspection	FD + V	−.05
Negative self-image	MOR	.12
Interest for others	SumH	−.15

Note: *p < .05, **p < .01.

Graphologists' Judgment and Rorschach Variables

For this stage of the study, we calculated the average score based on both graphologists' evaluations for each graphological variable. The results appear in Table 2. Only two correlations were significant: available resources ($p < .01$) and conventional thought ($p < .05$). This means that the 10 other graphological variables are independent of the related variables of the Rorschach test. The average correlation was equal to .05.

Graphical Variables and Rorschach Variables

Are the variables of Rorschach correlated with certain properties of the handwriting ($p < .05$)? The number of answers R ($M = 22.6$, $SD = 13.6$) correlated with two graphic variables: spacing between lines ($r_s = -.36$, $p = .02$) and height of the middle zone ($r_s = -.44$, $p = .002$).
– EA correlated with spacing between lines ($r_s = -.46$, $p = .002$).
– $Lambda$ correlated with the motionlessness of the handwriting ($r_s = -.32$, $p = .03$).
– $FC - (CF + C)$ correlated with the slant of the letters ($r_s = -.33$, $p = .04$).
– $X+\%$ correlated with spacing between lines ($r_s = .35$, $p = .02$).
– $Wsum6$ correlated with three graphic variables: the right margin ($r_s = -.35$, $p = .02$), spacing between lines ($r_s = -.37$, $p = 02$), and the width of the letters ($r_s = -.30$, $p = .05$).
– Ego correlated with spacing between lines ($r_s = .33$, $p = .03$).
– The $FD + V$ index correlated with two graphic variables: the top margin ($r_s = .39$, $p = .01$) and motionlessness ($r_s = .41$ $p = .01$).
– MOR correlated with two graphic variables: the left margin ($r_s = .32$, $p = .03$) and continuity of the graphic thread ($r_s = .34$, $p = .04$).
– $SumH$ is correlated with two graphic variables: the height of the middle zone ($r_s = -.31$, $p = .04$) and the height of the upper extension ($r_s = -.31$, $p = .04$).
– Afr, Zd, P were independent of the graphic variables.

In addition, we wondered if there was a link between the motion expressed by the handwriting and the number of M in the Rorschach test. The Spearman's correlation between our motionlessness variable and the number of M is equal to .27 ($p = .07$), which is not significant.

On the whole, we obtained 16 significant correlations ($p < .05$). Some must be due to type I errors. For 13 graphic variables and 13 Rorschach

33

variables (169 correlations), the probable number of type I errors is 8.5. Chance could not explain all these results.

Among the graphic variables, spacing between lines is correlated with five Rorschach variables: *R, EA, X+%, Wsum6*, and *Ego*. The influence of the number of answers *R* on the other Rorschach variables is known (Exner et al., 1984) and remains problematic. To look further into the relation between these six variables, we calculated linear equations according to a hierarchical method (we include *R* as first predictor, then the most correlated variables in descending order). We obtained five models of linear regression that we compared. We note that neither the number of answers *R* (the partial correlation between *R* and spacing between lines was close to 0), *X+%*, nor *Wsum6* provided additional information when *EA* was already included in the model. The most relevant and economic regression equation included *EA* and *Ego* (see Table 3) to predict spacing between lines.

Table 3. Summary of hierarchical regression analysis for variables predicting spacing between lines (*N* = 45)

Variable	*a*	*B*	*SE B*
Step 1	13		
EA		–.24**	.07
Step 2	11.6		
EA		–.21**	.07
Ego		3.3*	1.5

Note. R^2 = .21 for Step 1; ΔR^2 = .08 for Step 2 ($p < .05$). R = .54, p = .001 for Step 2. *$p < .05$, **$p < .01$.

The height of the middle zone was correlated (negatively) with the number of answers *R* and the sum of the human answers *SumH*. This time, the comparison of the linear models showed that *R* was the best predictor and that SumH did not have a direct link with the dependent variable (the partial correlation was equal to –.01).

The motionlessness of the writing was correlated with *Lambda* and the sum *FD + V*. A comparison of two linear models showed, however, that preference should be given to the one with only one predictor: *FD + V*. Indeed, the value of *Lambda* would not provide significant additional information.

Concerning the *WSum6* Rorschach variable, three graphic variables seemed to predict it. The comparison of three linear regression models, however, excluded the relevance of the letter width when the spacing between lines and the right margin were taken into account (both negatively correlated with the predicted variable). We chose to keep the variable right margin because it was very close to the significance threshold, $F(1, 40) = 3.61$, $p = .07$. The model with two predictors seemed relevant and economic ($R = .41$, $p = .01$).

Concerning the number of *MOR*, two graphic variables were good predictors: continuity of the graphic thread and left margin, $R = .46$, $p = .02$.

The link between *SumH*, the height of the middle zone, and the height of the upper extension disappeared when we introduced R as first predictor.

Discussion

The results concerning the reliability of the two graphologists show a common trend in rating. It should be noted that the graphologists, although not familiar with the Rorschach variables, which can be difficult to understand, reached relatively similar ratings. However, the average reliability of .43 calls for great caution. Even if Nevo (1989) finds this value satisfactory, especially compared with the reliability of projective techniques, it restricts validity. For certain variables, the two graphologists obtained uncorrelated (but never opposite) results. Concerning validity, i.e., the correlation between the graphologists' judgments and Rorschach variables, only two of the possible twelve were significant: the evaluation of the subjects' internal resources and their propensity to share common thoughts with the others. A first remark is essential here: The variable best predicted (available resources) by the graphologists is also the least reliable. This result is surprising and contradictory. Independence between the 10 graphologists' judgments and the 10 equivalent Rorschach variables calls for great caution and casts doubt on the validity of at least one of the two methods. However, scientific literature on the Rorschach test is extensive (Meyer & Archer, 2001), which is not the case for graphology (Beyerstein & Beyerstein, 1992). It should, however, be noted that the logic of $X+\%$ seems to have more satisfactory results in terms of reliability and validity. From the handwriting, graphologists seem to be able to deduce the capacity to share a common thought with others. In other words, the mediation cognitive process – detected by the Rorschach test – is also found within the handwriting. That is not very surprising: handwriting is, by definition, an activity of consensual communication. Learning how to write requires the assimilation of a strictly defined code. This code is by no means innate, it is transmitted to the individual during a long training process calling upon several spheres: motor, neurological, cognitive, and linguistic but also relational and emotional (Ajuriaguerra et al., 1956). The activity of writing is, in essence, a mediation activity. Our results seem to show that graphologists are able to detect signs of conventional thought in the characteristics of handwriting.

If we focus on the objective variables of handwriting, we find other interesting results that do not seem to be exclusively the result of chance. The correlation between the number of answers R and the height of the middle zone is difficult to interpret. Participants whose middle zone is smaller tend to give more answers than the others. The slant of the letters would be related to emotional control. The more tilted to the right the handwriting, the more the emotions tend to be released without control. This assumption is compatible with certain graphological assumptions (Stein Lewinson, 1961) that relate the right slant of the handwriting to *expansion*, in particular of the emotions, whereas a left slant relates to *contraction* i.e., control. By this same logic, the increase of *WSum6* with the reducing of the right margin is also consistent. Writers breaking lines before reaching the edge of the sheet give less special scores (or less important) than those who don't. *WSum6* can be interpreted as an indicator of cognitive failures and, thus, of a lack of control. The reduction of the right margin could have the same significance (at least at a rate of 12% of explained variance). It is, however, the combination of the reduction of the right margin and the spacing between lines that is the best predictor of the emergence of cognitive failures. According to the law of analogy (Delamain, 1949), graphology interprets space between the lines as follows:

> Relatively large spacing between the lines means reflection, emotions and feelings weighted by thought. The closer the lines, the less the subject takes distance and the more subjective he is. [Free translation] (Peugeot, Lombard, & de Noblens, 1986, p. 242)

This synergy between *expansion* and *loss of distance* can be conceived as compatible with the interpretation of *Wsum6*, i.e., as an index of temporary loss of control of cognitive processing.

Another synergy appeared in our results: left margin and continuity of the graphic thread related to the number of *MOR* in the Rorschach test. When the writer leaves a space on the left of his text and binds the letters, this shows an inclination toward self-depreciation. This result does not find obvious correspondence in the graphological literature. Personal depreciation is perhaps compensated by a tendency to bind the letters.

Concerning spacing between lines, its increase is accompanied by a fall of available resources and by a greater self-concern. It should be noted that *EA* and *Ego* are not correlated within our sample. Spacing between lines would be an indication of self-centeredness at the cost of the adaptive resources of the individual. We have also discussed the link between spacing between lines and the emergence of cognitive failures. Reduced spacing would, hus, be an indication of better adaptive resources.

These results bring us to certain findings: (a) graphologists' judgments show a relative, but weak consensus, (b) relevant graphologists' predictions of Rorschach variables exist but are rare, (c) correlations exist between certain handwriting variables and Rorschach variables, (d) only three of these correlations are compatible with existing graphological theories, and (e) other correlations are the result of chance or difficult to understand.

The results of this study are more favorable to graphology than those trying to bring graphology closer to the variables of self-report questionnaires (Furnham et al., 2003; Thiry, 2008). Graphology does not seem to adequately predict variables of the five-factor model. Rorschach variables, however, seem closer to the graphological variables, although the link between these two types of variables remains weak and/or obscure. Our results do not allow us to support the idea that graphology assesses personality the way Rorschach tests do.

This study has certain weaknesses that should be underlined. First, the relatively small sample mainly consists of prisoners. Consequently, it is not representative of the general population and can be the source of unexpected results. Second, we decided to keep the Rorschach protocols with less than 14 answers, reducing the reliability of some Rorschach variables (Exner, Viglione, & Gillespie, 1984). Third, the reduction of the number of Rorschach variables to 13 and their analytical use largely reduce the complex approach of this test. Fourth, the use of regression equations presents a logical problem: Graphologists predict personality based on handwriting but, actually, it is personality that could influence handwriting. The cause and the effect are reversed. The linear models suggested here reflect this ambiguity. Nevertheless, we share our results because they are rare in the current scientific literature. To our knowledge, handwriting variables have never been compared with the Rorschach variables of the comprehensive system. Replication research is necessary.

References

Ajuriaguerra de, J., Auzias, M., Coumes, F., Denner, A., Lavondes-Monod, V., Perron, R. et al. (1956). *L'écriture de l'enfant, tome I* [Handwriting of the child vol 1?]. Lausanne: Delachaux et Niestlé.

Anderson, H., & Anderson, G. (1951). *An introduction to projective techniques.* New York: Prentice Hall, Inc.

Anzieu, D. (1991). Test projectif [projective test]. In R. Doron & F. Parot (Eds.), *Dictionnaire de psychologie* [Psychology dictionary] (p. 682). Paris: PUF.

Asp, T., Yalon, D., & Turk, B. (2004). Poor handwriting as a psychological problem – a summary of a Finnish Ph.D. thesis by Paivi Onionen, 1960. *Global Graphology, 1,* 84–89.

Backman, B. (2001). *Graphology in America.* Retrieved September 8, 2008 from http://www.graphology.ws/2169-graphology-america.htm.

Belin, C.J., & Aubert, M.F. (1989). La personnalité des violeurs au travers d'expertises psychologiques et d'examens graphologiques [Personality of rapists through psychological and graphological assessments]. *Psychologie Médicale, 21*(1), 73–75.

Bergeret, J. (1974). *La personnalité normale et pathologique* [Normal and pathological personality]. Paris: Editions Dunod.

Beyerstein, L.B., & Beyerstein, D.F. (1992). *The write stuff. Evaluations of graphology. The study of handwriting analysis.* New York: Promotheus Books.

Binet, A. (1906). *La graphologie. Les révélations de l'écriture d'après un contrôle scientifique* [Graphology: Revelations of the handwriting following a scientific controle]. Paris: L'Harmattan.

Bruchon-Schweitzer, M. & Lievens, S. (1991). Le recrutement en Europe. Recherches et pratiques [Recruitment in Europe. Research and practices]. *Psychologie et Psychométrie, 12,* 7–71.

Castelnuovo-Tedesco, P. (1948). A study of the relationship between handwriting and personality variables. *Genetic Psychology Monographs, 37,* 167–220.

Costa, P.T., & McCrae, R.R. (1985). *The NEO personality inventory manual.* Odessa, FL: Psychological Assessment Resources.

Crépieux-Jamin, J. (1889). *L'écriture et le caractère* [Handwriting and character]. Paris: PUF. (1951 14ème éd.).

Crépieux-Jamin, J. (1930). *ABC de graphologie.* Paris: PUF.

Crumbaugh, J.C., & Stockholm, E. (1977). Validation of graphoanalysis by "global" or "holistic" method. *Perceptual and Motor Skills, 44,* 403–410.

Dean, G.A. (1992). The bottom line: Effect size. In L.B. Beyerstein & D.F. Beyerstein (Eds.), *The write stuff. Evaluations of graphology. The study of handwriting analysis* (pp. 329–341). New York: Promotheus Books.

Delamain, M. (1949). Réflexion sur l'intuition [Discussion about intuition]. *La Graphologie, 35,* 9–11.

Demarche, A. (1982). *Graphologie et structure de personnalité. Etude comparative en vue de dégager des profils graphométriques spécifiques des grandes structures de personnalité* [Graphology and personality structure. Comparative study in order to draw graphometric patterns related to major personality structures]. Unpublished manuscript, Institut de Psychologie et des Sciences de l'Education, Université de Liège.

Exner, J.E. (1982). *The Rorschach: A comprehensive system.* New York: Wiley.

Exner, J.E. (1996). *Manuel de cotation du Rorschach pour le système intégré* [A Rorschach workbook for the comprehensive system] (2nd ed.). Paris: Edition Frison-Roche.

Exner, J.E., Viglione, D., & Gillespie, R. (1984). Relationships between Rorschach variables as relevant to the interpretation of structural data. *Journal of Personality Assessment, 48*, 65–70.

Fluckiger, F., Tripp, C., & Weinberg, G. (1961). A review of experimental research in graphology, 1933–1960. *Perceptual and Motor Skills, 12*, 67–90.

Furnham, A., Chamorro-Premuzic, T., & Callahan, I. (2003). Does graphology predict personality and intelligence? *Individual Differences Research, 1*(2), 78–94.

Gacono, C.B., Meloy, J.R., & Bridges, M.R. (2000). A Rorschach comparison of psychopaths, sexual homicide perpetrators, and nonviolent pedophiles: where angles fear to tread. *Journal of Clinical Psychology, 56*, 757–777.

Gilbert, P., & Chardon, C. (1989). *Analyser l'écriture* [Analyzing handwriting]. Formation permanente en sciences humaines, ESF Editeur. Paris: Entreprises moderne d'édition.

de Gobineau, H., & Perron, R. (1954). *Génétique de l'écriture et étude de la personnalité* [Genetic of the handwriting and study of the personality]. Lausanne: Delachaux et Niestlé.

Hull, C.L., & Montgomery, R.P. (1919). Experimental investigation of certain alleged relations between character and handwriting. *Psychological Review, 26*, 63–74.

Huteau, M. (2004). *Écriture et personnalité. Approche critique de la graphologie* [Handwriting and personality. Critical approach of graphology]. Paris: Dunod.

Lemke, E.A., & Kirchner, J.H. (1971). A multivariate study of handwriting, intelligence, and personality correlates. *Journal of Personality Assessment, 35*, 584–592.

Lockowandt, O. (1992). The present status of research on handwriting psychology as a diagnostic method. In L.B. Beyerstein & D.F. Beyerstein (Eds.), *The write stuff. Evaluations of graphology. The study of handwriting analysis* (pp. 55–85). New York: Promotheus.

Mandeville, R.G., Peeples, E.E., & Stutler, D.L. (1990). Students' involvement as indicated by personality and graphological factors. *Perceptual and Motor Skills, 71*, 1359–1363.

Mandeville, R.G., Peeples, E.E., & Stutler, D.L. (1992). Students' rating of college services and their scores on handwriting areas. *Perceptual and Motor Skills, 75*, 1227–1232.

Meyer, G.J., & Archer, R.P. (2001). The hard science of Rorschach research: What do we know and where do we go? *Psychological Assessment, 13*, 486–502.

Michaux-Granier, C., Vrignaud, P., & Ohayon, T. (1999). Validité factorielle de la graphologie. Une étude exploratoire [Factorial validity of graphology. An exploratory study]. In M. Huteau & J. Lautrey (Eds.), *Approches différentielles en psychologie* [Differential approaches in psychology] (pp. 309–314). Paris: PUF.

Nevo, B. (1986). Reliability of graphology: A survey of the literature. In B. Nevo (Ed.), *Scientific aspects of graphology*. Springfield, IL: CC Thomas.

Oinonen, P. (1960). *Huono käsiala psykologisena ongelmana – kansakoululapisilla suoritettu tutkimus* [Poor handwriting as a psychological problem – An investigation carried out among primary school chlidren – in Finnish]. Doctoral thesis, University of Jyväskylä, Finland: Acta academiae pedagogicae Jyväskyläensis XXI.

Petot, J.-M. (2004). Le modèle de personnalité en cinq facteurs et le test de Rorschach [The five-factor model and the Rorschach test]. *Psychologie Française, 49*, 81–94.

Peugeot, J., Lombard, A., & de Noblens, M. (1986). *Manuel de graphologie* [Handbook of graphology]. Paris: Editions Masson.

Stein Lewinson, T. (1961). The use of handwriting analysis as a psychodiagnostic technique. *Journal of Projective Techniques, 25*, 315–329.

Stein Lewinson, T. (1991). Comment on an article by Mandeville, Peeples, and Stutler. *Perceptual and Motor Skills, 72*, 742.

Tett, R.P., & Palmer, C.A., 1997. The validity of handwriting elements in relation to self-report personality trait measures. *Personality and Individual Differences, 22*, 11–18.

Thiry, B. (2008). Graphologie et personnalité selon le modèle en cinq facteurs [Graphology and the five-factor model]. *Psychologie Française, 53*, 399–410.

Zulliger, H. (1957). *Le test Z collectif* [The collective Z test]. Paris: PUF.

Benjamin Thiry
Faculté de Psychologie et des Sciences de l'Education
Place du Cardinal Mercier 10
B-1348 Louvain-la-Neuve
Belgium
Fax +32 2 349-7563
E-mail benjamin.thiry@just.fgov.be

Appendix A

Slant of the letters. Five words are measured: the first word from the first line, the last word from the first line, a word in the middle of the text, the first word of the last line, and the last word of the last line. The first two letters of each word are considered. The prolongation of each letter is drawn. A protractor is used to evaluate the angle formed by this line with the base of the word. Letters that are exactly vertical form an angle of 90° with the base of the word. The letters slanting to the right have an angle greater than 90° and the left slanted writings have an angle that is less than 90°.

Slope of the lines. The angle is measured for all the lines of the text by means of a transparent sheet of A4 format placed on the white sheet in a parallel manner. The cross is placed at the base of the first letter of each line. The end of the last letter represents the end of the line. The position of this "final point" is evaluated by the angle that it forms with a horizontal line.

Spacing between words. Four lines are measured: the second line, the fourth line, the fourth line before the end, and the penultimate line. Spaces between all the words are measured (.1 mm). An average is then calculated based on all these measurements.

Spacing between lines. Using a graduated ruler, the distance between the base of the first letter of each line and the base of the first letter of the following line is measured. This measurement is repeated for all spaces between two lines.

Average height of the middle zone. The height of three letters in five zones of each handwriting is measured using a graduated magnifying glass (.1 mm): at the top on the left, at the top on the right, in the central part, at the bottom on the left, and at the bottom on the right. The average is then calculated. The measured letters must be the first three (in the left and central zones) or the last three (for the zones on right-hand sides).

Average height of the lower extensions. Fifteen jambs are measured: five jambs starting from the 2nd line, five jambs starting from the line at the middle of the text, five jambs starting from the penultimate line (if the two last lines contain less than five jambs, measure jambs of the preceding lines). The distance from the lower edge of the jamb to the baseline of the handwriting is measured using a graduated magnifying glass. Respect the slope of the letter. Measurements are made to .1 mm.

Average height of the higher extensions. Fifteen poles are measured: five poles starting from the 2nd line, five poles starting from the line at the middle of the text, five poles starting from the penultimate line (if the two last lines contain less than five buckled poles, measure poles of the preceding lines). Using a graduated magnifying glass, the distance that separates the top of the pole from the baseline of the handwriting is measured. Respect the slope of the letter. Measurements are made to .1 mm.

Average width of letters. The width of all the words of the fourth line and line n-4 are measured, which are divided, each time, by the number of letters constituting the words.

Left margin. The distance between the left edge of the sheet and the first written mark of each line of the text is measured with a graduated ruler. It is important that subparagraph lines not be measured.

Right margin. The distance between the right edge of the sheet and the last written mark of each line of the text is measured with a graduated ruler. If a sentence finishes at the beginning or at the end of the line and is accompanied by one return to the line, the distance between the last word and the flat rim of the page can be important. This is likely to cause a skew of measurement. Consequently, do not measure the right margin for the ends of "paragraphs."

*Top margin.*The distance between the higher edge of the sheet and the base of the first traced letter is measured with a graduated ruler. Make only one measurement per writing.

Appendix B

Available resources *EA*	Effectiveness of mental activity. Capacity of the individual to control his behavior. Capacity to adequately address day-to-day problems. Tolerance of stress.
Tendency to simplify reality *L*	Natural way to treat stimuli at a simple and economic level. Psychological tactic that consists in being unaware of the complexity and/or the ambiguity of a field, even when these aspects have been perceived. Only basic or obvious aspects of the field are considered. "Avoiding" style.
Emotional control *FC: CF + C*	Expression of emotions is modulated or reduced. Discretion of feelings. Greater "coldness."
Interest in emotional stimuli *Afr*	Interest in emotional stimuli or environments. The subject seeks emotional situations.
Cognitive processing *Zd*	Effectiveness of scanning activity during operations of data processing. Need to process data in an exhaustive way. Meticulous approach to the surrounding world (incorporation).
Inclination toward banality *P*	Tendency to adopt obvious, awaited, and socially admitted behaviors. Capacity to act like everybody else. Unusual concern for conventions or correction.
Conventional thought *X+%*	Subjective thought is reduced in favor of conventionality. Thoughts adhere to a certain social consensus. Individuality is sacrificed.
Thought disturbance *Wsum6*	Difficulties in conceptual thought. Thoughts are not clear to others. The thread of thought is disturbed by odd and very personal phenomenon. Erroneous judgments.
Self-concern *Ego*	Attention paid to oneself (positive or negative). This narcissistic concern can lead to withdrawal from the external world.
Introspection *FD + SumV*	Capacity to examine oneself, to become aware of internal phenomena. Capacity to question oneself. Can be painful.
Negative self-image *MOR*	Self-image includes negative impressions or characteristics that the subject resents. Feeling of failure. Disappointments. Pessimism.
Interest in others *SumH*	Interest in people. Subject regards others as equals. Search for social interactions.

Summary

Since its official birth in 1872, graphology has claimed to assess the whole personality by looking at one's handwriting. Its basic postulate is that the characteristics of the handwriting are the reflection of conscious and unconscious dynamics that are expressed according to a law of analogy (Delamain, 1949). To date, empirical research has not supported the graphological claims. Recent studies (Furnham, Chamorro-Premuzic, Callahan, 2003; Thiry, 2008) have shown that the graphological variables are independent of the five-factor model (FFM) variables. Graphologists (e.g., Stein Lewinson, 1991), answer that graphology is a projective technique and must not be compared to self-reported inventory variables. In our study, we take this point into account and compare graphological variables with the Rorschach test variables, which is currently the most used and validated projective test. We asked 45 people to write a free text containing no personal information. Our sample was composed of 14 voluntary participants and 31 imprisoned people who were tested for a psychological assessment. These 45 people took the Rorschach test. Passing and protocol noting followed Exner's instructions (1996). The 45 handwritten texts were independently evaluated by two graphologists. These graphologists evaluated (from 0 *absence* to 5 *very present*) 13 variables directly inspired by the comprehensive system (e.g., available resources). The mean reliability of these 13 judgments for both graphologists was .43. The mean validity of these 13 judgments with the Rorschach test variable was .05. This validity can be described as very weak and does not support the exhaustive claims of graphology.

Only one type of judgment produced by the graphologists was significantly reliable ($r_2 = .32$) and valid ($r_s = .30$): that relating to X+%. The graphologists seemed to be able to evaluate thought conventionality from the handwriting. Handwriting, by definition, is a meditational activity because it requires a consensual activity and allows the sharing of ideas.

Beyond the qualitative judgments carried out by the graphologists, we measured certain handwriting characteristics with a sufficiently reliable method (Thiry, 2008). The slant of the handwriting would be linked ($R = -.33$) to emotional discharge. The more tilted to the right the handwriting, the more the emotions tend to be released without control. The reduction of the right margin and of the space between the lines allows a certain prediction ($R = .41$) of the emergence of cognitive failures Rorschach (WSum6). Graphologists classically interpret these graphic characteristics as lack of anticipation and distance indices. However, the link between the WSum6 and these two variables requires additional study.

These results are interesting; nevertheless, in the best case, they only explain 17% of the variance, which remains low. This may be the result of sampling biases (small sample and presence of many inmates). They do not support the claim that graphology is an assessment technique similar to the Rorschach test.

Résumé

Depuis sa naissance officielle en 1872, la graphologie affirme pouvoir cerner de manière exhaustive la personnalité profonde d'une personne base de son écriture. Son postulat de base est que les caractéristiques de l'écriture sont le reflet de dynamiques conscientes et inconscientes qui s'extériorisent selon une loi d'analogie (Delamain, 1949). Jusqu'à présent, les recherches empiriques solides sur le plan méthodologique ne soutiennent pas les ambitions graphologiques. Des études récentes (Furnham, Chamorro-Premuzic, Callahan, 2003; Thiry, 2008) invitent à penser que les variables graphologiques sont indépendantes des traits de personnalité du modèle en cinq facteurs. Les graphologues (e.g., Stein Lewinson, 1991), répondent que la graphologie est une technique projective et ne doit donc pas être comparée à des variables issues de questionnaires auto-rapportés. Dans le cadre de notre étude, nous tenons compte de cet argument et comparons des variables graphologiques avec des variables du test de Rorschach, qui est l'épreuve projective la plus utilisée et validée actuellement.

Nous avons demandé à 45 personnes d'écrire un texte libre ne contenant pas d'informations personnelles. Notre échantillon se compose de 14 participants volontaires et de 31 personnes incarcérées qui furent testées dans le cadre d'une évaluation psychologique. Nous avons administré le test de Rorschach à ces 45 personnes en respectant la méthodologie du système intégré d'Exner. Les 45 textes manuscrits furent évalués par 2 graphologues de manière indépendante. Ces graphologues devaient évaluer de 0 *absence* à 5 *très présent* 13 variables directement inspirées du système intégré (par exemple: ressources disponibles). La fiabilité moyenne de ces 13 jugements pour les 2 graphologues est égale à .43. La validité moyenne de ces 13 jugements avec la variable correspondante au test de Rorschach est égale à .05. Cette validité peut être qualifié de très faible et ne rejoint pas les prétentions exhaustives de la graphologie.

Un seul type de jugement produit par les graphologues est significativement fiable (r_2 = .32) et valide (r_s = .30): celui relatif au X+%. Les graphologues semblent capables d'évaluer la conventionalité de la pensée par le biais de l'écriture. L'écriture, par définition est une activité de type médiationnel car elle est par définition consensuelle et permet le partage d'idées.

Au-delà des jugements qualitatifs effectués par les graphologues, nous avons mesuré certaines caractéristiques des écritures manuscrites à l'aide d'une méthode suffisamment fiable (Thiry, 2008).

L'inclinaison de l'écriture serait liée (R = −.33) avec la décharge émotionnelle. Plus l'écriture est inclinée vers la droite, plus la décharge affective serait grande. La réduction de la marge de droite et de l'espace interlignes permet une certaine prédiction (R = .41) de l'émergence de ratés cognitifs au Rorschach (WSum6). Les graphologues interprètent classiquement ces caractéristiques graphiques comme des indices de manque d'anticipation et de manque de recul face aux événements. Cependant le lien entre le WSum6 et ces deux caractéristiques psychologiques devrait encore être clairement approfondi.

Ces résultats sont intéressants et méritent que l'on s'y intérèse. Ils ne permettent toutefois, dans le meilleur des cas, de n'expliquer que 17% de la variance, ce qui reste peu.

Ils sont peut-être le fruit d'un biais d'échantillonnage dû au faible effectif (n = 45) et à la surreprésentation de personnes incarcérées. Ils ne permettent pas d'affirmer que la graphologie est une technique d'évaluation de la personnalité similaire au test de Rorschach.

Resumen

Desde su nacimiento oficial en 1872, la Grafología trata de evaluar la personalidad basándose en la escritura individual. Su postulado básico es que las características de la escritura a mano son un reflejo de la dinámica consciente e inconsciente y que se expresan siguiendo una ley de analogía (Delamain, 1949). Hasta ahora, las investigaciones empíricas no han podido demostrar estas afirmaciones. Recientes estudios (Furnham, Chamorro-Premuzic, Callahan, 2003; Thiry, 2008) han demostrado que las variables grafológicas son independientes de las variables descritas en el Modelo de los Cinco Factores (FFM). Los grafólogos

(Stein Lewinson, 1991), responden que la Grafología es una técnica proyectiva y no debe compararse con variables de inventarios o autoinformes. En nuestro estudio, tuvimos en cuenta estos aspectos y comparamos ciertas variables grafológicas con variables del Test de Rorschach, que es actualmente el test proyectivo más usado y validado. Solicitamos a 45 personas que escribieran un texto libre que no incluyera información personal. Nuestra muestra estuvo compuesta por 14 participantes voluntarios y 31 personas que cumplían condena en una prisión y de las que se había solicitado una evaluación psicológica. A estos 45 sujetos también se les administró el test de Rorschach, siguiendo las instrucciones de Exner (1996). Los 45 textos escritos a mano fueron evaluados por 2 grafólogos de manera independiente. Estos expertos valoraban en una escala de 0 (ausencia) a 5 (muy presente) la aparición de las 13 variables directamente inspiradas por el Sistema Comprehensivo (p.e. recursos disponibles). La fiabilidad media para esos 13 juicios de los 2 grafólogos fue de .43. La validez media de esos 13 juicios con las variables del test de Rorschach fue de .05. Esta validez puede entenderse como bastante débil y no apoya los postulados básicos de la Grafología.

Sólo un tipo de juicio generado por los grafólogos apareció como significativamente fiable (r2 = .32) y válido (rs = .30): el relativo a X+%. Los grafólogos parecieron muy capaces de evaluar el grado de convencionalidad a través de la escritura. La escritura a mano, por definición, es una actividad mediacional porque requiere una ejecución consensuada y permite compartir ideas.

A través de los juicios subjetivos elaborados por los grafólogos, se pueden medir algunas características de la escritura de manera aceptablemente fiable (Thiry, 2008). La inclinación de la escritura puede vincularse (R = –.33) con el tipo de descarga emocional. Cuanto más se inclina a la derecha, más se tiende a dejar las emociones fuera de control. La reducción del margen derecho y del espacio entre las líneas, permite hacer una predicción (R = .41) sobre la aparición de fallos cognitivos en Rorschach (WSum6). Los grafólogos interpretaron clásicamente estas características como índices de distancia y falta de anticipación. Sin embargo, la relación entre WSum6 y estas dos variables requiere otros estudios.

Estos resultados son interesantes y permiten mantener el interés por este tema. No obstante, en el mejor de los casos, sólo explican un 17% de la varianza, lo que resulta insuficiente. Quizá han influído los sesgos de la muestra (número pequeño y presencia de muchos presos). De momento, no parece apoyarse el supuesto de que la Grafología sea un método de evaluación semejante al test de Rorschach.

1972年の正式な誕生以来、筆跡学は筆跡を見ることによってパーソナリティ全体に接近することを主張している。その基本的な仮定は、筆跡の特性は、類似性の法則によって表現される意識的および無意識的力動の反映ということである（Delamain,1949）。現在まで、実証的な研究は筆跡学の主張を支持していない。近年の研究（Furnham, Chamorro-Permuzic, Callahan,2003;Thiry,2008）においては筆跡学の変数は5因子モデル（FFV）の変数と関連がないことを示している。筆跡学者（例えば、Stein Lewinson, 1991）は、筆跡学は投映技法であり、自己報告のインベントリーの変数と比較されるべきではないと反論している。我々の研究では、この点を考慮に入れて筆跡学の変数を、現在最もよく使われており妥当性が認められているロールシャッハテストの変数と比較した。我々は45名に個人的な情報を含まない自由な文を手書きするように求めた。我々のサンプルは14名のボランティアの研究協力者と31名の心理学的なアセスメントのためにテストを受けた収監された人々から構成されている。これらの45名はロールシャッハテストを施行されている。施行とプロトコルの記録はエクスナー（1996）の教示によっている。45の手書き文は2名の筆跡学者によって別個に評価された。筆跡学者は包括システムから直接もたらされた13の変数（例えば、利用可能な資源）について、0（ない）から5（とてもある）の評価をおこなった。二人の筆跡学者のこれら13変数に関する信頼性の平均は.43であった。また、ロールシャッハテストの諸変数に関するこれら13の変数の妥当性の平均は.05であった。この妥当性は大変低いものであり、筆跡学者の徹底した主張を支持しない。

筆跡学者によってなされたわずかにひとつのタイプの判定は有意な信頼性（r2=.32）と妥当性（rs=.30）があり、それはX+%と関連していた。筆跡学者は筆跡により思考の慣習性を評価することが可能なようである。手書きは共感的活動を必要とし、観念の共有を許容するので、明らかに思考過程である。筆跡学者によってなされた質的判断を超えて、我々は十分に信頼のおける方法（Thirty,2008）をもちいて確かな手書きの特徴を測定した。筆跡の傾斜は情緒的な解放と関連している可能性がある（R=-.33）。筆跡が右に傾けば傾くほど、情緒はより統制を失って解放される。右側の余白と行間のスペースの減少はロールシャッハの認知的失敗（WSum6）の出現をある程度予測する（R=.41）。筆跡学者は伝統的にこれらの文字の特徴を見通しが欠如している、そして距離の指標が欠如していると解釈する。しかしながら、WSum6とこれらの二つの変数との関連には別の研究が必要である。

これらの結果は興味深いものであり、関心を向けられる価値のあるものである。しかしながら、これはせいぜい分散の17%を説明するに過ぎない。おそらくサンプリングの偏りによる問題（サンプル数が少ないことと多くの収監者が入っていること）も存在するであろう。筆跡学はロールシャッハテストと類似したアセスメント技法であるという主張は本研究によっては支持されていない。

Rorschachiana 30, 48–72
DOI: 10.1027/1192-5604.30.1.48

The Logical Axis in the Rorschach

A Study on Alternative Ways of Organizing the Sensory Universe

Etel Schvartzapel de Kacero

Universidad del Salvador (USAL), Buenos Aires, Argentina

Abstract. The paradigm of complexity that rules the current conception of knowledge proposes to observe and understand reality through multiple perspectives. This paradigm emphasizes relations and interactions, leading us to pay special attention to transformations that take place over time. These concepts are particularly valid when reading a subject's Rorschach productions, inasmuch as the goal is to make visible psychic motions, modalities thereof, as well as the subject's defense strategies and effectiveness. After having analyzed the spatial, temporal, and bonding perspectives elsewhere, as well as the linguistic resources used in responses, the author focuses in this paper on the logical axis, trying to show subjects' prevailing codes for attributing meaning and significance to the realities they are seeing. An attempt is made to find out the rules constraining subjects to see and think in a certain way, thus, determining their behavior. From this angle, the goal lies in making plain the problems that subjects have regarding each plate-specific configuration, the way and words they resort to when rationalizing their responses, and the kind of solutions they reach.

Keywords: paradigm of complexity, logical axis, cognitive affective patterns, thought, significance, behavior

Introduction

This paper is an outcome of ideas developed by the paradigm of complexity (Morin, 1994), born out of the quantum physics discoveries during the 1960s, when Heisenberg made public his formulation of "indeterminacy" relations. At the beginning of the 20th century, Einstein had already stated that knowledge about any material phenomenon depends on the observer's viewpoint. New perspectives on "knowing knowledge" have since emerged in many different branches of learning: philosophy, epistemology, cognitive science, neurophysiology, etc. All these views point to the multiple dimensions of knowledge, and there is no privileged perspective. Complexity emphasizes links, articulations, interaction, and the effect of irreversible time. Articulation of factors is organized through *processes* linked to each other both in serial (successive) networks and in parallel, and give rise to *emergent* properties or products just because of their multiple interactions with environment and context.

In our case, subjects' contact with the Rorschach plates connect them directly with a sensory universe; Rorschach images are not representations of things: instead, they provide marks that each subject will organize according to his/her own recognizing codes. In turn, such codes are the result of a particular interweaving of each subject's own body experiences, bonds, and values with the cultural codes.

As Hermann Rorschach (1964) stated, the test is based on perception. The perceptual process not only encodes data, it also gives birth to an order – the order the representation system developed by subjects makes possible. I would like to express my support to Debray's (1994) expression: "To look at is not to receive: it is to put in order what is visible, to organize what has been experienced."

Once a given subject has looked at the different visual structures of Rorschach plates, the subject gives a verbal response. So, his/her constructions allow us to observe the processes and transformations that have taken place. Either those constructions or organizations show us the articulation modes, the grades of stability achieved, the points wherein the subject has paused, what aspects he/she has either made visible or needed to leave aside. In sum, we are shown the different forms of rationality every subject resorts to when looking at the plates.

Conditions for a Sound Knowledge in Psychology from the Complexity Point of View

In the field of psychology, we are allowed to build complex skills out of diverse sources of information, taking into account at the same time each subject's history, his/her organizing epistemologies, and bonding modalities.

49

The multifaceted perspective presented by the complexity paradigm is only possible if Rorschach researchers are open to types of knowledge likely to widen their observation field. As far as I am concerned, when it comes to the present paper, I have been influenced by
- Psychoanalysis, when it comes to paying attention to dynamic processes and interactions;
- A concept proposed by Eco (1997), according to which there exists a mutual feedback between perception and knowledge, while, at the same time the role of language in these processes has to be taken into account (Eco, 1997);
- Logic (Minkowska, 1978; Husain., Merceron, &, Rossel,. 2001; Rebourg, 2001, Barthélémy, 1987; Ducrot, 1986; Searle, 1980; Austin, 1998
- Image semiotics (Groupe μ, 1993, Vilches, 1983).

A Device for Knowledge: Axes

On the basis of the foregoing, and from the above mentioned fundamentals, I suggest the use of a tool that is apt at allowing the multifaceted perspective as well as considering psychical dimensions at the same time. This tool is based on the construction of what I have named *axes*.

Axes are angles of vision offering a Rorschach researcher "lenses" with which they can identify typical features of subjects' psychical constitution, the way they operate as well as the way they relate to other people.

So, each axis would represent a reading performed from a focalization; thus, an observation vertex could be constituted for generating hypotheses related to any aspect in question, inasmuch as the axis brings out a subject's *functioning lines*. Those functioning lines are likely to be observed when subjects utilize their spatial, temporal articulations, the causality modes they resort to, as well as the way they make links, and the way they have to put thoughts into words by means of discourse while they are interpreting a card. A different dimension of mental functioning is taken into account by each axis and this allows us to observe whether transformation occurs, whether a fixation or variation occurs in the dimension, whether articulations achieved follow a direction more or less evolved, as well as integrated. Thus, a more precise mapping of mental functioning can be obtained.

To date, I have studied the bounding (Kacero, 1993), the spatial (Kacero, 1996), the temporal (Kacero, 1999), the discursive (Kacero, 2009), and the logical axes. In this paper, I am going to explore this last axis.

We temporally refrain from analyzing and encoding the end product – namely, the response – and, instead, we pay attention to the implicit processes of construction, of "gestation " The mind can be seen as a working device that classifies, combines, and internalizes experiences and affects – that is, a set of *information transformation* processes. This is a sort of *metabolizing* work, within which data, as such, is remodeled (Aulagnier, 1975).

The Logical Axis

In perceiving and acting[1] – that is, in giving a response – subjects enforce an order on the visual structure of the Rorschach plate: They give it a *form* and a *meaning,* turning it semiotic through different strategies, such as:
– emphasizing or neutralizing contrasts;
– creating or reinforcing contours;
– equating or differentiating fields;
– ignoring or exaggerating some areas.

This is not a random process; rather, it depends on the conditions of each plate (open, compact, scattered, colored, nuanced, etc.) and on how they affect the psychical organization.

It should be noted that while some features have "objective" characteristics, their grouping in structural units is based on the way the mind metabolizes them. In this regard, some studies have shown the importance of limits and, even more, of angles (Noton & Stark, 1971). Exner (1998) has also investigated how small visual-information components have a critical value in the choice of responses. Choice, rejection, and/or neutralization of some visual characteristics are determined by subjects' experience, needs, wishes, and defenses.

If we consider Rorschach visual structures as signs to be interpreted, a "reader" will have his/her own way of organizing reality, and will prefer certain mechanisms to perceive reality. Thus, logical forms would be models for bestowing meaning.

---

1   I hereby take the concept of language pragmatics that considers language as a form of action that is known as *acts of speech.*

51

E. Schvartzapel de Kacero

Any attempt at studying the logical dimension in Rorschach productions is aimed at demonstrating subjects' organizing perspective of the world and reality, making both visible in subjects' enunciation acts. The way we think is crucial; it could be said that an interplay of relations is generated between data, describing and manifesting perception patterns, giving rise to different approaches on actual situations, and interpreting diverse circumstances, so that several lines of action are likely to be either activated or inhibited. The logic operating within each individual leads to decisions and affective experience, and privileges certain contents.

Discourse analysis is one way of accessing the subject's perspective on reality and is based on the idea that at the root of the production of any sentence there is an unseen logic that attests to the underlying production rules present within the individual who makes the statement.

Every discourse implies relations that follow these rules, though they may be unknown to the subject. Discourse analysis helps to make explicit how the subject perceives reality.

The viewpoint from which we interpret a subjects' production is based on the conviction that their statements and attributed meanings depend on inner laws or codes that constitute conditioning factors that are apt at fostering a resolution mode. Should it be possible for us to make those ordering patterns explicit, we could be in a position to give a Rorschach researcher – through his/her own recognizing codes– some basic, specific standards as to how subjects organize experience and acquired skills, what their investments are, what the patterns are that guide their way of looking, as well as other patterns that are likely to be missing (Castoriadis, 1998).

Establishing different classes of significance could pertain to archaic ways stopped somewhere in time, or evidence more complex and evolved forms. Significance can be either fixed or flexible; it can appeal to sensory, actual, rational, or abstract signifiers. It may cover several aspects or just one. It may take outer references as a guarantee, or operate with its own referents without resorting to reality testing.

In my opinion, the kind of verisimilitude enacted by subjects, the kind of causes they resort to so that their responses are *justified* gives account of:
– The structural dynamics of their psychical functioning,
– What aspects of the object are central in their perception or how these aspects organize subjects' perception, and which references subjects privilege,

– What other aspects are either ignored by subjects or what other aspects subjects find difficult to deal with or explain,
– Whether subjects adjust their perceptions to either the principle of reality or the pleasure principle, and at what point on the continuum between both principles the subjects are located.
– What are the classes, properties, and relationships that might limit thinking or determine their ways of solving problems.

Possible Alternative Ways for Ordering the Sensory Universe of Rorschach Plates

The following examples are from subjects observed in various clinical settings.

Using the *Analogical Code*

This type of response is when subjects say "it seems . . .," "this is similar to . . . ." This implies a reference to images including the basic, structural characteristics of the plate.

No analogy is identical to the object. Analogy is based on establishing a relationship between the spatial proportions of the plate's visual structure and proportions of the object involved. Considering a Rorschach plate as an iconic sign, analogy implies that, in Peirce's opinion (quoted by Eco,1986, p. 234) is "a relationship model homologue to the perceptual relationship model we construct when getting in touch with and remembering a given object." The iconic sign properties are not shared with any object involved but with the perceptive model of the object. An iconic sign may be similar to the object in its optical (visible), ontological (presumptive), or conventional properties (Eco, 1986, p. 228).

A case in which optical properties prevail is when a subject says, with respect to the D black inferior of Plate III, "Ovaries, they have the rounded form of ovaries, like small beans." If the aspect that is considered to be similar refers to ontological properties, subject would have said: "They are like ovaries, those parts of a woman's reproductive system where eggs grow." However, should similarity be determined by a conventional encoding, subject could have said: "These are ovaries, because there are two of them, just like in the female sexual organ."

53

Conventional encoding is very clear in the response: "a small lake" to the central green area on Plate VIII, since in every map lakes are drawn that way.

However, analogy or similarity may be construed not only based on shapes but also on qualities, function, movement, and state. It should be stressed that no analogy is identical to the reference object as a mirror-like image: Such a large variety of responses is obtained because new analogies are always expected.

Causality as a Determinant

Responses that contain a syllogism structure, and an irrefutable conclusion:

> Plate I: "Eagles raising dust when leaving the ground; dust is raised *because* when birds take off they rustle the air, and the air rustles the soil."
>
> Plate II: "A buffalo running ahead with its head down, *implying* a rapid movement."

Insistence on the cause-consequence process is so strong that it neutralizes the intense motion in the content. This is because the subject's whole value system, linked to some logical preferences, gets in the way of how meaning is attributed. Causality is substituted for a story. Such an intention appears clearly in the following response to Plate VI: "An asparagus with sauce. When I *thought* about an asparagus (Dd), I *thought* that this (side thing) could be some sauce. And seeing spilled sauce that *gave me the idea* of an explosion."

Emphasis Placed on Relations of Correspondence, Enumeration, and Measurement

Here, action is reduced to a logical-mathematical operation implying a distance relationship with little or no emotional involvement. This is a type of organization of the sensory world wherein different, heterogeneous, qualitative components do not matter. *Frequencies* do matter – that is, those periods from which symbolic equivalences are spun. A numerical world substitutes for the symbolic one (Maldavsky, 1997) so that numbers come to represent a perceptual universe understood as a series of frequencies. However, with a fixed point of anchorage, the perception of more complex links is interfered with.

Plate I: "There are four people, two in the middle and two at sides."
Plate I: "I see four little ghosts" (white spaces).

The emphasis is on a quality-free universe. Let us remember that qualities make for differences. Thus, a speculative, numerical way of thinking prevails and, hence, symbolic-emotional components are not seen.

The degradation of what is alive, what promotes diversity, could lead to psychic inertia. Some homogenizing peace is achieved at the price of trivializing differences. The same effect is pursued through the well-known phenomenon of perseveration.

The *isonomy* concept is applicable here. This concept implies organizing the world through coherent relations ruled by numerical correspondences so that equality, symmetry, and reciprocity relationships can be established, thus, constructing a *cosmos*, a seemingly homogeneous universe with no hierarchies, neither positive nor negative investments; a world in which there are neither levels nor any differentiation.

It is a well-known fact that among psychosomatic patients the missing symbolic world is replaced by a numerical world, and that the number (that is, frequency) has a greater value for patients than any other specific sensory quality (Maldavsky, 1994). However, it should also be emphasized that counting is a way to look for coherence, to formalize the sensory matter. Therefore, underlining at what frequency things appear might have a double value: On the one hand, this process points out either the avoidance or lack of development of the "quality" register. On the other hand, however, this process reveals an attempt to overcome a state of greater psychic helplessness.

As can be seen in subjects responding to the Rorschach instructions, the notion of similarity is always present. This aspect is likely to be given by a material, numerical, or purely conventional analogy, and also through a comparison (by either coexistence, remembrance, or confrontation).

"Semanticization" from Contiguity Relationships (Copresence)

The subject gives contiguity as a reason for their concepts. Subjects do not examine the multiple variables offered to them, but just construe the meaning from the nearest space available. This type of functioning obeys the topological space *reasons*, wherein proximity and inclusion relations prevail. There is no organized and stable system to use as reference point; in that case there would exist, indeed, a Euclidean, rational space.

If, when looking at Plate X a subject says "substances (D side blue), because they *accompany* this body, you can see the windpipe and the lungs," or, when looking at Plate II this same subject says "an airplane, because *it is emerging* from clouds." Here, the thinking process is based on elements fortuitously present in the current field of vision, rather than founded on relationships and logic as complex thinking would be, which takes more complex variables into account.

These forms of organization can be related to responses known as *position responses*.

Position Responses

Plate III: "Two children playing with a ball (?), because the ball is *under* their feet"
Plate III: "Two little angels (side red), because they are *above* each child (D side black)."
Plate IV (inverted position): "The eyes of a mosquito, that are *within* those sphere-like hings."
Plate VIII: "The North Pole (superior grey), because it is *above*."

This same subject's perceptual construction axis derives from the relative positions between elements. There could be a need to search for an explicit, effective spatial ordering aimed at establishing reference in spaces. It also could be possible that an organized spatiality has not yet been acquired, or that the subject has to reinforce his/her reference parameters when facing either new or critical situations.

It is important to find out whether relations are established based on the oppositions below-above, center-side, or container-contents, as in the following construction:

Plate III: "A fish tank (outer contour of human figures), because there is a fish (?) *within*, it seemed to me that this (central red) thing was floating *in the middle of it*, and this (side red) could be a cover you put *on top* of it."

Thus, such reference modes could be connected, then, with the privileged bounding relationships, so whoever is above represents authority; anyone to the sides means peers, and anything underneath represents subordinate positions. A relationship could also be related to hierarchical values, as this response to Plate VI: "Christ the Redeemer, because he is *on the top of* the mountain."

Affective Logic. Defining Through the "State" of the Object

The most significant features are the affective components.

> Plate III: "A *broken* butterfly" (side red).
> Plate II: "Something fell down and these little stains remained (Ddi in side black), it seems full of *smudges*, then someone rubbed a finger on it; it is leaking and it began to fall off until *it got dried.*"
> Plate I: "It's a bat *in decay*, its color is uneven, it's polka-dotted and gives the impression of *being aged.*"
> Plate II: "The face of a person . . . not someone who is *ruined*, I rather see him as *fallen*, as *bad*. The eyes are like those of a *destroyed* person, not for being bad but for not *feeling well*. Cheeks are *wrinkled.*"
> Plate VII: "An *old, half corroded* bone, with an uneven surface."

We can also observe the affective logic in the following responses given by the same subject:

> Plate IV: 1) "A young male goat, a kid, *chopped into two halves*"; 2) "Here it might be two *mutilated* hands (superior side) . . . it gives me the heebie jeebies."

When seeing Plate VI, the same female patient who gave the two last responses said: "All of them are *cut in half* . . . as if it was the digestive tract, and this that bothers me (pointing to her windpipe)."

Clearly, the emphasis on the *state* of the object (not on its *being*) somehow implies a lack of distance through a rapprochement to the object on which states of feeling or fear are projected. This "shortening of distances" betrays a very sensitive person likely to be specifically impacted by some bodily manifestations from the Other, thus, partly loosing one's ability to observe other aspects that were also present. It could be said that subject's ability to "objectify" the situation is lessened. This mode of processing is also likely to reveal a concern for one's own physical health, as was the case with this female patient, who had been recently operated on for an ovarian tumor.

> Plate I: "A butterfly with no colors . . . it has *holes* in its wings, it's not pretty, it's a *slob*, it's almost *dead*, like a *fossil*, it's *disintegrating.*"
> Plate II: "The heart of a human being, it's *cut in two*, it's *ill.*"
> Plate IV: "A tree that is *growing wrong*, that has been *deformed*, *it hasn't the shape of a normal tree, it's loosing its vitality.*"

57

Here, the object is formed by a temporary state, and conceptual rationality is not used in defining it. The prevailing feature is an intrabody distance that, pursuant to Maldavsky (1976), is likely to be found in psychosomatic, addicted, or epileptic patients.

Canceling out the Succession of Time

This is an organization pattern ignoring the succession of time by turning it out into simultaneity. The evidence of that mode of functioning is a contamination response ruled by condensation, which is inherent in the primary process.

In these constructions, the temporal and spatial merging of two or more images prevents the images becoming articulated, inasmuch as any articulation requires the setting up of cutting points, differences, rhythms, and sequences.

In contaminated responses, a type of "temporal short-circuit" is found, affecting both the sight of images and their verbal description. (Grillat, 1998). Such a temporal and conceptual short-circuit is evident in the following sequence:

> Plate I: "A female butterfly (D central), a woman . . . well, a female butterfly, and these are the wings (D side) . . . a woman's wings, like breasts (superior center), wings and part of the rear (woman's feet)."
> Plate I: "On the other side of the butterfly, this bat is partly a pigeon."
> Plate III: "It could be a skeleton around the hip area, the kind of boots that black women wear. The skeleton is nude, because there are two woman's breasts like a cow's udders . . . well, the breasts, the hip is like the breasts . . . it could be the nude body of a person."

Representations are condensed and not ordered in accordance with chronological time. Transformations do not entail that time has gone by, since everything happens in the same place, at the same time.

Here we have specific "mind states" rather than "mind products" (Roitman, 1993). States are linked to perceptual fragments emerging into awareness without achieving any articulation or any confrontation with data at hand. Instead of organizing a story based on the spatial indicators, another story is superimposed. The result seem like a broken kaleidoscope made with small pieces of paper trying to structure ephemeral forms. Therefore, neither places nor the duration of those forms matter. Time is canceled out by a type of automatic acceleration that turns succession into simultaneity.

There is a regression to more archaic stages, or perhaps what is lacking is a psychical complexity interspersing differences (Maldavsky, 1994). However, we could also be facing the fact that trauma has been so deeply and violently implanted that psychical life has been reduced to fragments of reality unlikely to be metabolized, as if the mind were "out of place" (Kacero, 2000).

Emphasis is Placed on the Context Wherein the Object Is Included

The rationality of responses is linked to the action, as if part of a scenario. In this way of organization, scenario and drama form a whole unit, as a text and its context would do. Context is not truly outside, inasmuch as it has been merged with the object-text that, for any reason whatsoever, has not been left isolated.

> Plate III: "Two children playing with a ball in a park."
> Plate I: "A fox's head (W) hung on a wall (S) by the hunter who was willing to decorate his living room. There are some other trophies around."
> Plate V: "A gull (W) flying through the sky." (space white)
> Plate III (inverted): "A monster raising his hands as if he had defeated the city (?), I can't see the city, I imagine it, I ascribe a purpose to this triumph."

The peculiarity of these logical constructions lies in the fact that context is the *raison d'être* of the object; the blank space either accompanies or completes the concept the subject is speaking of, as if it is a prosthesis. Neither the figure nor its supporting space could be separated. Being is "with reference to."

It has to be determined whether context containing function is either protective or destructive, either supportive or dependent, or if context merely plays the role of a "doorframe" that completes the scene décor. It should be determined whether this "doorframe" is contemporaneous with the object action or pertains to a past working, so to speak, as an instituting reference of the present. This last quality is displayed as follows:

> Plate VI: "It reminds me of an image I kept from my childhood . . . a rabbit's skin, at my grandmother's, when we skinned rabbit to eat it . . . I helped taking off all its leather, and then it was spread out in the sun to dry."

Here, context is build upon the temporal aspect. At any rate, however, the role of the scenario lies in either capturing the sight or stopping the image; freezing movement by giving the scene only one well-defined contextualization, thus preventing the scene to happen in any other "possible" contexts that, as such, could not be resorted to as a prevision object. There would be, then, some difficulty in doing without the background or we would be still at the organizing stage of a space akin to topology, inasmuch as the abstract, differentiated mental space has not been wholly internalized as yet. Traveling from that quasi-topological space to another space with its own autonomy and movement implies changing the relationship between one's own body and the body of one's own mother. We still have an archaic image of the body. Somehow, there still exists a physical symbiosis that has not already reached the representational dimension giving access to the symbolic realm. Let us observe how this archaic image appears to the same person who saw a fox in Plate I:

> Plate VII: "I see something like the two breasts of a mother (1/3 inferior) and, from here up, two busts in contact with her, sustained by her. This isn't a reality by itself but one of the mother's thoughts . . . as she had a determined child model in her mind and can't escape from that . . . like molds according to which she wants to build things, instead of looking for other possibilities."

Of course, this object, *glued* to the original background space, tells us about an intermingling of the bond, which still plays the role of spatial support. Merging with the object is both needed and feared, which makes the subject's deployment and growth, as well as the subject's ability to construct a future based on selfhood, even more difficult.

Resorting to a Generalization that Brings a Law to Mind

This law is external to the actual, present object alluded to in the response.

> Plate VIII: "A symbol of a past civilization (?). Latin American pre-Columbian symbols *generally* include animals, tombs, friezes . . ."
> Plate V: "Smoke, because it's dusky, as *when* something is burnt down . . . *When* wood catches fire it is dusky like this."

The law keeps distance. We would be at the antipodes of affective logic. Subjects are, thus, allowed to keep an out-and-out objectivity, so that any personal involvement is avoided. Subjects are merely the users of a law that transcends them. The law reflects concept – not subject. This type of logical processing is connected with an important feature in the Spanish language, namely the use of the infinitive, which is not only most usual, but also most correct. An expression such as: "un ave, por el volar" would normally be rendered in English as "a bird, because of its way of *flying.*" What the subject actually said, in Spanish, is "a bird, for its [way] to fly." The fact is that the infinitive does not permit discerning the subject's position. It marks the lack of evolution of a discourse enabling the subject to assume his/her own uniqueness.

This is what happens in obsessive patients who, by resorting to the law to justify a concept they have just uttered, emphasize the reference function while ignoring their own subjective involvement. In ascribing an explanatory value to an element endowed with the highest level of abstraction, they go beyond any individual features.

Reference to Others (Alorreferencia)

There is a reference to others *(alorreferencia*; (Kacero, 1983) when subjects explain their response alluding to some experience they have shared with other people.

All the following responses pertain to the same subject, a 40-year-old man:

Plate I: (1) "Something like the Romans'eagle, on their standards. It might be because yesterday was Family Day and all parents we went with our children to the country, and we were dressed up as Roman gladiators and Caesars . . . One of the parents had made a banner like that with a cane." (2) "It is a very strange, small animal . . . It reminds me of Lovecraft's books, of Cthulhu's mythological beings emerging from the mist or from the sea depths."
Plate II: "A perfect butterfly, as if it were a photograph . . . Perhaps because yesterday I saw a lot of them attached to a board at the Forestry Institute . . . they . . . were pinned on a board."
Plate III: "Blood, the small red thing with white . . . When I did my military service they took blood from me and spread it on a small white card. I still remember how it looked like when it was dissolving."
Plate IV: "A blot like blots children do at the kindergarten, they pour some paint on a paper, then fold it and open it again, and there is a blot there."
Plate V: "It looks like a butterfly this thing; spending the day in the country with some people yesterday has influenced me."
Plate VI: "The photograph of a mountain zone from the air, like the one they showed me at the Forestry Institute."
Plate VII: "I don't find any identifiable thing. I'm surely frustrating the designer of Plate VII."
Plate VIII: "It reminds me those little creatures in science-fiction, those critters . . ."
Plate IX: "I don't see anything. It's like trying to explain the drawings my son makes at the kindergarten . . . No idea . . ."

As we can see, the subject's explanations are not merely references to personal experiences, but to a particular type of experience in which other people are always present. Thus, the subject says "*we* dressed up ... *one of the parents* had made a banner ...". The photograph was showed to him by *others*, butterflies had been attached to a board by *others*, "*they* took blood from me..." When looking at Plate IV, he mentions blots "*children do*"; as regards Plate V, he says that he has been influenced by "spending the day in the country with *some people*." With reference to Plate VII, he alludes to a third person (the one who has "made" the plate). With regard to Plates I and VIII, he makes reference to what "*they*" (the authors of science-fiction books) narrate.

Clearly, there is no link between the visual configuration and some unique personal experience. Whenever the subject alludes to any experience of his, there are always other people (or at least some other individual) present. Whatever would have been any personal involvement, any personal responsibility about his perception or his lack of any interpretation, is carried over to others. This excessive dependence on the social world either inhibits or substitutes for the development of the specifically personal realm. That is, the ability to look into oneself is rarely, if ever, enacted. The subject depends on others to assess the accuracy of his perceptions.

Sometimes, the only guarantor for value and truth is to be found in the voice of culture, the mass media, or of the social imagination.

Plate IX: "It looks like the nuclear mushroom cloud; I've seen *a TV program* in which *they showed* what happened in Hiroshima."

Self-Reference as a Conceptual Foundation

In all these constructions, the subject's own experience prevails. Any other, more comprehensive confrontation with the marks on the plate is left aside.

Plate I (D central): "It's a little bear, because when *I* was a child, *I* used to draw it this way."
Plate III: "Waiters in a restaurant, the bow tie is the logotype of the restaurant (?). *I* like going out for dinner ... A friend *of mine* is going to get married soon, so that ..."

The subject becomes the focus of the scene, the world organization turns around him/her, the points of reference are his/her own experiences, and any other elements needed to recognize the object as such are left aside. This is the case of a female patient who says when looking at the following plates:

Plate I: "When I was a child I had a doll that was exactly like this."
Plate II: "It reminds me a very affectionate little dog we had at home."

The way this organizational semiotic mode works is typical of childhood, when a child is still immersed in the self-centered stage (Piaget, 1961). At this stage, words are not yet concepts. For a child, the word "cat" is the same as *his/her cat*. Children go from one unique thing to another; they have not reached that stage at which behavior is based on concrete, logical, reversible operations. Thus, their thinking might also evidence other characteristics pertaining to that preconceptual, self-centered stage: Thinking is likely to appear somewhat artificial, animistic. All and every phenomena will be associated to the child's own ways of action.

However, it is not only necessary to observe how often any Rorschach reader resorts to such resources, but also what are the formal, sensory organizations the subject reacts to by means of those types of justifications, inasmuch as any other developments the subject is likely to reach at within the same protocol should not be ignored. Time periods used by the subject as personal references (past, present, or future) should also be analyzed as well as any object references (parental, social, or intellectual). All this material is bound to give us information about epistemological and emotional supports the subject requires when operating within the realm of reality.

The Object Function as a Structuring Code

In this case, objects are characterized by their use value. The object does not act as an mediator favoring human contact, it does not become a libidinal object;but, the object has to show how *functional* it is.

Plate I: "A bird which *can fly and stop*."
Plate VIII: "A flag, because *it flutters* at flagpoles."
Plate IV: "An animal the skin of which has been completely removed. I don't know the name of this kind of skin *you hang on a wall* or *you lay to cover* the floor with."

Reality is organized in terms of use. Functionality of any object is its raison d'être. An object is only a means to achieve a goal.

Plate I: "A jet-like plane *used with different purposes*, it's equipped with intelligent devices for military actions."

The Other loses his/her condition of being a subject and is only looked upon to check out whether this individual *is useful or functional* in the way one needs him/her to be.

Action and Movement as Organizers

Here, action either cancels out or replaces the object, or obscures the action-performing subject. A driving force prevails.

Plate III (D inferior): "Something is *shaking*."
Plate IX: "A fountain with dancing waters. The fountain is not seen, the water *jet* is central. A water surface where you can see how drips *fall down* after *surging up*."
Plate VIII: "This means *speed* and *dynamism* to me, as if an animal, or some organic thing, *moved very quickly*. Colors represent *different speeds*."
Plate VI: "A quiet lake . . . soil. Something is *moving quickly*. There are lots of dust, it raises dust . . . It's something organic, it might be an animal or a person in a car, it's so *quick* you cannot catch it, cannot discern it."
Plate II: (within the blank space) "Those things that *go around or spin* on the floor, I don't know their name."

It is not the object that matters, but the movement of the object. Reality is a scenario set up for transforming, dizzyingly rapid action. The object is merely an instrument for exercising an intense motor activity. Time is conceived as a constant present, the time in which action is performed (Maldavsky, 1997). This way of interpreting the Rorschach images gives preeminence to the kinetic component.

As Rebourg (2005) said, these subjects find their sense of existence in action and it does not matter whether such an action is against physical laws.

Such responses, which show a state of motor excitement, are quite frequent nowadays.

I associate speed, unrest, a constant dance, with the logical architectures prevailing in our current society, a trend to the dissolution of object consistency. For example, digital technologies allow any texts to be flowingly contoured, built in a malleable way; electronic connections make it possible to link images, sounds, and texts. There is no longer a Euclidean time: digitalization, networks, and speed have brought about a crisis. However, a price is paid for microelectronics and simulations: namely, disappearance of the body into the virtual world, together with the disintegration of reality as a place you were able to live safely in – before. (Piscitelli, 1998).

Technology does not merely act on a single field. It also generates an epistemological mutation affecting our ways of thinking and organizing reality as well as our body.

Harmony

The response is based upon a need for stability, permanence, or maintenance of the status quo. To do so, the subject will place an emphasis on (a) symmetry and (b) repetition.

> Plate X (male subject, 60-year old): "That's always the same thing, one drawing is placed on top of the other and the result is always the same. There are simply two parts of the same thing, both on the right and on the left. It is a part in itself, open in this way. What is seen at the right is the same of what is seen at the left, so that it is a single whole, a whole in itself."

We see how symmetry and repetition are mutually reinforced in this response so as to achieve unity.

A careful search for harmony leaves aside any difference, any possible intrusion from any type of diversity. Symmetry sets up a nonrandomized order, it creates a rhythm based on regularity. However, both symmetry and repetition imply that time has been stopped. You could ask whether is there any need in the subject involved that forces him to do this. What could be psychically at risk for him if there were any hint of heterogeneity? Or what sensations, what physical or psychological factors provoke this time-stabilizing mode?

> Plate VIII: "A volcano, because I see the channel through which lava bursts out to the surface, where eruption takes place. There is an incandescent mass under the ground ... bears emerge from that incandescent mass. All figures, they always seem *symmetrical*, to me, *both to the right and to the left.*"

This response shows what are the different types of heterogeneity (mobilizations, explosions) the subject protects himself from by means of the comforting order of symmetry in an attempt at controlling instincts. The same subject gave the following responses:

> Plate I: "Symmetry, in which, perhaps there is the shape of a bird."
> Plate VIII: "A symmetry of some kind of animal ... as if on alert."

Whenever relationships are in harmony there is no conflict, no opposition, no confrontation whatsoever. This can be observed in the following sequence (subject is a young woman):

> Plate II: "Two friends in an affectionate exchange, they seem to be shaking hands and laughing."
> Plate III: "This is symmetrical too . . . Two birdies like those in Walt Disney's films, they are *joined* by a bowknot, as if their hearts were *tied*. A love card, a Valentine Day's card . . . as if they were *two people in love*."
> Plate IX: "I like it, it gives me an idea of equilibrium, plenitude . . . tenderness (?). I don't see blots or animals . . . Well, yes, I see spots but all is . . . as within a closed, a compact circle . . . I see no pet, no structure whatsoever . . . I see colors I like"

The search for harmony is sometimes equivalent to a need for maintaining unity – such a need is only achieved if relationships are idealized. A space threatened by dispersion, bursting out, or disorganization could appear as a basically inharmonious space.

Conclusions

This article was an attempt at defining some variables as well as producing a certain class of enunciation. I did not attempt to classify the multiple forms and shapes into which the mind could process the marks of the visual Rorschach configuration, and what does the mind does with them. Does it evacuate, destroy, ignore, or distort them? Does it explore their emotional qualities? Does it adhere to their sensory resonances or does it construct new meaningful forms? Does it join inarticulate elements so as to give it some feeling of unity, or does it disintegrate the whole unit into more manageable fragments?

Each mode of imbrications and relevance gives preeminence, somehow, to those senses through which reality is instituted.

As in my previous work, I have attempted to combine theoretical ideas with empirical findings, leading to inferences on the subjective structuring process that, in its turn, provides information on any subject's way of living, bonding, and operating.

The idea lies not in measuring the frequency of appearance of such-and-such phenomenon. The idea lies in *building a network* wherein we are in a position to observe how phenomena influence each other significantly while bearing in mind that even an apparently missing phenomenon occupies a place in the network.

References

Aulagnier, P. (1975). *La violencia de la interpretación* [The violence of interpretation]. Buenos Aires: Amorrortu.

Austin, J. (1998). *Cómo hacer cosas con palabras* [How things are done with words]. Barcelona: Paidós Ibérica.

Barthélémy, J.M. (1987). *L'analyse phénoméno-structurale dans l'étude psychologique des alcooliques* [A phenomenal-structural analysis in the psychological study of alcoholics]. Lille: Eres.

Castoriadis, C. (1998). *Los dominios del hombre* [Domains of humans]. Barcelona: Gedisa.

Debray, R. (1994). *Vida y muerte de la imagen* [Life and death of image]. Barcelona: Paidós.

Deleuze, G. (2004). *En medio de Spinoza* [In mid-Spinoza]. Buenos Aires: Cactus.

Ducrot, O. (1986). *El decir y lo dicho* [The way you say things, and what was said]. Barcelona: Paidós.

Eco, U. (1986). *La estructura ausente* [The absent structure]. Barcelona: Lumen.

Eco, U. (1997). *Interpretación y sobreinterpretación* [Interpretation and over-interpretation]. Madrid: Cambridge University Press.

Exner, J. (1998). Piezas críticas en el proceso de respuesta al Rorschach [Critical pieces in Rorschach responses]. *Abreletras, 2,* 9–24. La Plata: De la Campana.

Grillat, D. (1998). Étude différentielle des réponses contaminées: Retour à H. Rorschach [A differential study on contaminated responses: Going back to H. Rorschach]. *Bulletin de Psychologie, SI* (4), 436.

Groupe μ. (1993). *Tratado del signo visual* [Treaty of the visual sign]. Madrid: Cátedra.

Husain, O., Merceron, C., & Rossel, F. (2001). *Psychopathologie et polysémie* [Psychopathology and polysemy]. France: Payot Laussane.

Kacero, E. (1983). *Alo-referencia* [Reference to others]. Unpublished manuscript.

Kacero, E. (1995, July). *Los vínculos en el Rorschach* [Bonds in the Rorschach test]. Paper presented at the 9th Latin-American Congress of the Rorschach and Other Projective Techniques, Quito, Ecuador.

Kacero, E. (1996). The Rorschach: From formal factors to forms or organization. A study of the spatial axis. *Rorschachiana, 21,* 127–152. Cambridge and Göttingen: Hogrefe & Huber.

Kacero, E. (1999). *A la recherche d'un temps à construire au Rorschach: Des facteurs formels aux liens qui les régissent* [In search for a time to build in the Rorschach test: From formal factors to binding rules thereof]. *Psychologie Clinique et Projective, 5,* 143–163.

Kacero, E. (2000, August). *Historia y subjetividad en las respuestas combinatorias confabulatorias* [History and subjectivity in confabulatory, combined responses]. Paper presented at the 5th Congress "Rorschach en la Universidad,8 Buenos Aires.

Kacero, E. (2009). *Rorschach: Transformaciones entre la imagen y la palabra* [Rorschach: A transformation between image and word]. Buenos Aires: Lugar.

Maldavsky, D. (1976). *Teoría de las representaciones* [Theory of representations]. Buenos Aires: Nueva Visión.

Maldavsky, D. (1994). *Pesadillas en vigilia* [Wakeful nightmares]. Buenos Aires: Amorrortu.

Maldavsky, D. (1997). *Sobre las ciencias de la subjetividad* [On the sciences of the subject]. Buenos Aires: Nueva Visión.

Minkowska, F. (1978). *Le Rorschach, à la recherche du monde des formes* [The Rorschach test in search of the world of forms]. Paris: Desclée de Brouwer.

Morin, E. (1994). *Introducción al pensamiento complejo* [An introduction to complex thinking]. Barcelona: Gedisa.

Noton, D., & Stark, L.(1971). Eye movements and visual perception. *Scientific American, 224*(6), 35–43.

Piaget, J. (1961). *La formación del símbolo en el niño* [Formation of symbols in children]. Mexico: Fondo de Cultura Económica.

Piscitelli, A. (1998). *Post/Televisión* [Post-TV times]. Buenos Aires: Paidós.

Rebourg, C. (2001). *Identification et qualification au Rorschach* [Identification and qualification in the Rorschach test]. *Bulletin de Psychologie, 54*, 487–492

Rebourg, C. (2005). *Le contenu animal* [Animal contents]. In O. Husain, C. Merceron, & F. Rossel (Comp.), *Les phénomènes particuliers au Rorschach* [The Rorschach Test's phenomena]. Lausanne: Payot.

Roitman, C. (1993). *Los caminos detenidos* [Interrupted ways]. Buenos Aires: Nueva Visión.

Rorschach, H. (1964). *Psicodiagnóstico* [Psychodiagnosis]. Buenos Aires: Paidós.

Searle, J.(1980). *Actos de habla* [Acts of speech]. Madrid: Cátedra.

Vilches, L. (1983). *La lectura de la imagen* [Reading the image]. Barcelona: Paidós.

Etel Schvartzapel de Kacero
Universidad del Salvador (USAL)
Asociación Argentina de Estudio e Investigación
en Psicodiagnóstico (ADEIP)
Zavalía 2174, 3°P.
1428 Buenos Aires
Argentina
Fax +54 11 4783-9986
E-mail etelkacero@yahoo.com.ar

Summary

The traditional way to study the Rorschach productions has always been by codifying the responses once subjects have verbalized responses. This approach has been enriched by Rorschach-specialized scholars for more than 80 years.

Without neglecting this method, the author's interest has focused on analyzing the ways of acting that subjects evidence when giving their responses, as well as analyzing the building processes taking place from the moment subjects look at the plates, so carefully constructed by Hermann Rorschach, until subjects verbalize their response. The idea lies in paying attention to subjects' observation, selection, combination, canceling out, categorization, and organization of reality once they have been shown the visual information.

In perceiving and acting at our request, subjects not only receive sensorial data but also put into order the material they have just looked at. In other words, subjects organize, set up relationships, and attribute meaning pursuant to their psyche's representational-cognitive process.

From the logical axis, it can be said that subjects' constructions bear witness to the mechanisms and strategies they rely on to know the real world, to live in it, and give it a meaning. Different logical forms could be considered as potential options. However, such options always imply personal decisions, evidence personal experiences, privilege some contents more than others, and show the values with which subjects face life. Whenever productions are observed from this perspective, the classes, relationships, and properties guiding subjects' interpretations, how significances are colored, so to speak, and how the subject involved either confronts or solves problems, are likely to be observed.

In this paper, some alternatives and variations as to the way of processing the markes on each plate are presented. The goal does not lie in assessing either the deviant or the pathological – the idea is evidencing inner models or patterns determining a subject's cognitive and emotional functioning.

Résumé

Traditionnellement, la production du Rorschach a été étudiée une fois codifiées les réponses du sujet, cotation qui s'est enrichie de l'expérience des Rorschachistes tout au long de plus de quatre-vingts ans de travail.

Sans vouloir rejeter cette méthode, nous aimerions, en cette occasion, centrer l'analyse sur le mode d'opérer propre à chaque sujet au moment de donner sa réponse; veiller aux processus de construction qui ont lieu dès qu'il pose le regard sur les planches, si soigneusement construites par Hermann Rorschach, jusqu'à ce que, finalement, le mot soit émis et constitue ce que l'on dénomme "réponse." Il s'agit donc de nous demander quelles sont les activités d'observation, de choix, d'annulation, de catégorisation et, finalement, d'organisation de la réalité ayant lieu dans le sujet quant aux données visuelles que nous lui avons présentées.

Le sujet qui perçoit et agit répondant à notre requête, a reçu non seulement des données sensorielles mais encore il en ordonne les aspects visibles, les organise, établit des relations, des signifiants, en accord avec les processus cognitivo-relationnels qui structurent son psychisme. Les construits que le sujet établit, considérés depuis l'axe logique que nous proposons deviendront les témoins de mécanismes et stratégies que le sujet met en jeu afin de connaître, vivre la réalité et lui donner du sens. Les différentes formes logiques peuvent être prises en tant qu'alternatives possibles; cependant, elles impliquent toujours des décisions, mettent des expériences en évidence, octroient des privilèges à certains contenus et témoignent des valeurs depuis lesquelles le sujet observe la vie.

Ainsi, considérer les productions sous cet angle nous rend visibles les classes, les relations et propriétés qui, chez le sujet, guident son interprétation, en colorient le signifié, en déterminent les modes qu'il a de résoudre ou d'affronter ces questions.

Nous présentons ici quelques alternatives et variations possibles auxquelles peut se livrer le sujet quant aux modes destinés à traiter les marques présentées par les planches. Il ne s'agit point ici d'évaluer ce qu'il peut y avoir de dévié ou de pathologique mais bien de mettre en évidence les modèles internes, les structures qui déterminent, chez le sujet, son fonctionnement cognitif et émotionnel.

Resumen

Tradicionalmente se ha estudiado la producción Rorschach a través de la codificación de las respuestas una vez emitidas. Codificación que se ha enriquecido con la experiencia de los rorschachistas a lo largo de más de ochenta años de trabajo.

Sin desechar este método, mi interés es, en esta ocasión, focalizar el análisis en el modo de operar del sujeto cuando da una respuesta; atender a los procesos de construcción que tienen lugar desde que posa la vista en las imágenes – tan cuidadosamente construidas por Hermann Rorschach – hasta que finalmente la palabra es emitida en lo que se denomina "respuesta." La idea es atender a qué trabajos de observación, selección, combinación, anulación, categorización y finalmente organización de la realidad, se desarrollan en relación con la información visual que le presentamos.

La persona que percibe y actúa respondiendo a nuestro requerimiento no sólo recibe datos sensoriales, sino que ordena lo visible, organiza, relaciona y significa, según qué procesos cognitivo representacionales configuran su psiquismo.

Las construcciones que hace el sujeto, miradas desde el eje lógico que propongo, serán testimonio de los mecanismos y estrategias que pone en juego para conocer, vivir la realidad y adjudicarle sentido. Las diferentes formas lógicas pueden ser tomadas como alternativas posibles, pero siempre implican decisiones, evidencian experiencias, privilegian contenidos y testimonian valores desde los que el sujeto mira la vida.

Observar las producciones desde este vértice hace visible, para nosotros, qué clases, relaciones y propiedades guían su interpretación, colorean la significación y determinan sus modos de resolución o de afrontamiento.

Presento en este trabajo algunas alternativas y variaciones posibles de los modos de procesar las marcas que presentan las láminas, por parte de cada sujeto. No se trata de evaluar aquí lo desviado o lo patológico sino de hacer evidente los modelos internos, las pautas que determinan su funcionamiento cognitivo-emocional.

71

　ロールシャッハにおいて産出されるものについて研究する伝統的な方法は、常に、被検者によって一度言語化された反応を記号化することによってなされる。この研究方法はロールシャッハを専門とする研究者らによって 80 年以上の間、その質が高められてきている。

　著者はこの方法をおろそかにすることなく、被検者がヘルマン・ロールシャッハによって慎重に構成された図版を見た瞬間から、反応を言語化するまでの間に行われた反応成立の過程についての分析と同様に、被検者が反応を生じた際にどのようにその根拠とかかわっていたかについて分析することに関心を持っている。この考えは、ひとたび視覚的情報を提示された後、被検者が現実を観察し、選択し、組合せ、埋合せ、分類し、構成することに注目することにある。

　知覚することや我々の要求に応える中で、被検者は感覚的情報を受け取るのみならず、まさに見た素材に秩序を与えるのである。言い換えれば、被検者は心的表象認知過程に従って、構成し、関係性を構築し、意味を付与するのである。

　論理的な軸から、被検者の説明は、被検者が現実の世界を知り、そこで生活し、そこに意味を与える仕組みと方略を証言していると言うことができる。種々の論理的形態は、可能な選択であるとみなすことが出来る。しかしこのような選択は常に、個人的な意思決定を意味し、個人的経験を明示し、ある内容には他のものよりも重きを置き、被検者が人生に直面した際、何を重視しているかを示している。被検者についての解釈を導くこれらの展望、分類、関係、特性が反応に見られた場合にはいつでも、どのような意味が着色されたか、いわば被検者が問題への直面または解決にどのように関わったかを観察することが出来るだろう。

　本論文では、各図版のしみを処理する方法についての新しいやり方や変法を示した。逸脱や病理を査定することを目標とするのではなく、被検者の認知的、感情的機能を決定する内的なモデルやパターンを証明することが目的である。

Rorschachiana 30, 73–96
© 2009 Hogrefe & Huber Publishers

DOI: 10.1027/1192-5604.30.1.73

The Use of the Defense Mechanism Test to Aid in Understanding the Personality of Senior Executives and the Implications for Their Careers

Olya Khaleelee

London, UK
Corporate psychologist, organizational consultant, and psychotherapist in private practice

Abstract. This paper describes the use of the Defense Mechanism Test as an aid in helping to assess senior executives in four areas: for selection, development, career strategy, and crisis intervention. The origins of this test, developed to measure the defense mechanisms used to protect the individual from stress, are described. The paper shows how it was used to predict the capacity of trainee fighter pilots to withstand stress and its later application to other stressful occupations. Finally, some ideal types of the test are shown followed by four real test profiles, two of them with their associated histories.

Keywords: defense mechanism, psychoanalysis, conflict, senior managers, development

Introduction

This paper examines the context in which the Defense Mechanism Test (DMT) is used, how the test examines the perceptual process, and its application in two cases. Knowledge of psychoanalytic theory and how defense mechanisms protect the personality from stress are taken as given.

The Context

I work in a partnership called Pintab Associates, which specializes in psychological assessment for senior managers, mostly in the commercial sector. We see executives for four different reasons: for selection, when they are short-listed for a top job; for development, as a way of assessing potential within an organization's change program or as a result of a takeover and merger; for career strategy, where the executive is either out of role already or will shortly be so and is working with an outplacement firm in order to re-present himself or herself to the market; and finally, for crisis intervention, when the individual is, perhaps, failing in the current role for no obvious reason.

Our approach is integrative in the sense that we are interested in understanding how the individual has made choices that have helped to map out his or her life and the implications of being in or wanting a particular work role. We focus on the fit between the individual and the role and we try to understand the function of anxiety and conflict whether it is intrapsychic and/or external in relation to the organization. In this way, we aim to augment these individuals' capacity to function effectively at work. Although I am going to talk about the use of this methodology and the use of the DMT in commercial settings, it has been successfully applied in many mental health settings and elsewhere, for example at the Cotswold Community (Khaleelee, 1994, 1997), in order to reduce staff turnover. It can, therefore, be used predictively as well as diagnostically.

The assessment process in the commercial setting for any of the reasons described above consists of data gathering and hypothesis formation through participation in four exercises and two discussions, finishing with feedback. The assessors, both psychoanalytically trained, are also, during the course of the process, using transference and their counter-transference to help formulate hypotheses about the individual, how he or she operates within the oedipal constellation evoked by working in a "threesome," relationship to authority, and so on.

The DMT is the core of this process, but embedded within a range of measures, all of which help to develop as complete a picture as possible about the individual.

Taken as data and put together with other information from test results, and discussions about work and formative experience, we are able to form good enough hypotheses to help the person understand better how they function and the reasons for what has happened to them most recently, thereby connecting up the past and the present. From this understanding we can either comment on the fit between person and role in a selection process; or we can highlight the factors that need to be incorporated into the developmental plan in order to maximize an executive's potential; or, for a career strategy, we would aim to maximize the possibility of future success and contentment for the executive. In crisis situations, we are able to formulate a key hypothesis to bring some insight into the current situation.

The Defense Mechanism Test (DMT)

The DMT is a projective test that assesses resilience in the face of stress by examining the perceptual apparatus. It was originally developed by Kragh (1955) at the University of Lund in the mid 1950s as a diagnostic test to be used as a basis for psychotherapy. During the late 1960s it was applied to stressful occupations such as air force pilots (Neumann, 1971) and air traffic controllers (Svensson & Trygg, 1991). Up to this point, the selection of young men as trainee fighter pilots for the Royal Swedish Air Force by traditional interview methods was producing a two-thirds failure rate. The problem appeared to be that under the stress of flying, gross perceptual errors about the environment were affecting performance. Analysis of the DMT showed that the defense of *reaction formation* appeared to play a particularly prominent role in the process linking DMT scores and the cause of accidents. Statistical analysis proved a highly significant connection between DMT prognosis and accident-proneness (Neumann, 1971).

Various follow-up studies have taken place with workers in different industries, especially those who have to manage high levels of stress during the course of their work. The DMT was subsequently used for selecting others for dangerous occupations, such as deep sea divers (Kragh, 1962) and air traffic controllers (Svensson & Trygg, 1991). It has also been used for the assessment of subjective fear in training for parachute jumping (Vaernes, 1982) and in research on the assessment of serious drinking and driving offenders. During the 1970s it was increasingly used in senior management selection and development.

The DMT is based on an examination of the perceptual process using a tachistoscope. Percept-genetic analysis works on the basis that perception is a process that extends over time and is not something instantaneous.

The individual is shown a series of 18–20 exposures of a stimulus that contains a peripheral threat, designed to provoke conflict and stress. The conflicts are those to which all of us are exposed during our formative years, those of aggression, authority, separation, and loss. The pictures shown in the test are segmented into a set of observations, initially for a very short time of $1/100$ s and gradually increasing to a maximum of 2 s in the final exposure. This kind of test series is called a percept genesis, and enables an examination of the various developmental phases of perception. Two processes are believed to be operating, the first we can call "construction," which is the preconscious awareness of the stimulus, followed by "reconstruction," which is the process through which some aspects are re-worked and enter conscious experience. Thus, what is consciously perceived is not what has been preconsciously perceived, and we hypothesize that the difference is accounted for by the mobilization of defense mechanisms. As with other projective tests, the DMT is designed so that the viewer will identify with the central figure and will react to the threat present in the picture in the same way as they might have reacted to actual threat in their own lives.

From the verbal and visual feedback supplied by the viewer, a profile is developed, which indicates both how the individual developed over time and how the defense mechanisms, mobilized by the ego to cope with the anxiety generated in stressful situations, have impinged on the individual's emotional development. The DMT identifies the pace of an individual's development, derived from the points at which the nine elements of reality in the test are perceived, and at what stages in their development the defenses emerge. The defenses are categorized as integrative (sometimes called autoplastic) and assertive (sometimes called alloplastic). These terms – autoplastic and alloplastic – referred to by Ferenczi (1919) and Freud (1924), distinguish between two kinds of adaptation at an early stage of development, one directed toward the subject himself, the other directed toward the outside world, both of which allow the ego to maintain its equilibrium (Laplanche and Pontalis, 1973).

For example, if we take the defense mechanism of introaggression, the direction of the defense is against the subject and the equilibrium is maintained by the subject absorbing the feeling and taking it inside. This is an autoplastic or "integrative" response. With the defense of reaction formation, the subject converts a threatening reality in the environment into its opposite; the experience is a form of denial actively asserted in relation to the environment. This is an alloplastic or "assertive" response. In each instance the subject controls the threat in a different way.

These categories – alloplastic and autoplastic – are, in turn, made up of various types of defense mechanisms such as those Anna Freud (1946) described of repression, isolation, reaction formation, denial, projection, introjection, regression, and introaggression or turning against the self. Some defenses, mobilized in different ways, can be common to both types of adaptation. Each defense is scored according to when it appears on the individual's profile and for how long it remains in place. This provides hypotheses about the age at which a defense was mobilized, which can be discussed in relation to an individual's life history. It is then possible to score an individual's defenses with an overall score, with an assertive (alloplastic) and integrative (autoplastic) score and with scores of specific defenses within the assertive and integrative bands.

The test is scored strictly according to a manual, which minimizes the impact of subjective assessment by the tester. Within the test, there are nine elements of reality that can be perceived, and the various distortions, omissions, or additions reported by the viewer provide hypotheses about emotional reactions and defense mechanisms influencing the perceptual process. The elements coded by the tester are the deviations from the correct content of the picture.

According to psychoanalytic theory, defense mechanisms are needed in order to retain stability when in a state of anxiety, so as not to become overwhelmed. These defense mechanisms function like shock absorbers, warding off painful perception, so that the individual can survive and continue to function. Constitutional factors and formative experiences contribute to distinct differences in the individual's ability to tolerate and manage stress. Therefore, each DMT result is unique.

Where an individual is sensitive to stress or has a low tolerance, the experience of stress will affect specific functions, such as memory or the capacity to process information. The individual may slow down or demonstrate dysfunctional behavior such as difficulties in making decisions. Where denial has been mobilized as a defense, there is a particular danger because the perception of external reality is so distorted that judgment is very seriously impaired. The amount of energy needed to maintain psychic stability also affects how much is available for engaging with the outside world and is linked to inner resilience.

We work on the assumption that the development of resilience within the personality is based on the internalization of a good love object in infancy, leading to a capacity to cope with ambivalence. In adulthood, this, in turn, will likely lead to the individual having a more accurate perception of reality and a greater capacity to tolerate uncertainty. The test is very useful in a commercial setting, because the higher the individual progresses within an organizational hierarchy, the more resilience is required to cope with the increasing ambiguities and political processes that operate at that level. The capacity to continue to lead effectively and maintain competence in one's role in the face of such uncertainties is a central factor in our assessment of the individual.

Below are a set of diagrams that illuminate how the test works. The first five DMT diagrams illustrate profiles of emotional development over time in the form of ideal types, but without the defense mechanisms being listed. Following these are four actual test results where the defense mechanisms that have been mobilized are noted. The last two DMT results will be elaborated on with two case studies.

Diagram 1 shows the ideal type of a typical managerial profile. Of the various possibilities, this is the most healthy, being continuous in descent. What this means is that, each step in the profile indicates perception of a reality that was there to be perceived. The fact that the progression is continuous and steady through the 20 columns of the test will reflect the emotional development of the individual during his or her formative experiences. In this diagram it can be seen that the pace of development speeds up from Column 13.

The second diagram (Diagram 2) shows the profile of an entrepreneur, characterized by fast early development. In this example, the individual has perceived many elements of the reality before column 9, that is, during their formative years. Such individuals are good at initiating projects, they are people who "do" rather than "feel." But once their organization has developed beyond what they themselves can control, difficulties frequently arise because they tend to be highly assertive, autocratic and distrustful of others. The entrepreneur tends to make high demands on him/herself and, often insensitively, on others. As bosses, they begin from the rational goal and ask themselves what objectives should be achieved, then they tend to "go for it" and feel frustrated and irritated if their goals are not achieved. While the assertiveness and dynamism of the entrepreneur is to be appreciated, in larger organizations, their insensitivity and lack of diplomacy leads to the risk of being fired.

Diagram 3 shows the profile of an intuitive person. Here the development is "up and down," characterized by several regressions. This means that the individual loses reality despite being shown the picture for longer. It suggests that the individual is in touch with their feelings but that there is a lack of consolidation and resilience. This means that although they might rely on their feelings, they would not necessarily feel very confident about them. This would affect their capacity to take action.

The fourth diagram (Diagram 4) shows a sensitive person who developed quite quickly early on, that is from frames 1–7, but then the indi-

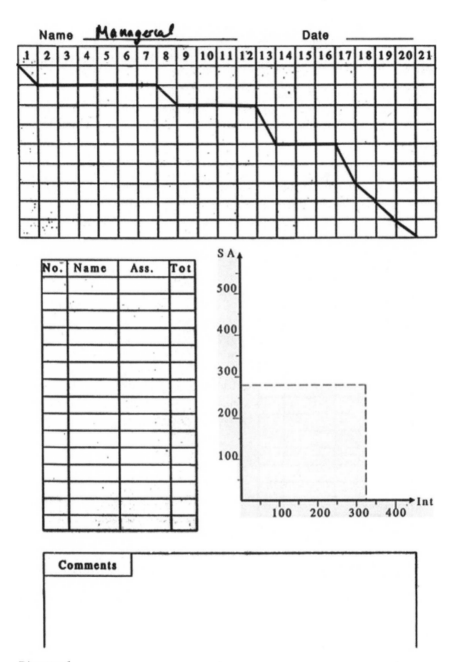

Diagram 1.

O. Khaleelee

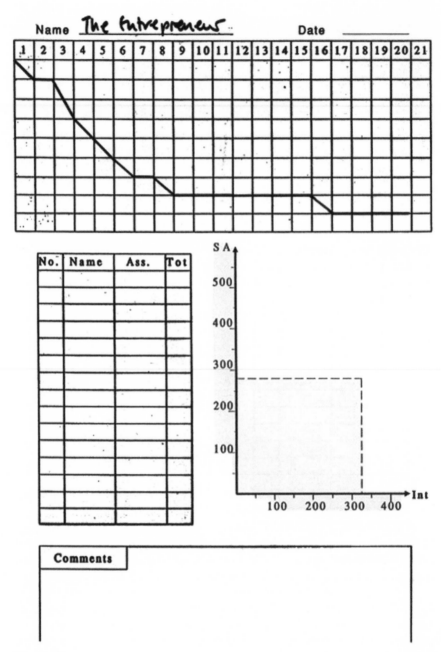

Diagram 2.

80

vidual has regressed because their capacity to sustain this emotional development is limited. Because of their sensitivity to environmental stimuli, such individuals tend to be rather cautious. They may be highly skilled but they are not ideal for a managerial post because they perceive threats in the environment too early and may then overreact.

Diagram 5 shows the typical profile of a late developer. In this instance the person perceives few elements of the realities present until column 15. Such individuals often grow up in a sheltered family situation, therefore with a sense of being very special. The omnipotent structure in the personality remains and they tend as a result to be immature or rather naïve. They are not ideal in managerial situations, because they perceive reality and threats in the environment rather late. However, in staff roles, they may well be good at completing tasks and can therefore be an effective complement to initiators such as entrepreneurs.

The following diagram, Diagram 6, shows not only Phil's profile of emotional development over time but also the defense mechanisms mobilized to protect him from stress. His profile indicates a resilient personality, since there are no regressions. It is similar to the managerial ideal type described above, except in this case his development speeded up earlier. However, the defense mechanisms mobilized to protect him from stress – repression, isolation, and introjection – are mostly assertive or alloplastic. Furthermore, he perceives the threat in the test rather late, which is not ideal. While his results place him where we would expect general managers to be (within the dotted line box on the chart and with moderate defenses), his position in the chart, close to the assertive dimension, will mean that his task focus will dominate over his orientation to people and therefore he would not be an effective general manager. He would be most likely to be effective in a more technical role, such as Finance Director.

Diagram 7 shows that Lesley developed very rapidly during her formative years and has a profile similar to the entrepreneurial ideal type described above. The dotted lines indicate a hint of regression in column 11 and indications of striving for greater maturity in columns 12, 16 and 18. Her defense mechanisms include isolation, that is, cutting off from feelings and turning away from the threat, introjection suggestive of an old head on young shoulders and therefore a tendency to take a great deal of responsibility; and reaction formation, indicating a tendency to deny the threat to some extent and put a brave face on difficult situations. Her results place her within the general management box but with few defenses. While the positive aspect of this is likely to be clarity of

O. Khaleelee

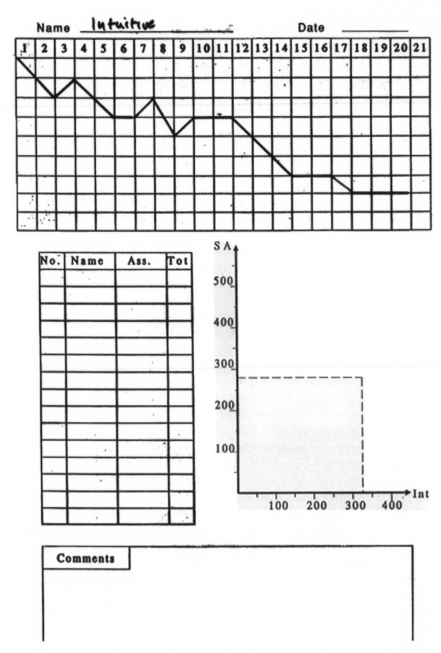

Diagram 3.

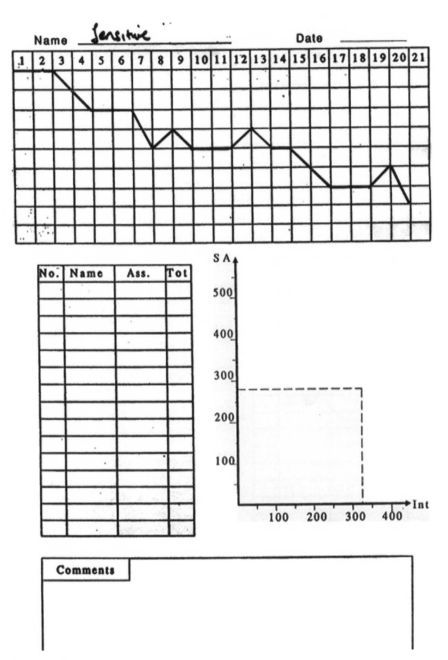

Name _Sensitive_   **Date** _____

No.	Name	Ass.	Tot

Comments

Diagram 4.

O. Khaleelee

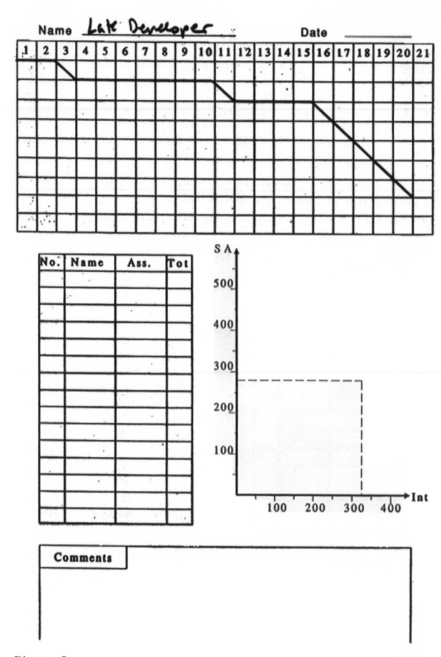

Name *Late Developer* **Date** _____

No.	Name	Ass.	Tot

Comments

Diagram 5.

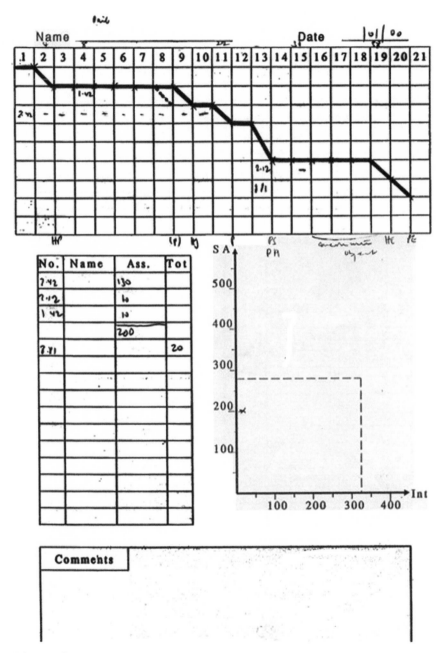

Diagram 6.

85

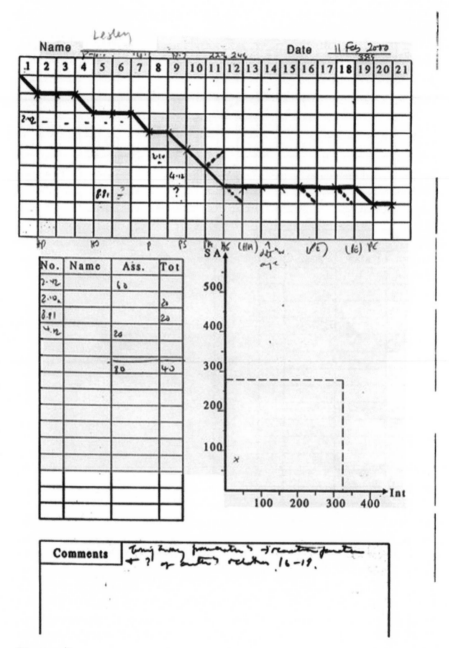

Diagram 7.

judgment and a capacity to innovate, the negative aspect might be a lack of sensitivity to others.

The same could be said for Diagram 8, which shows Arturo's emotional development. Arturo was an overseas candidate who was assessed for the role of chief executive. He had a DMT profile showing the rapid early emotional development characteristic of entrepreneurs and he also had few defense mechanisms. He was therefore very "thin-skinned," which implied a sensitive and open personality. His conceptual capacity, measured with another test, was well developed and he thought about issues in the relevant political and strategic context. The candidate was dynamic and charismatic in his self-presentation with a direct and forthright style. He was cultured, had many and varied interests, and was, in addition, witty, fun and extremely articulate. He was immediately able to take charge of difficult or uncertain situations and turn them to his advantage. This produced a mixed reaction to him: on the one hand he was perceived as charming and engaging and, on the other, as somewhat controlling. Both aspects underpinned his dynamic managerial style, which was also characterized by a strong focus on task and action.

Arturo came from a politically active and well-educated family in Latin America. His father was a self-made man from a powerful Conservative family, who had been extremely successful prior to radical political change, at which point his business was confiscated. Arturo had a close relationship with his mother, who was a well-educated, professional woman. She was always there for him and made it clear that he was her favorite child. He was not conscious of experiencing many frustrations in his early life and he internalized a strong sense of self, which gave him confidence to the point of omnipotence. The harmony and pleasure of his early life was marred only by the loss of his nanny at the age of 6, with heavy "isolation" appearing on his DMT profile. His early development led to the experience of himself as very special.

Later, his father was exiled for conspiring against the government. Arturo was sent away for his own safety in his early teens and then re-joined his family, where he found his father penniless and in a state of breakdown. Seeing his family in exile contributed to his already fast emotional development, in particular the shock of seeing his once successful father temporarily a broken man. His mother got a job and sustained the family while father recovered. As his family had to re-make its fortune, this contributed to Arturo becoming a good initiator of projects. And perhaps because part of his early adolescence was spent in poverty selling home-made sweets on street corners, he developed early on an important capacity to negotiate

O. Khaleelee

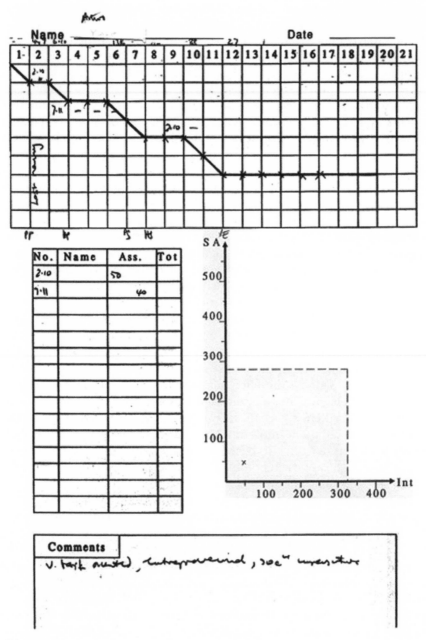

Diagram 8.

successfully with others. As a manager, he had gradually become more participative, although under pressure, his natural authoritarianism and "macho" way of working asserted itself and he then exhibited a more aggressive and commanding attitude.

One interpretation of his DMT profile was that his task focus was so strong and he had so few defenses, that his sensitivity to the environment was exceptionally high. As a result, he tended to act precipitately in relation to the task, at those times exhibiting a corresponding insensitivity to others. He became a successful managing director, operating on greenfield sites and in companies undergoing very rapid growth. However, when there was a need to move into a different phase of development, which involved more attention to detail, reduction of expenditure and a curtailment of growth, including making employees redundant, his negative qualities predominated and he was much less successful. To continue to be successful in these circumstances, he would have needed focused role consultations so that he could relate his managerial behavior to his understanding of his personality. This would have helped him deal with the managerial issues involved in the next phase of development within his organization.

Finally, Diagram 9 shows Malcolm's profile, which is rather different. Comparing it to the ideal types described above, it can be seen that he is a "late developer" with many ways of protecting himself from stress. Malcolm was a technical director, who was invited to have a developmental assessment, because he had every expectation of becoming chief executive but had not got the post. Although he was perceived as extremely competent in the technicalities of his role, he had a reputation for being arrogant, abrasive and difficult to relate to as a manager. Some people found him intimidating. His DMT profile suggested that he was a "slow starter" emotionally and had many defense mechanisms, in particular repression and isolation. More surprising was that the DMT indicated considerable sensitivity and a female identification from the age of 8, which suggested a softer, more nurturing but hidden part of his personality. This seemed in strong contrast to his dismissive and cynical self-presentation, represented through his capacity to "isolate" his more sensitive feelings from the scrutiny of others. His test results showed that he would use primarily assertive ways of protecting himself from stress. The strong "isolation" in his DMT profile meant that he would be so task focused that he would be unaware of his impact on others.

An interview elucidated that his mother was ill from early on in his life and in fact had died when he was 8, which coincided with the onset of

O. Khaleelee

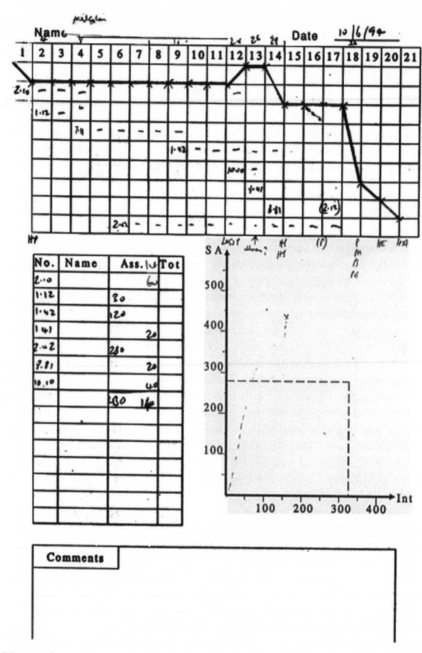

Diagram 9.

90

female identification in his DMT profile. At this point, his father sent him to boarding school, where he became extremely rebellious, bucked against all discipline out of feelings of insecurity and was often caned as a result. He described his father as strict and dictatorial, someone he saw little of and who seemed to be indifferent to him. He felt intimidated by him. When his father remarried, he remembered feeling resentful and jealous. He recalled that he behaved badly out of envy. He felt that, as a result of his parenting, he became an institutionalized child with a truculence that covered over his extremely sensitive feelings. Despite being highly intelligent and originally having been able to read and write at a very early age, he failed his examinations.

In our view, this manager had developed a very assertive and intimidating style, which both unconsciously protected him from further hurt and conveyed to others his own experience of authority figures. His fundamental mistrust of other people's motives, which derived from early experiences of parental abandonment, meant that it would be difficult for him to progress further.

While he demonstrated a high level of intelligence and conceptual ability and his time span of discretion - that is, his capacity, - was sufficient to work at the level of technical director, it was not high enough for him to work at the level of a managing director of a medium sized industrial company with a time span of 5-10 years. In spite of having considerable sensitivity and hidden concern for others, his life experience meant that, firstly he was unable to provide the necessary "containment" for subordinates' concerns and anxieties. Secondly, his lack of trust gave rise to a difficulty in delegating, and this hindered him from motivating and energizing others over the longer term required in the role of chief executive.

Although Malcolm was intelligent and able to conceptualize a strategy to pursue a vision, his lack of emotional intelligence meant that he would not be able to perform at the level required. His capacity to live with uncertainty, which is the consequence of having a resilient personality based on inner security, was lacking. For him to have been able to move into the chief executive role, he would have needed to engage in a program of personal development, which would have enabled him to work through the issues of distrust and bitterness resulting from his formative experiences, rather than continuing to enact them.

I hope these examples will help to flesh out and clarify how a projective technique such as the Defense Mechanism Test – in combination with other measures – can be used to understand the personality and career prospects of senior executives.

References

Cooper, C. (1988). Predicting susceptibility to short-term stress with the defense mechanism test. *Work and Stress, 2*(1), 49–58.

Ferenczi, S. (1919). The Phenomena of hysterical materialization. Thoughts on the conception of hysterical conversion and symbolism. *Further Contributions*, 96.

Freud, A. (1946). *The ego and the mechanisms of defense.* New York: IUP.

Freud, S. (1924). *The loss of reality in neurosis and psychosis, XIX.* London: Hogarth Press.

Freud, S. (1926). *Inhibitions, symptom,s and anxiety. Standard edition* (Vol. XX). London: Hogarth Press.

Hessle, S. (1990). The Defense Mechanism Test: A personality test for studying changes in defense organization and self-identity with clients in psychotherapy. *Journal of Psychology, 31,* 81–88.

Khaleelee, O. (1994). The Defense Mechanism Test as an aid for selection and development of staff. *Therapeutic Communities, 15*(1), 3–13.

Khaleelee, O., & Tomlinson, P. (1997). Intrapsychic factors in staff selection at the Cotswold Community. *Therapeutic Communities, 18,* 255–269.

Kragh, U. (1955). *The actual-genetic model of perception-personality: An experimental study with nonclinical and clinical groups.* Lund, Sweden: Gleerup.

Kragh, U. (1962). Prediction of success of Danish attack divers by the Defense Mechanism Test (DMT). *Perceptual and Motor Skills, 15,* 103–106.

Kragh, U., & Smith, G. (1970). *Percept-genetic analysis.* Lund, Sweden: Gleerups.

Laplanche, J., & Pontalis, J.-B. (1973). *The language of psychoanalysis.* London: Hogarth Press.

Neuman, T. (1971, September). Perceptual defense organization as a predictor of the pilot's adaptive behavior in military flying. In J.D. Anderson (Ed.), *Report of the 9th Conference for Aviation Psychology,* Cambridge, UK.

Olff, M., Godaert, G., & Ursin, H. (Eds.). (1991). *Quantification of human defense mechanisms.* Berlin: Springer-Verlag.

Svensson, B., & Trygg, L. (1991). *Personality characteristics of candidates for air traffic controller training.* Lund, Sweden: University of Lund.

Torjussen, T., & Vaernes, R. (1991). The use of the Defense Mechanism Test (DMT) in Norway for selection and stress research. In M. Olff, G. Godaert, & H. Ursin (Eds.), *Quantification of human defense mechanisms* (pp. 172–206). Berlin, Heidelberg, New York: Springer-Verlag.

Vaernes, R.J. (1982). The Defense Mechanism Test predicts inadequate performance under stress! *Scandinavian Journal of Psychology, 23,* 31–43.

Winnicott, D. (1956). *Primary maternal preoccupation in through pediatrics to psychoanalysis.* London: The Hogarth Press and the Institute of Psycho-Analysis.

Olya Khaleelee
10 Golders Rise
London NW4 2HR
UK
Tel. +44 208 202 7097
E-mail olyakh@tiscali.co.uk

Summary

This paper describes the use of the Defense Mechanism Test as an aid in helping to assess senior executives in four areas: for selection, development, career strategy and crisis intervention. The focus is on understanding the function of anxiety and conflict in enabling or hindering performance in role, especially where a role may be stressful and where it demands a clear perception of reality or of threats in the environment. This is especially important with roles such as commercial and fighter pilots, air traffic controllers, deep sea divers, parachutists and so on. The history of the DMT is outlined from its original use in successfully predicting the performance of trainee Swedish fighter pilots during the 1950s to its current use with senior managers. The test has also been used to predict staff turnover in mental health settings. The paper describes how the test works, firstly in terms of its theoretical basis in measuring perception, which is believed to be a complex process rather than an instantaneous event. Secondly, the administration of the test is described in detail and how defense mechanisms, believed to protect the individual from stress, are elucidated from the test data. Finally a (200) set of diagrams illustrates profiles of emotional development over time, both in terms of ideal types, followed by examples of actual test results. Two of these are elaborated with case study material demonstrating how the test can be used effectively in the assessment of senior managers. The first example is of an entrepreneurial manager who found he was less successful once he had to consolidate the business. The second example is of a technical director who aspired to be chief executive but, because of difficult formative experiences, had not developed a sufficient level of emotional intelligence to take up this role. 301 In both cases, suggestions were made about the developmental requirements that would enable each executive to move on.

O. Khaleelee

Résumé

Cet article décrit comment le Test des Mécanismes de Défenses (Defense Mechanism Test, DMT) peut être employé dans avec des chefs d'entreprise dans quatre domaines: la sélection, le développement professionnel et stratégique, et l'intervention en temps de crise. Le but de l'évaluation à l'aide du DMT est de permettre de comprendre les conflits et angoisses qui peuvent entraver les prises de décisions et les performances des dirigeants ou des rôles qui nécessitent des prises de décisions importantes. Le but est aussi d'évaluer les compétences d'individus qui opèrent dans des milieux stressants qui demandent une perception accrue de la réalité ou des risques. Ceci est particulièrement important pour les personnes qui travaillent comme pilote d'avion, aiguilleur du ciel, plongeur sous-marin ou parachutiste. L'historique du DMT est décrit dans cet article. Ce test a été développé dans les années cinquante en Suède pour sélectionner et évaluer les candidats souhaitant devenir pilote d'avion de chasse. Il a été ensuite utilisé dans les sélections de cadres pour entreprise. Il a aussi été utilisé pour étudier les changements fréquents de personnels en milieu psychiatrique. Tout d'abord, cet article décrit l'utilisation et le fonctionnement du DMT d'un point vue théorique et discute les processus complexes en jeu dans la perception de la réalité. La passation du DMT est ensuite expliquée en détail et l'auteur montre comme le test peut mettre à jour les mécanismes de défense qui permettent aux individus de ce protéger contre un environnement stressant ou à risque. Finalement, un certain nombre de diagrammes sont utilisé pour illustrer différents profils affectifs. Deux de ces exemples sont décrits de manière détaillée pour montrer comment le test peut contribuer à l'évaluation de cadres et dirigeants d'entreprise.

Resumen

Este artículo describe el uso del Test de los Mecanismos de Defensa (DMT) como un instrumento útil para evaluar ejecutivos de alto nivel en cuatro áreas: selección, evolución, estrategia de trabajo e intervención en crisis. El foco de la prueba consiste en comprender la función de la ansiedad y el conflicto a la hora de permitir y de obstaculizar la representación del propio rol, especialmente cuando ese rol puede ser estresante o cuando exige una clara percepción de la realidad y de las amenazas existentes en el entorno. Todo esto adquiere especial importancia en roles como, por ejemplo, el de piloto comercial o militar, controlador aéreo, submarinista, paracaidista, etc. La historia del DMT abarca, desde su diseño para preceder con éxito la actuación de pilotos militares en Suecia durante la década de 1950 hasta su uso actual con directivos de otras áreas. Este test también se ha utilizado para predecir los cambios de profesionales en contextos de salud mental. El artículo explica el funcionamiento del test, sobre todo en términos de su base teórica como instrumento para medir la percepción, que se considera como un proceso complejo más que como un acontecimiento momentáneo. Además, se describe la administración del test en detalle y el modo en que los mecanismos de defensa, que actúan para proteger al individuo en situaciones de estrés, se pueden observar en los datos aportados por la prueba. Finalmente, una serie de diagramas (200) ilustra perfiles de desarrollo emocional a través del tiempo, en términos de tipos ideales seguidos de ejemplos con resultados reales del test. Dos de ellos fueron elaborados con material de estudios de casos, demostrando cómo este test puede usarse de manera efectiva en la evaluación de directivos. El primer ejemplo es el caso de un directivo empresarial que parecía menos exitoso una vez que se había consolidado la empresa. El segundo ejemplo es el de un director técnico que aspiraba a ser el jefe ejecutivo pero, a causa de experiencias formativas difíciles, no había alcanzado suficiente nivel de inteligencia emocional para llevar a cabo ese rol. En ambos casos, se aportó orientación y asesoría para que los objetivos a alcanzar permitieran a cada ejecutivo realizar los cambios oportunos.

　本論文は上級管理職を４つの領域：選抜、発達、キャリア戦略、危機介入、においてアセスメントするための防衛機制検査の利用を記述している。とりわけ役割がストレスフルであり、環境の現実と脅威の明確な知覚が要求される役割の遂行を可能にするあるいは妨げる不安や葛藤の機能の理解に焦点が当てられている。これは、商業および軍事パイロット、航空管制官、深海潜水夫、落下傘兵などといった任務においてとりわけ重要である。1950年代のスウェーデンの軍事パイロット訓練生の成績をうまく予測した最初の利用から、上級管理職への最近の利用まで、DMTの歴史が概説されている。この検査はメンタルヘルスの設定におけるスタッフの交替を予測するのにも用いられてきている。本論文では、第一に、それは一時的な事象というよりは複雑な課程であると信じられている、知覚の測定におけるこの検査の理論的根拠という観点から、どのようにこの検査が機能するのかを説明している。次に、この検査の施行が詳しく記述され、個人をストレスから防御すると信じられている防衛機制が検査データより解明されている。最後に、理想的なタイプの観点から、200組のダイアグラムが時間の経過にともなう情緒的な発達のプロフィールを例示し、実際の検査結果の例が続いている。これらのうちの２つは、上級経営者の査定にいかにうまく利用することができたかを例示しているケース検討資料とともに詳しく解説されている。最初の例は、かつてはあまり成功していないと見られ、仕事を強固にしなければいけなかった起業家マネージャーのものである。第二の例は、最高経営責任者になることを熱望しながらも、困難な発達上の経験によって、この役割をとるのに十分なレベルの情緒的理解力を発展させられなかった技術責任者のものである。どちらの事例においても、それぞれの重要職に出世することを可能にするであろうと思われる発達上必要とされることについて示唆がなされている。

Rorschachiana 30, 97–100
© 2009 Hogrefe Publishing

DOI: 10.1027/1192-5604.30.2.97

Special Section: Psychotherapy Outcome

Fernando Silberstein

Professor at the University of Buenos Aires; Editor of Revista Psicodiagnosticar;
Vice-President, Asociación Latinoamericana de Rorschach and founder member of the
Asociación Argentina de Estudio e Investigación en Psicodiagnóstico, ADEIP

The test created by Rorschach started out as a tool which was used both in a clinical sense and for researching some of the theoretical ideas of its author. This is why, from the beginning, the link between the test and patients in psychotherapeutic treatments was established. We can consider as the first of these published comparisons the seldom mentioned case number twelve of the casuistry, which accompanies the original publication of the *Psychodiagnosis*. Here Rorschach studies the changes in an obsessive patient after undergoing psychoanalytical treatment, comparing the protocols obtained at the beginning and end of his treatment. Reading his results today still feels like something very close and alive.

The best known among the first cases is the protocol published posthumously of an engineer, who was analyzed by E. Oberholzer, in which Rorschach tries to understand the patient's behaviour in front of the plates. He introduces new ideas and suggestions which, as we know, even if they were not developed by him, opened up paths for reflection and subsequent studies. Among these we find Rorschach's thoughts on shading and "programmatism in the thinking process" (Rorschach, 1921, English translation by Paul Lemkau, 1942, 5th ed., pp. 196–197). This latter idea, initially a characteristic form of choosing the place of the responses in the figure, leads to and flows towards the concept of style, initially a characteristic form original to a subject. The concept of style has become a way for defining or to proceed assuming what is more stable in a personality. The idea of style stems from literary and artistic studies and moved into the realms of psychology and psychoanalysis. Within the Rorschach camp it was studied by numerous historical authors from different perspectives (among others, D. Shapiro, F. Minkowska, R. Mucchielli) in order to think about the characteristic attitudes, the modifications, and the consistency of the results following the different experiences a patient has gone through. We are indebted to J.E. Exner for his central perspective in studies on stable and variable characteristics observed in patients from the protocols in order to define his or her personality. The article which we present by Vera Campo used this to think, in a very suggestive manner, about the results in the tests and retests within a group of thirty patients treated with psychoanalytical therapies.

From the start, the Rorschach Test has proved its efficacy through the changes that can be seen thanks to the sensitivity of its variables. Even more interesting, as Justine McCarthy Woods highlights in her article in this Special Section, is that it allows access to the existence of transformations in the subject which are not obvious otherwise for the psychotherapist. This same observation is made by Naomi Inoue in her case study of a trauma survivor.

Many years have gone by since the first Rorschach studies, during which the validity and reliability of the test have been fully proven. Now we seek less to prove the efficacy of the test by comparing the transformations obtained with the differences in the second protocol; beforehand and inversely we can validate and broaden our understanding of what has occurred during the treatments by the results obtained in the test. We have become so used to the test's great sensitivity that we consider it an obvious fact. However it is still important to ask questions.

If we look back at history, we must remember that the foundations for the Rorschach Test arose with the antecedent of the perceptive studies linked to a model of symbolization that its author had begun eleven years before and as an investigation of the processes which this approach allowed within the clinical context of his work as a psychiatrist. From the start, Rorschach tried to join the experience of perceptive organization and the processes of symbolization. He studied these by trying to understand the functioning of different subjects and also to find out how they would behave with regard to the basic variables of the test-movement, introversion, associativity and creative ability opposed to colour, extraversion, reproductive capacity. The variables he chose – determinants, localization – express or attempt to express the theoretical concerns that moved him and which refer, partly within the Germanic psychology scheme of his professor Eugen Bleuler, to the search of this attitude before the world, antecedent of the phenomenological position, which several of his disciples studied under different denominations. In Rorschach this attitude takes form under categories which, after his death, have been considered just an empirical listing capable of showing, with unequalled fineness, the variations of the subject's psychic transformations. These have been later studied from concepts which could have many differences among themselves. This situation, considered an obvious fact, brings forward an epistemological and methodological question which we should not evade by sheltering within the habit of the daily use of ideas which we are accustomed to think about.

In the first place, we could hypothesize that the processes found by the variables in the test are so broad that they permit us to look into others, which by definition would be included in this very sensitivity. Secondly, that the processes conceptualized by the theories either find or share common empirical bases in spite of the possible theoretical and methodological differences and approaches in their respective theoretical contexts of origin. That is to say that the processes of the variables in the test considered through habit of thinking as only empirical are based on or tend to describe a process common to the subsequent psychopathological theories, and to show a central process of the emotional functioning, at least as we can consider it still today.

It is worth adding, however, that the above consideration finds its own space from within the context of construction of the hypothesis, more than from the empirical contrasting. The latter validates the existence of this link, which constitutes the efficacy of the test.

The follow-up study and results in psychotherapeutic treatments clearly show the ductility of the variables in the test. With the matter of the validation of the study itself and also of the test, we see a complex existence arise of the thought processes concerned, which hold up these possibilities and which make possible the broadness and richness of description.

The four papers submitted in this Special Section cover in their different ways the methodological and technical problems of psychotherapy outcome analyzed from the test. In each we see the complexity of the processes under study, which seem to add something more to what is already known by therapists. Vera Campo studies the concept of style of the variables in the test in order to be able to think about the changes and traits which are most stable in subjects who were treated psychoanalytically. Adriana Lis gives us an exhaustive analysis of an early adolescent and the changes which were observed thanks to the treatment and studied through the administration of the Rorschach and other tests. Justine McCarthy Woods presents a comparative study of adolescents using the Rorschach and a special approach scheme of four consultations. Naomi Inoue presents the case of a woman affected by a traumatic situation and treated with Eye Movement Desensitization and Reprocessing (EMDR) therapy and who was administered the Rorschach, TAT, and the IES-R scale. In each of these four articles, we see the variations obtained and the traits which appear to be the most stable in the subjects. But also the processes observed from the classifications allow us unique access to the thinking and emotional processes of these patients. We might think that it is a matter of good translation or rather that the Rorschach provides us, from behind the theories that we have become accustomed to read and relate to, with an exciting look upon the potent mental functioning processes, which are only partly capable of being described along with the great well-known theories.

If the psychopathological theories and the psychotherapeutic practices found an efficient ally in the Rorschach for studying the variations in a subject comprised within them, perhaps it is up to us to look more deeply at the possibility of continuing the variables of Rorschach's symbolization model in the field of psychotherapy. Up until now only the phenomenologists have made attempts in this direction.

Rorschachiana 30, 101–128
© 2009 Hogrefe Publishing

DOI: 10.1027/1192-5604.30.2.101

Variations of Rorschach Variables
in Therapeutic Follow-Up

Vera Campo

Professor of Rorschach of the Barcelona Rorschach School, Catalan Rorschach Society, Barcelona, Spain

Abstract. This paper studies some of the basic Rorschach styles and diagnostic indexes, most of which are considered to be stable over time in the Comprehensive System (EB and EBPer, EA, Lambda, Form Color Ratio, Afr, Mp > Ma, $3r + (2)/R$, Reflections, Zd+–, X+%, SCZI, DEPI and CDI and AP). It compares the Rorschach protocols of 30 adult patients before and after 1 year of psychoanalytic therapy. The concept of style, a simple description of the patterns of changes observed (%'s), the descriptive group statistics together with a comparison of paired groups (Wilcoxon), a Pearson correlation, and a comparison with the Weiner and Exner (1990) study are described and discussed, with the aim of clarifying and briefly illustrating how these styles and indexes behave in follow-up research with the Rorschach, and how their stability is over time. Results showed that, with the exception of EA, EBPer, Afr, the directionality of the Form Color Ratio, high W and Dd, S responses, and a high Lambda – styles that appeared as most stable – no definite patterns could be observed in the remaining styles and indexes studied after only 1 year of treatment.

Keywords: styles, indexes, stability, therapy

This study observes the changes that take place after 1 year of long-term psychoanalysis or psychoanalytic psychotherapy in 30 subjects (8 men and 32 women, between 20 and 51 years of age, mean age: 29.0), who consulted for many different reasons, had various personality structures, were treated by different therapists, and had different numbers of treatment sessions (between 2 and 4 per week, whereas only 5 had less than 4; see Table 1, which very briefly describes each individual case).

Although these external variables could not be controlled, this being a posttreatment study, nevertheless continuing interest in treatment effects and follow-up (Botbol, Campo, Dow, & Galan, 1987; Campo, 1988, 1995; Campo & Dow, 1993; Campo, Dow, & Tuset, 1993) and particular-

V. Campo

Table 1. Age, sex, number of treatment sessions, personality data, and therapeutic evolution (derived from the Rorschach protocols and clinical data) of 30 patients after 1 year of long-term psychoanalytic psychotherapy

Case	Age	Sex	Sessions	Personality traits	Therapeutic evolution and diagnostic features
1	23	F	2	Reactive depression in hysteroid personality, paranoid base DEPI = 4, CDI = 4, L = 3.25	Clinically improved DEPI = 4, CDI = 3, HVI, L = 1.00
2	34	F	2	Schizophrenia SCZI = 6	Clinically improved SCZI = 4
3	43	M	4	Depression in obsessive personality DEPI = 6, CDI = 5, L = .52	Clinically improved DEPI = 5, CDI = 3, L = 1.17
4	36	F	4	Depression, somatization, lesbian SCZI = 4, DEPI = 6	Clinically improved SCZI = 3, DEPI = 4
5	22	F	4	Depressive moods, interpersonal problems in hysteroid personality DEPI = 5, CDI = 5, L = .63	Clinically improved DEPI = 4, CDI = 3, L = 1.38
6	24	F	4	Depressive moods, somatization DEPI = 5	Clinically improved DEPI = 3
7	21	F	4	Anxiety, depression S-CON = 10, SCZI = 6, DEPI = 6, Fr = 1	Doubtful evolution S-CON = 9, SCZI = 6, DEPI = 5, Fr = 1
8	21	F	4	Anxiety, depressive moods, interpersonal problems S-CON = 8, DEPI = 5, CDI = 4, Fr = 1	Doubtful evolution S-CON = 7, SCZI = 4, DEPI = 7, CDI = 4, Fr = 0
9	31	F	4	Depressive moods DEPI = 5	More disorganized? but less depressed SCZI = 5, DEPI = 4
10	22	F	4	Anxiety, depression S-CON = 10, DEPI = 6, CDI = 4	Doubtful evolution, now 5 borderline contents S-CON = 9, DEPI = 6, CDI = 2
11	21	F	4	Depressive moods, rage, somatization DEPI = 5	Clinically improved DEPI = 4
12	25	F	4	Depressive moods S-CON = 8, DEPI = 5	Clinically improved DEPI = 4
13	37	F	4	Borderline SCZI = 5	Clinically much improved SCZI = 1
14	36	F	4	Depressive moods, interpersonal problems SCZI = 4, DEPI = 5, CDI = 5, Fr = 1	Clinically improved SCZI = 3, DEPI = 4, CDI = 3, Fr = 0

Variations of Rorschach Variables in Therapeutic Follow-Up

Case	Age	Sex	Sessions	Personality traits	Therapeutic evolution and diagnostic features
15	34	M	4	Depression DEPI = 4	Doubtful evolution DEPI = 6
16	28	M	4	Depression DEPI = 6	Clinically improved DEPI = 3
17	32	F	4	Depression S-CON = 8, DEPI = 6	Slight improvement? S-CON = 5, DEPI = 6
18	25	F	4	Paranoid depression S-CON = 8, SCZI = 4, DEPI = 7, HVI	Doubtful evolution S-CON = 7, SCZI = 1, DEPI = 6
19	21	F	4	Immature personality S-CON = 8, CDI = 4	Doubtful evolution S-CON = 7, DEPI = 6, CDI = 3
20	24	F	4	Depression, interpersonal problems DEPI = 7, CDI = 4	Therapeutic regression SCZI = 6, DEPI = 7, CDI = 3
21	24	M	4	Anxiety, phobic and obsessive traits, depression S-CON = 8, SCZI = 6, DEPI = 6, OBS = 3	Doubtful evolution S-CON = 5, SCZI = 6, DEPI = 5, OBS = 4
22	20	F	2	Schizoid character L = 1.70	Clinically improved, but now DEPI = 5, CDI = 4, L = 1.42
23	22	M	2	Paranoid schizophrenia, drug abuse, suicide attempts SCZI = 5, L = 3.00	Clinically much improved SCZI = 2, HVI, L = .31
24	28	M	2	Obsessive ideation, phobic traits L = .33	Clinically improved but now Fr = 2, L = 1.06
25	25	F	4	Hysteroid personality, psychotic ideation, SCZI = 6, DEPI = 5, L = 1.44	Doubtful evolution S-CON = 6, SCZI = 3, DEPI = 5, L = 1.14
26	51	M	4	Major depression in phobic personality with obsessive traits DEPI = 4, L = 1.08	Clinically improved but now L = 1.53, DEPI = 5
27	33	M	4	Major depression in depressive personality S-CON = 8, DEPI = 6	Clinically slightly improved? S-CON = 7, DEPI = 6, CDI = 4
28	44	F	4	Hysteroid personality, schizoid base, depression and somatic complaints DEPI = 6	No change DEPI = 6
29	25	M	4	Borderline schizophrenia, alcohol abuse SCZI = 6	Doubtful evolution S-CON = 9, SCZI = 5, DEPI = 5
30	20	F	4	Emotional problems in obsessive personality	Clinically much improved

ly in the stability of certain Rorschach variables and styles – as shown by the fundamental Weiner and Exner (1990) study – led to the observations presented below.

But what is a *style*? Exner (1993) refers to it as the "more basic features of personality ... although historically they have also been identified as traits ... (that) give rise to psychological and behavioral response tendencies ..." (p. 404), creating "one of the strengths of the Rorschach, as a test – its reliability over time" (p. 44). He describes the characteristics of several styles: Lambda, introversive and extratensiveness, the EB, the EBPer, reflection responses, the "Snow White syndrome," etc. His many investigations on the temporal stability of styles – mostly in nonpatients – showed that, for instance, the directionality of the FC:CF + C Ratio is quite remarkably stable, as are the retest correlations for Afr, the egocentricity index (3r + 2), or the S responses elevated beyond the mean; and that Zd+ subjects are more stable than Zd– ones. (While the Experience Actual – EA – is not a style, it appears to be rather unstable over time in the sense of its observed increase, particularly in long-term interventions.). This lead him to the following conclusion: "In most instances, the basics of the person do not change" (p. 50).

Nevertheless, psychological *states* can and do influence the temporal stability of styles as Exner has shown in his studies on stress (m + Y), loss (T), and major depression (DEPI).

So what occurs during and/or after treatment? As is shown by the Weiner and Exner study (1990) on psychotherapeutic change after 1 year, in the long-term treatment group (N = 88) the positive changes registered concerned a number of variables. Those also chosen for this study were: CDI, Zd–, Lambda, X+% < .70, DEPI = 5, Afr < .50, CF + C > FC + 1, and Mp > Ma.

After only 1 year of treatment – and according to the Weiner and Exner study – no fundamental changes were expected in the D scores, X–% (keeping in mind that the Barcelona normative, 1993, mean is .19), T (presence or absence since this Barcelona normative mean is less than 1), and FD (normatively low, too). Furthermore, in order to avoid "cluttering up" the present study, some variables were excluded, while the SCZI index – since local experience had shown that it was not very reliable (Alvarez et al., 1993) – seemed interesting enough to be observed again and included as well.

The variables that did *not* change in the Weiner and Exner study after 1 year were: EA < 7, the ambient style, DEPI > 5, Fr + rF > 0, and 3r + (2)/R.

One question raised by these data concerns the relationship between styles (or traits, a concept preferred by this author), states, personality structure, the degree of pathology, *and* the therapeutic relationship (which does not always work). We will not attempt to solve this very complex puzzle, but rather only mention that in a smaller study on the ORT and the Rorschach (Campo & Dow, 1993) with only 10 patients, it seemed quite clear, for instance, that the more pathological subjects changed less than the more "neurotic" ones.

Another part of the puzzle concerns the often difficult translation of the many Rorschach styles into clinical, psychological, or psychiatric theories of psychopathology, not only because these employ a different language, but also because they have tended to change over time.

Method

The 60 Rorschach protocols of the study were administered at the "Dr. Enrique Racker" Clinic of the Argentine Psychoanalytic Association, which offered 1 year of "orthodox" psychoanalytic treatment – 4 sessions a week – to economically limited subjects in the social professions (teachers, social workers, psychiatric nurses, and the like) as a first step in an interrupted pilot study on treatment effects. The five subjects with only two sessions a week belonged to the same institution, but to another organizational division, dedicated to psychoanalytical psychotherapy.

The protocols were scored twice (with the Comprehensive System), once by the author, who had administered 29 of the 30 cases, and once by another Rorschach specialist (with thanks to N. Vilar) with an overall coincidence of better than 80%. (As usual, difficulty was greatest regarding the Special Scores.)

According to the aim of the study – to observe the variations of the principal Rorschach "styles" – the following 14 variables were chosen and recorded twice for comparison – initially in percentages – before and after 1 year of treatment; all subjects were re-tested between 12 and 18 months after the initiation of therapy:

1. **AP***: The Perceptual Approach (W, D, Dd, and S), which according to Beck (1960) is rather impervious to change if it is centered on either W, D or Dd, that is to say, unbalanced.

---

*   The reason for including the perceptual approach – **AP** – is derived from Beck's (1960, p. 202–203) considerations regarding its very early installation and its scant change over time.

2. **EB** and **EBPer**: The Experience Balance, considered to be very stable by most Rorschach authors including Exner (1993), which reflects a person's characteristic coping style, oriented either toward ideation, toward affective manifestation, or toward an oscillation between these two basically complementary (Rorschach, 1948) styles. And the EBPer, which reflects their pervasiveness, i.e., their rigidity (Exner, 1993).

3. **EA**: Beck's (1960) "experience actual," which reflects a person's total emotional reactivity and mobility. It "may be the road either to Waterloo or to Olympus" (p. 204) as regards the possibility of change.

4. **Lambda**: By means of which a subject simplifies and narrows the stimulus field – from another point of view separates = dissociates and represses or denies parts of reality – although it remains unclear when Lambda is not a style but the effect, for instance, of a melancholic depression (Rapaport, 1968; Kohler & Bernhard, 1970; Liberal, 1987; Rorschach, 1948).

5. **Form-Color Ratio** (FC:CF + C) or the modulation of affect.

6. **Afr**: Responsiveness to affectively toned stimuli.

7. **Mp > Ma**: The "Snow White" syndrome by which a subject avoids and denies unpleasant situations through flight into fantasy.

8. **3r + (2)/R**: related to self-centeredness and self-esteem.

9. **Reflection responses**: These are consistently interpreted by Exner (1993) as a narcissistic feature, although no Rorschach author appears to have studied the numerical significance of this response. Gacono and Meloy (1994) dedicate a whole chapter of their recent book to it without coming to any conclusions regarding this aspect, although they do point out that "its presence should be contextualized by frequency, location, form level, other determinants, and special scores to advance its meaning for a particular patient" (p. 258), also pointing out that the most frequent reflection response occurs to Card VIII.

10. **Zd+–**: Reflecting over and under incorporation of stimulus cues, this also has stylistic features (Exner, 1993): While Zd– people can be taught to pay more attention to them, Zd+ subjects are more impervious to change, and psychological treatment tends to reinforce this cautious and careful perceptual attitude.

11. **X+%**: Normatively (see Exner's data on child development, 1993) and in nonpatients X+% is a quite stable Rorschach feature; this aspect, related to precise reality perception, was also included in this study.

12. **SCZI**: Was included because of its lack of preciseness and stability, often registered in clinical experience (Campo, 1993, 1994)*.
13. **DEPI**: Included because so many of the 30 subjects had a positive depression index.
14. **CDI**: Known to be unstable (Exner, 1993); nevertheless, this index was also included in order to observe said instability.

Furthermore, and from a more statistical point of view, means and standard deviations were calculated for the 14 variables in the two sets of protocols (see Table 3), as well as a comparison of paired groups (Wilcoxon, see Table 4) and a Pearson correlation (see Table 5).

Results

A simple review of these 14 compared variables (see Table 2) showed the following:

1. **AP**: In only 11 of the 30 subjects (37%) did the AP vary substantially; in 9 of these toward a more balanced distribution, particularly centered on D responses. 7 of the 30 subjects maintain a high W approach (23%), in 9 the style is a large number of Dd's (30%), whereas 12 increase their Dd's even more. As regards the S responses, little change is found, for of the 18 subjects (60%), who had 2 or more space responses, 16 keep them (53%).
2. Concerning the **EB**, the results are most varied: Of the 11 introversive subjects 7 remain the same, but 3 become ambitent and 1 extratensive. Of the 6 extratensives 1 turns ambitent. And of the 12 ambitents, 4 do not change, but 5 become introversive and 3 extratensive. Only 1 case had a very coarcted EB which became introversive. As to the **EBPer**, in 20 subjects (66%) this variable remains unchanged, either high – 8 subjects – or within the "normal" range – 12 subjects – while in the rest – 10 subjects – it becomes either rigid or "normal." But if we relate these data to the changes registered in

---

* Note 2008: This point of view seems to be in accordance with the Comprehensive System's development in the sense of the substitution of the SCZI index by the PTI, which in the author's experience appears to be much more reliable and also less "psychiatric" – that is to say, more clinically and psychologically descriptive as the Rorschach is meant to work.

Table 2a. 14 compared variables in 30 subjects: first Rorschach

No.	W	D	Dd	S	EB + EBPer	EA	FC:CF + C	Afr	Ma:Mp	L	Zd	EGO
1	3	30	3	1	1:0	1	0:0	.31	1:0	3.25	−1.5	.24
2	10	0	0	0	8:2high*	10	0:2	.43	3:5	.33	+10.0	.50
3	3	15	7	1	4:0high	4	0:0	.37	2:2	.78	0	.52
4	12	5	3	6	8:45	12.5	5:2	.43	4:4	.25	−2.0	.43
5	7	10	9	0	1:6high	7	2:4	.37	0:1	.63	−1.0	.27
6	7	3	2	0	3:3, 5	6.5	1:3	.33	2:1	.50	+7.0	.33
7	33	11	3	4	21:15	36	2:14	.48	13:11	.07	+11.5	.55
8	5	20	5	3	3:4.5	7.5	2:3	.50	2:1	.50	+8.5	.47
9	10	5	2	3	5:1.5high	6.5	1:1	.42	4:1	.42	+4.0	.65
10	22	20	5	8	5:10.5	15.5	3:8	.55	0:5	.62	+4.5	.13
11	7	5	3	1	4:4.5	9.5	1:4	.25	3:1	.36	+5.5	.40
12	11	0	0	1	3:4.5	7.5	2:3	.38	2:1	.10	+4.0	.36
13	7	6	1	1	5:2	7	4:0	.56	3:2	.27	−4.0	.36
14	5	19	6	4	7:0.5high	7.5	1:0	.36	4:2	.43	−1.0	.36
15	7	3	8	1	6:1 high	7	2:0	.80	3:3	.50	−1.0	.67
16	6	10	2	2	4:5	9	3:3	.29	1:3	.13	+7.0	.22
17	11	15	10	9	8:6.5	14.5	2:4	.71	4:4	.38	+11.5	.28
18	14	7	2	6	6:5	11	2:4	.44	5:2	.28	+6.5	.30
19	11	3	1	2	1:4 high	5	1:3	.50	0:1	.67	+6.0	.13
20	8	19	2	5	3:7.5	10.5	5:4	.45	2:1	.38	+6.5	.24
21	6	18	18	9	5:5	10	7:1	.54	1:4	.34	+6.5	.45
22	9	14	4	3	7:05high	7.5	1:0	.29	5:2	1.70	+2.0	.30
23	12	2	1	3	4:0 high	4	0:0	.25	2:0	2.00	+0.5	.33
24	9	5	2	2	6:1 high	7	0:1	.33	4:3	.33	−4.0	.44
25	10	12	0	0	2:4.5	6.5	2:3	.69	1:1	1.44	−3.0	.55
26	3	16	8	1	4:1.5 high	5.5	0:1	.35	1:3	1.08	−.5	.09
27	13	5	4	4	3:6	9	1:5	.57	2:1	.38	+.5	.27
28	9	5	3	0	4:4.5	8.5	1:4	.31	1:3	.55	+3.0	.35
29	17	0	3	7	12:8.5	20.5	4:6	.67	4:8	.05	+12.0	.40
30	9	26	11	3	14:4 high	18	2:3	.48	7:7	.39	−3.0	.26

*high = > 2.5

Table 2b. Additional 5 compared variables of 30 subjects: first Rorschach

No.	Fr	X+%	SCZI	CDI	DEPI
1	0	.70	0	YES	4
2	0	.30	6	NO	4
3	0	.64	0	YES	6
4	0	.40	4	NO	6
5	0	.38	3	YES	5
6	0	.58	1	NO	5
7	1	.32	6	NO	6
8	1	.53	2	YES	5
9	0	.71	1	NO	5
10	0	.36	1	YES	6
11	0	.67	0	NO	5
12	0	.45	1	NO	5
13	0	.36	5	NO	2
14	1	.56	4	YES	5
15	0	.39	3	NO	4
16	0	.72	1	NO	6
17	0	.50	1	NO	6
18	0	.52	4	NO	7
19	0	.27	1	YES	3
20	0	.41	1	NO	7
21	0	.33	6	NO	6
22	0	.56	1	NO	4
23	0	.47	5	NO	3
24	0	.56	0	NO	2
25	0	.36	6	NO	5
26	0	.44	3	NO	4
27	0	.64	0	NO	6
28	0	.41	3	NO	6
29	0	.45	6	NO	4
30	0	.57	2	NO	4

Table 2c. 14 Compared variables in 30 subjects: second Rorschach

No.	W	D	Dd	S	EB + EBPer	EA	FC:CF+C	Afr	Ma:Mp	L	Zd	EGO
1	3	12	2	0	7:2.5high	9.5	2:1	.44	3:4	1.0	−9.0	.28
2	8	3	1	1	6:3	9	0:3	.33	5:1	.33	+10.0	.33
3	3	23	11	0	3:3.5	6.5	3:2	.42	2:1	1.17	+3.5	.42
4	18	6	4	5	5:7.5	12.5	6:4	.75	3:2	.21	+3.5	.36
5	5	7	7	1	1:3 high	4	2:2	.58	0:1	1.38	−1.0	.32
6	4	8	2	0	2:4	6	0:4	.75	1:1	.27	+2.5	.50
7	16	12	18	6	20:10	30	6:6	.50	12:11	.12	−12.0	.52
8	7	26	11	1	5:5.5	10.5	4:3	.42	2:3	.33	−1.0	.42
9	8	23	5	1	9:3.5high	12.5	5:1	.57	4:5	.56	+1.5	.50
10	39	9	2	11	4:12.5high	16.5	4:9	.47	1:3	.47	+10.0	.14
11	8	11	1	0	3:6	9	3:4	.43	4:0	.33	+1.5	.40
12	9	11	1	0	4:5.5	9.5	3:3	.31	2:2	.40	+1.0	.43
13	6	18	3	0	5:7	12	5:3	.93	3:2	.35	−1.5	.33
14	7	16	4	3	6:6.5	12.5	4:3	.50	5:1	.50	−1.0	.33
15	6	16	12	3	6:1.5high	7.5	1:1	.55	4:2	.79	−1.0	.44
16	5	21	2	3	3:5.5	8.5	7:2	1.15	3:0	.40	+6.5	.43
17	5	17	26	12	8:3.5	11.5	5:1	.66	3:5	.45	+1.0	.31
18	13	16	8	2	9:5	14	3:3	.46	4:5	.30	+6.5	.54
19	11	7	5	3	2:7.5high	9.5	2:5	.35	1:1	.44	−5.0	.17
20	8	13	5	4	3:3	6	3:1	.37	1:2	.86	+3.5	.54
21	4	19	27	10	11:1high	12	2:0	.43	3:9	.72	+5.5	.42
22	4	14	11	5	6:05high	6.5	1:0	.16	2:4	1.42	+6.5	.21
23	11	3	3	2	8:1.5high	9.5	1:1	.55	7:1	.31	+7.0	.41
24	10	21	6	2	4:2.5	6.5	1:2	.48	4:0	1.06	−8.0	.43
25	8	6	1	0	1:2.5	3.5	0:3	.67	0:1	1.14	−4.5	.47
27	10	7	4	5	1:6 high	7	2:4	.50	1:0	.40	+2.5	.29
28	12	5	0	3	6:6	12	3:4	.31	5:2	.06	+1.5	.35
29	16	4	3	5	17:9	26	4:6	.77	10:8	.05	+15.0	.61
30	6	23	11	4	12:3high	15	2:2	.48	7:5	.48	+2.0	.38

*high = > 2.5

Table 2d. Additional 5 compared variables of 30 subjects: second Rorschach

No.	Fr	X+%	SCZI	CDI	DEPI
1	0	.55	3	NO	4
2	0	.50	4	NO	4
3	0	.57	1	NO	4
4	0	.43	3	NO	4
5	0	.47	3	NO	4
6	0	.50	2	NO	3
7	1	.28	6	NO	5
8	0	.47	4	YES	7
9	0	.47	5	NO	4
10	0	.30	3	NO	6
11	0	.60	1	NO	4
12	0	.71	0	NO	4
13	0	.44	1	NO	4
14	0	.44	3	NO	4
15	0	.50	3	NO	6
16	0	.61	2	NO	3
17	0	.35	2	NO	6
18	0	.54	1	NO	6
19	0	.39	2	NO	6
20	0	.31	6	NO	7
21	0	.28	6	NO	5
22	0	.55	2	YES	5
23	0	.41	2	NO	2
24	2	.49	1	NO	2
25	0	.33	3	NO	5
26	0	.33	3	NO	5
27	0	.52	1	YES	6
28	0	.65	3	NO	6
29	0	.30	5	NO	5
30	0	.60	1	NO	4

the EB, no definite patterns can be detected: Only 6 subjects (20%) – 2 extratensives and 4 introversives – maintain the directionality of their EB and their rigid EBPer. Among the 14 subjects (47%) in whom the EBPer stays within the normal range, their respective EB's change direction except in 3 ambitents. In 5 rigid EBPer's who become normal, there was 1 extratensive, 2 introversives, and 2 introversives who become ambitent, while the remaining 5 subjects whose normal EBPer turns rigid, there are 2 extratensives, 2 ambitents who become introversive, and the 1 coarcted subject who turns into an introversive.

3. As regards **EA**, 18 subjects oscillate around the values (< 7) of their first Rorschach (60%): 5 increase their values to more than 7 points, 4 decrease them below 7, and only 3 remain below 7.

4. **Lambda**: Only 4 of 5 subjects had and maintained a high Lambda (> .99), but 3 patients acquired this style. The rest oscillate around low numbers with no discernible pattern.

5. **Form-Color Ratio**: 18 subjects (60%) do not change the directionality of this ratio, but in 17 subjects (57%) emotional control develops and/or increases positively: 11 subjects maintain their initial lability –CF + C > FC–, 2 remain unchanged and coarcted, 4 had adequate control from the beginning, and 1 remains supercontrolled.

6. **Afr**: In 19 subjects (63%) it either stays equally low (53% under .52) or within the normative range (10%), while among the remaining 11 subjects diverse changes are registered: Some open up to the normal range – 4 –, some close down – 3 –, only 1 goes from one [high] extreme to the other [low], 1 from high to normal, and the last viceversa.

7. **Mp > Ma**: Regarding this aspect in 15 subjects (50%) Ma > Mp. But of the remaining 50%, 5 Snow White subjects come out of their fantasy refuge, 2 remain in their private cave, and 3 turn into Snow Whites, while another 5 subjects tend toward this style (Mp > Ma by only one point) in their second Rorschach.

8. **3r + (2)/R**: Oscillates so much that no pattern can be discerned: 6 subjects stay within the expected mean, 7 remain below it, 6 go from a high to the "normative" level, 3 stay above it, 2 acquire it from a high percentage, 2 go from normal to high, 2 go from a high to a low mean, and 2 descend below the mean.

9. **Fr + rF**: Information regarding this narcissistic trait is meager since only 1 subject gave 1 reflection response to both protocols, another 2 subjects lost their Fr, and only 1 gained 2 in the second testing.

10. **Zd+−**: Again, no clear pattern can be seen: 5 subjects stay within the expected range, 7 subjects with high scores do not change, and 5 become overincorporators after 1 year of treatment, while in 9 Zd enters the normal range – from above or below it. But 4 become underincorporators (!), 2 of whom change from the high to the low extreme.

11. **X+%**: Since the 30 subjects of the study are all of Hispanic origin, the tentative data from the Barcelona normative investigation (Alvarez et al., 1993) were applied: **Mean X+% = .55 + −.13**. Otherwise, only 2 subjects would be considered to have an adequate perceptual accuracy (i.e., > .70 according to Exner's, 1993, normative data). Thus, 15 patients (50%) fall within the Barcelona "normal" range and 7 reach this level on their second Rorschach, thus showing some improvement, while 8 either stay below it (4) or lose it completely (4).

12. **SCZI**: 10 subjects showed a positive index (4–6). Thereof, 6 lost it, 4 maintained it (2: 6 → 6 and 1: 6 → 5) without being considered clinically schizophrenic, while 1, who had been psychiatrically diagnosed as schizophrenic, improved (6 → 4), but 3 subjects acquired a positive index, 1 of whom showed a therapeutic regression (meaning a generalized state of disorganization and anxiety).

13. **DEPI = 7**: 2 subjects, 1 goes down to DEPI = 6; DEPI = 6: 9 subjects, of these 3 lose the index, 4 keep it, and 2 go down to DEPI = 5. DEPI = 5: of the 8 subjects, 6 lose it, 1 keeps it and 1 acquires an index of 7. The index was not significant in 10 subjects, but of these 5 acquire a positive index of 5 or 6 on their second protocols. Again, this index behaved in a haphazard manner, but in the subjects with a score of 6 or 7, DEPI tends to stay positive – as Exner (1993) also found.

14. **CDI**: While in 19 subjects this index was negative, in 6 out of 7 it disappears in the second testing, and in 2 it becomes positive.

A comparison of the two paired groups (Wilcoxon) (see Tables 3 and 4) showed that, on this group level, only four variables changed significantly: The D location, which increased (p .01), as well as the Dd location (p .002), while S remained unchanged. Also FC in the Color Ratio increased in the second testing (p = .01). Both W and Ma only tended to increase (p = .09).

The Pearson correlation (see Table 5) showed, at a p level of .05 (higher than .70), the following: a high correlation for high W subjects as well as for subjects with many Dd and S responses. Furthermore, a high correlation was also found for M in the EB but not for SumC, the same occurring for Ma but not for Mp, and finally for EA.

113

Table 3. Descriptive statistics of 14 Rorschach variables: Rorschach 1

Variable	Mean	SD	Kurtosis	Skewness
W	9.86	5.98	7.21	2.27
D	9.70	7.13	-.79	.46
Dd	4.23	3.98	3.69	1.72
S	2.96	2.74	-.13	.88
EB	5.56:4.11			
EA	9.75	6.44	9.04	2.58
FC:CF + C	1.83:2.86			
Afr	.44	.14	.05	.76
Ma:Mp	2.86:2.83			
Lambda	.63	.67	7.58	2.58
Zd	3.20	4.97	-1.07	.23
EGO	.53	.91	28.37	5.26
Fr	.10	.30	6.30	2.80
X+%	.48	.13	-.99	.27
SCZI	2.56	2.14	-1.23	.45
DEPI	4.86	1.30	-.13	-.53

Qualitative variables:
1. EBPer: High: 12
2. CDI: YES: 7
NO: 23

Table 4. Descriptive statistics of 14 Rorschach variables: Rorschach 2

Variable	Mean	SD	Kurtosis	Skewness
W	9.13	6.88	12.04	3.03
D	13.13	6.74	-1.10	.17
Dd	7.26	7.37	1.68	1.53
S	3.13	3.23	1.74	1.41
EB	6.13:4.73			
EA	10.86	5.62	4.93	1.95
FC:CF + C	2.80:2.86			
Afr	.52	.20	2.44	1.24
Ma:Mp	3.53:2.83			
Lambda	.59	.41	-.22	.90
Zd	1.28	6.03	.25	-.17
EGO	.39	.11	.13	.40
Fr	.10	.40	18.77	4.28
X +%	.46	.11	-.75	.04
SCZI	2.73	1.63	-.27	.61
DEPI	4.66	1.29	-.32	-.14

Qualitative variables:
1. EBPer: High 13
2. CDI YES: 3
NO: 27

Table 5. Comparison of Rorschach variables (means, Wilcoxon, paired groups)

Variables	Z	P		
W1–W2	–1.65		.0988 *	
D1–D2	–2.53		.0113 **	
Dd1–Dd2	–3.02		.0025 **	
FC:CF + C1–FC:CF + C2	–2.51	–.58	.0119**	.5590
Ma:Mp1–Ma:Mp2	–1.68	–.16	.0990*	.8710

Table 6. Pearson correlation for 14 Rorschach variables (*p* .05), Rorschach 1 – Rorschach 2

Variables		Correlation
1.	W 1–W 2	.7018 *
2.	Dd 1–Dd 2	.7688 *
3.	S 1–S 2	.8540 *
4.	EB 1–EB 2 (1st proportion)	.8306 *
	EB 1–EB 2 (2nd proportion)	.6446
5.	EA 1–EA 2	.8330 *
6.	FC:CF + C (1st proportion)	.3770
	FC:CF + C (2nd proportion)	.6800
7.	Ma:Mp 1–Ma:Mp 2 (1st proportion)	7255*
	Ma:Mp 1–Ma:Mp 2 (2nd proportion)	6683

Discussion

1. As expected, following Beck, the perceptual approach – **AP** – did not vary substantially in the 30 subjects of this study. Both high W and high Dd subjects resort to the same style. The noted increase in usual details (D) suggests a positive change toward a better appreciation of the obvious, concrete and practical aspects of reality, while the space response (S) appears to be the most stable aspect of the AP (53%), coinciding with Exner's (1993) observations.

2. The **EB**'s appear much less stable in general, and also less stable than the **EBPers**'s, which may not be so striking; but 1 year of therapy may be too brief a period to reach any conclusions regarding the stability of the Experience Balance. In any case, it was expected that the EB would be *less* affected by only 1 year of treatment.

115

3. Meanwhile, the **EA** remains practically unchanged in 60%, which, in light of the general findings of the study, points to a certain stability coinciding with Weiner and Exner's (1990) experience in their long-term group after 1 year of treatment.

4. As regards **Lambda**, there were 4 subjects who maintained this style (80%): One was a hysterical character who suffered a reactive depression, clinically improved; another a rather rigid schizoid woman who showed little change; the third a hysteroid personality with psychotic ideation and a doubtful evolution; and the last a phobic personality with obsessive features who consulted for a major depression, improved. In all of them the second Rorschach showed few basic changes, thus pointing to a rather rigid and stable style. Of the 3 patients who acquired a high Lambda, one was again severely obsessive, improved; one hysterical, improved; and one phobic, improved. But the distinction between Lambda as an either hysterical or obsessive defensive style or under the influence of a severe depression could not be satisfactorily clarified because of the small number of cases and treatment time. In any case, the high Lambda subjects of this study appear to be less modifiable than Weiner and Exner's (1990) subjects. The fact that some patients acquire the high Lambda style on their second protocol might be explained by its being obscured by other features in the first Rorschach, or by its being increased as a response to a greater defensiveness at second testing.

5. The directionality of the **Form-Color** ratio reached a stability of 60%. What does seem clear – and expected from a clinical point of view, as Weiner and Exner (1990) also found – is that emotional modulation changed and improved in slightly more than half of the 30 cases.

6. The **Afr** seems a rather stable variable in this sample, *not* coinciding with Weiner and Exner's (1990) findings, since in 63% no changes were observed.

7. The only thing that can be said of the **Snow White** syndrome is that it does change with psychotherapy – as Weiner and Exner (1990) also found – but both in a positive and possibly even a negative sense.

8. **3r + (2)/R** proves to be very changeable, *not* coinciding with the Weiner and Exner (1990) study.

9. **Reflection responses**: That there were only 3 subjects with a narcissistic trait among the 30 patients does not come as a surprise from

116

a therapeutic point of view. What does appear of interest is that only one subject kept this trait, while in another it emerged in the second Rorschach.

10. **Zd+–** also seems rather unstable or apt to change, the most striking and obscure being the fact that only a few (4 subjects) become underincorporators, an unexpected reaction.

11. With the **X+%** it might be pointed out that, on applying the Barcelona data (1993), this variable seems to remain in a middle range of stability (50%), with some improvement after 1 year of treatment, not in contradiction with Weiner and Exner's (1990) findings.

12. As to the **SCZI** and with respect to the X+% and the Barcelona study (1993), considering the importance given in it to X+% < .50 and X–% > .40, it seems understandable that the 10 subjects showing a positive index may not be schizophrenic – except, supposedly, the one psychiatrically diagnosed as such even though this patient improved too (SCZI = 6 → 4). The 3 subjects who become positive on this index on their second Rorschach appear to display a perhaps *psychotic but not necessarily schizophrenic* phase in their respective treatments.

    The experience with this index suggests that, since it is too often positive *without* symptomatic or clinically valid accompanying data, and also keeping in mind that this occurs frequently with borderline and other subjects (Campo, 1994; Campo & Vilar, 1991), a tentative conclusion might be that the SCZI too often appears to identify false positives, at least in *Hispanic* subjects.

13. As regards **DEPI**, an index of 7 or 6 tends to change very little in 1 year of treatment, while an index of 5 does change in accordance with Weiner and Exner (1990).

14. As expected, the **CDI** was not stable in this study.

As shown above, the comparison of the paired groups (Wilcoxon) as well as a Pearson correlation tended to confirm what was previously registered in percentages.

Regarding the study of some specific patterns of change among the 14 variables, let us illustrate some of them with more information:

– Take the reactive depression in a hysteroid personality with paranoid features (Case 1) and a positive CDI but negative DEPI, whose EA was 1 and whose AP remains similar, mainly centered on D – despite the increased R in her second Rorschach – and whose Form-Color Ratio equaled = 0. This patient was able to change to an introversive

EA of 9.5, with a Form-Color Ratio of 2:1, a Lambda that goes down from 3.25 to 1.00 and a now negative CDI, but whose Ma:Mp is now 3:4 with a positive HVI index. Although the depression disappeared – clinically speaking – no clear "Waterloo" or "Olympus" in Beck's sense.

– Or take the psychiatrically diagnosed schizophrenic woman (Case 2, SZCI = 6)*, whose rigid introversive EA was 10, whose AP consisted of 10 W's, with an X+% of only .30, shows a similar introversive EA of 9, a SCZI index of 4, an X+% of .50, and an Ma:Mp that changes from 3:5 to 5:1 in the second testing. Improvement seems clear.

– Or take Case 20, a major depression with a DEPI of 7, a positive CDI, low X+% and 3r + (2), a similar AP centered on D and S, but a poorer EA: 10.5 vs. 6, first extratensive, then ambient, loses the positive CDI, keeps her high DEPI and acquires a high 3r + (2) together with a now positive SCZI index of 6!. A probable therapeutic decompensation or regression.

– Or take another doubtful picture at the time of the second protocol (Case 10, suicidal depression), who has a similar rich extratensive EA: 15.5 vs. 16.5 and a similar AP centered on W's, remains a Snow White, develops 5 Borderline contents (Campo & Vilar, 1991), retains a DEPI of 6 and a very low 3r + (2) –.13 vs. .14 – with a still high suicide constellation (10 vs. 9), but whose CDI is no longer positive.

– Or take one of the high Lambda cases (26) with an AP centered on Dd, whose major depression only registers in the second testing (DEPI = 4, now 5) despite his increased defensiveness (L = 1.08, now 1.53), in whom few changes can be observed. A possible "Waterloo"?

– Or take case 21, who shows a doubtful evolution and a difficult diagnosis with a DEPI of 6, then 5, a similar SCZI index of 6, an AP centered on Dd's and S's, maintains a supercontrolled Form-Color Ratio, a "normal" 3r + (2), a high Zd+ and the Snow White style, but whose similar EA – 10 vs. 11 – goes from ambient to rigidly introversive with a no longer positive suicide constellation.

– Or, finally, take Case 30, a mildly obsessive character who shows a similarly rich introversive and rigid EA: 18 vs. 15, a similar AP centered on D and Dd, an improved 3r + (2)/R, affective modulation and reality perception, and whose 2 Fd responses disappear. "Olympus"?

---

* Despite the CS "rules" regarding records that are too short, this case was included because of its interesting evolution.

The different combinations are so varied that no particular trends could be found.

Compared with a previous paper (Campo & Dow, 1993) on follow-up with the Rorschach and ORT with 10 cases, 6 psychoanalyses (3 terminated after 6, 10 and 5 years) and 4 terminated psychoanalytical psychotherapies in which the stability of some Rorschach variables and styles was also studied, the results were only slightly different: The EB's and AP's remained mostly stable – except in 2 very successful psychoanalyses – very unlike the data of the present study, of course with much shorter periods of treatment. X+%'s did not improve in general, which Geller's (1990) investigation showed too; Lambda tended to remain high, Zd was unstable, 2 of the 3 Snow Whites changed for the better, but the Afr's were very stable in general, while the Form-Color Ratio's seemed less so.

This would seem to show again that many things may change during treatment, but that the basic personality styles do not appear to change as much as might be expected after a *longer period of treatment*. What does change fundamentally – and is expected to change – is the *inner balance and relationships* among the different personality variables and styles.

Actually, what the Rorschach "measures" or, rather, registers and basically describes in follow-up research, are these inner movements occurring in each individual during therapy. To judge basic changes in the styles – or character traits – probably requires subsequent, posttreatment follow-up testing, when each personality has settled down again to its fundamental rhythms.

The comparison of the complete protocols of the 30 cases will be taken up in a future effort as well as – perhaps – their prognostic study, in the sense of Exner's latest (1995) very intriguing "crude data" (p. 7) regarding Rorschach features found among patients with very favorable treatment progress as opposed to those who terminate early. Or, it might be added, what about those whose progress is so doubtful that – perhaps – psychoanalytic psychotherapy was not the best type of treatment to be applied?

To conclude, the overall impression derived from this study would be that after 1 year of psychoanalysis or psychoanalytic psychotherapy, numerous changes do take place in many of the variables and styles considered by Exner (1993) and Weiner and Exner (1990) to be stable over time. In this study the sturdiest ones appear to be the high **Lambda** (though based on too few cases), the **EA**, in the **AP** particularly the **S** (space response), as well as the high **W** or **Dd** approach, the **EBPer**, the **Afr** and the directionality of the **Form-Color** ratio, as long as not much more than 60% of stability is expected.

119

It seems evident that only a much more rigid selection procedure – regarding presenting symptoms, basic personality structures, therapists, and number of sessions (an extremely difficult task!) – might throw further light on the question of the stability of the Rorschach styles studied in this sample in relation to psychological treatment and its effects.

References

Alvarez, M., Baeza, A., Campo, V., Garcia, J.M., Guardia, J., Montlleo, T. et al. (1993). First approximation to a normative study with the Rorschach of Barcelona and its surroundings. *Revista de la Sociedad Española del Rorschach y Métodos Proyectivos (SERYMP), 6,* 6–20.

Beck, S.J. (1960). *The Rorschach experiment.* New York: Grune & Stratton.

Botbol, M., Campo, V., Dow, N., & Galan, F. (1987). *Rorschach y seguimiento: Un método de análisis de las respuestas para la evaluación terapéutica* [Rorschach and follow-up: A method of response analysis for therapeutic evaluation]. Paper presented at the XII International Rorschach Congress, Guarujà, Brasil.

Campo, V. (1988). *Los niños y el Rorschach: Aspectos clínicos, investigación y aplicación* [Children and the Rorschach: Clinical aspects, research and application]. Chapter III. Valencia: Promolibro.

Campo, V. (1993). An old friend revisited: In the throes of the schizophrenia index. *British Journal of Projective Psychology, 38*(1), 2–18.

Campo, V. (1994). Rorschach, "cultura" y precisión perceptual [Rorschach, "culture," and perceptual accuracy]. *Revista de la SERYMP, 7,* 23–27.

Campo, V. (1995). *Estudios clínicos con el Rorschach en niños, adolescentes y adultos* [Clinical studies with the Rorschach in children, adolescents and adults]. Chapter I. Barcelona: Paidós.

Campo, V., & Dow, N. (1993). *Follow-up with Rorschach and ORT: An approximation to differences and coincidences.* Paper presented at the XIV International Rorschach Congress, Lisbon.

Campo, V., & Vilar, N. (1991). Acerca de los contenidos, defensas, y relaciones objetales borderline [On boderline contents, defences, and object relations]. *Revista de la SERYMP, 3*(3), 28–32.

Campo, V., Dow, N., & Tuset, A. (1993). *Assessment of change with the ORT (and the Rorschach) in a case of psychoanalytic treatment.* Studii Rorschachiani, Numero doppio. Roma: Edizioni Kappa.

Exner, J.E. (1993). *The Rorschach: A comprehensive system* (Vol. 1, 3rd ed.). New York: Wiley.

Gacono, C.B., & Meloy, J.R. (1994). *The Rorschach assessment of aggressive and psychopathic personalities.* Hillsdale, NJ: Erlbaum.

Geller, S.C. (1990). Objective measurement of change in psychoanalysis assessed by the Comprehensive Rorschach System. *British Journal of Projective Psychology,* 35(1), 67–77.

Kohler, C., & Bernard, F. (1970). *Les états dépressifs chez l'enfant* [Depressive states in the child]. Brussels: Dessart.

Liberal, C. (1987). *Rorschach y depresión mayor* [Rorschach and major depression]. Unpublished monograph. Sociedad Catalana del Rorschach y Métodos Proyectivos, Barcelona.

Rapaport, D., Gill, M.M., & Schafer, R. (1968). *Diagnostic psychological testing* (rev. ed. by R.R. Holt). New York: International Universities Press.

Rorschach, H. (1948). *Psicodiagnóstico* [Psychodiagnostics]. Buenos Aires: Paidós.

Rorschach Workshops. (1995). *Alumni newsletter.* Asheville, NC: Rorschach Workshops.

Weiner, I.B., & Exner, J.E. (1990). Cambios en el Rorschach en las psicoterapias a corto y largo plazo [Rorschach changes in long-term and short-term psychotherapy]. *Revista de la SERYMP, 3,* 4–16.

Vera Campo
Barcelona Rorschach School
Catalan Rorschach Society
Fernando Agullo 24
Barcelona 08021
Spain
Tel. +34 932 092-923
E-mail veracampo@gmail.com

Summary

The aim of this study is to observe what changes take place after 1 year of long-term psychoanalytical therapy in 30 subjects. The continuing interest in treatment effects and follow-up and particularly in the stability of certain Rorschach variables and styles – as shown by the fundamental Weiner & Exner (1990) study – led to the observations presented. The variables that did *not* change in the Weiner and Exner study (1990) after 1 year were: EA > 7, the ambient style, DEPI > 5, Fr + rF > 0, and 3r + (2)/R. The 60 Rorschach protocols were administered at the "Dr. Enrique Racker Clinic" of the Argentine Psychoanalytic Association, which offered 1 year of "orthodox" psychoanalytic treatment to economically limited subjects in the social professions. The following 14 variables were chosen and recorded twice for comparison – initially in percentages – before and after 1 year of treatment:

1. **AP**, 2. **EB** and **EBPer**, 3. **EA**, 4. **Lambda**, 5. **Form-Color Ratio**, 6. **Afr**, 7. **Mp > Ma**, 8. **3r + (2)/R**, 9. **Fr + rF**, 10. **Zd+–**, 11. **X+%**, 12. **SCZI**, 13. **DEPI**, and 14. **CDI**.

Furthermore, and from a more statistical point of view, the means and standard deviations were calculated for the 14 variables in the two sets of protocols, as well as a comparison of paired groups (Wilcoxon) and a Pearson correlation.

Discussion: 1. As expected, the perceptual approach – **AP** – did not vary substantially in the 30 subjects. The noted increase in usual details (D) suggests a positive change toward a better appreciation of the obvious, concrete, and practical aspects of reality, while the space response (**S**) appears to be the most stable aspect of the **AP**. 2. The **EB**'s appear much less stable *in general*, and also less stable than the **EBPer**'s, but it was expected that the **EB** would be *less* affected by only 1 year of treatment. 3. Meanwhile, the **EA** remains practically unchanged in 60% (< 7). 4. As regards **Lambda** the small number of subjects with a high **L** limits any conclusion. 5. The directionality of the **Form-Color Ratio** remained stable, but what does seem clear is that emotional modulation improved. 6. The **Afr** seems a rather stable variable in this sample (63%), *not* coinciding with Weiner and Exner's (1990) findings. 7. The only thing that can be said of the **Snow White** syndrome is that it does change with psychotherapy. 8. **3r + (2)/R** shows up to be very changeable, *not* coinciding with the aforementioned study. 9. **Fr + rF**: This variable appeared in too few subjects to allow any significant comment. 10. **Zd+–** also seems rather unstable or apt to change, the most striking and obscure being the fact that a few subjects became underincorporators, an unexpected reaction. 11. As to the **X+%**, it might be pointed out that on applying the data from the Barcelona normative study (1993), this variable seems to remain in a middle range of stability (50%), with some improvement after 1 year of treatment. 12. As to the **SCZI** and in relation to the **X+%** and the Barcelona study mentioned above, considering the importance given in it to X+% < .50 and X–% > .40, it seems understandable that the 10 subjects showing a positive index may not be schizophrenic. The three subjects who became positive on this index on their second Rorschach appear to portray a *psychotic but not necessarily schizophrenic phase* in their respective treatments. 13. As regards **DEPI**, an index of 7 or 6 tends to change very little in 1 year of treatment, while an index of 5 does change in accordance with the Weiner and Exner (1990) data. 14. As expected, the **CDI** was not stable in this study.

As shown before, the comparison of the paired groups as well as the Pearson correlation tended to confirm what was previously registered in percentages.

Resumen

El objetivo de este trabajo es observar que cambios ocurren después de un año de terapia psicoanalítica a largo plazo en 30 sujetos. El interés continuado en los efectos del tratamiento y el seguimiento, y particularmente en la estabilidad de ciertas variables y estilos Rorschach – demostrados en el estudio fundamental de Weiner y Exner (1990) – llevó a las siguientes observaciones.

Las variables que no cambiaron en ese estudio después de un año son: EA < 7, el estilo ambitendente, DEPI > 5, Fr + rF > 0, y 3r + (2)/R.

Los 60 protocolos fueron administrados en la "Clínica Dr. Enrique Racker" de la Asociación Psicoanalítica Argentina que ofrecía un año de tratamiento psicoanalítico "ortodoxo" a sujetos económicamente limitados en las profesiones sociales.

Se eligieron las siguientes 14 variables, doblemente registradas para su observación – para comenzar en porcentajes –, antes y después de un año de tratamiento:

1. **AP**, 2. **EB y EBPer**, 3. **EA**, 4. **Lambda**, 5. **Razón Forma-Color**, 6. **Afr**, 7. **Mp > Ma**, 8.**3r+ (2)/R**, 9. **Fr + rF**, 10. **Zd+–**, 11. **X+%**, 12. **SCZI**, 13. **DEPI**, 14. **CDI**.

Además. desde un punto de vista más estadístico, se calcularon las medias y desviaciones tipo para las 14 variables en los dos grupos de protocolos, como así también una comparación de gripos apareados (Wilcoxon) y una correlación Pearson.

Discusión: 1. De acuerdo a lo esperado el enfoque perceptual – **AP** – no varió substancialmente en los 30 sujetos. El incremento notado en los detalles usuales (**D**) sugiere un cambio positivo hacia una mejor apreciación de los aspectos obvios, concretos y prácticos de la realidad; mientras que las respuestas de espacio (**S**) aparecen como los aspectos más estables del **AP**. 2. Los **EB** parecen *en general* menos estables y también menos que los **EBPer,** pero se esperaba que los **EB** serían **menos** afectados por un solo año de tratamiento. 3. Mientras, el **EA** permanece prácticamente sin cambios en el 60% (< 7). 4. En cuanto al **Lambda,** el número pequeño de sujetos con un **L** alto limita cualquier conclusión. 5. La direccionalidad de la **razón Forma-Color** permaneció estable, pero lo que sí parece claro es que la modulación emocional mejoró. 6. El **Afr** parece una variable más bien estable en esta muestra (63%), *no* coincidiendo con los hallazgos del estudio de Weiner y Exner (199). 7. Lo único que se puede decir del síndrome de Blanca Nieves es que sí puede cambiar con la psicoterapia. 8. El **3r + (2)/R** se muestra muy cambiable, *no* coincidiendo con el estudio más arriba mencionado. 9. **Fr + rF:** Esta variable apareció en demasiado pocos sujetos como para permitir un comentario significativo. 10. **Zd+–** también parece bastante inestable o apto a cambiar, siendo lo más impactante y oscuro el hecho que unos pocos sujetos se volvieron subincorporadores, una reacción inesperada. 11. Del **X+%** se podría señalar que al aplicar los datos del estudio normativo de Barcelona (1993) esta variable parece quedar en un rango medio de estabilidad (50%), con alguna mejoría después de un año de tratamiento. 12. Respecto del **SCZI** y en relación al X+% y al estudio de Barcelona arriba mencionado, considerando la importancia dada en él a X+% < .50 y X–% > .40, parece comprensible que los 10 sujetos que mostraban un índice positivo pueden no ser esquizofrénicos.. Los tres sujetos que se volvieron positivos en este índice en sus segundos Rorschach, parecen representar una *fase psicótica pero no necesariamente esquizofrénica* en sus respectivos tratamientos. 13. En cuanto al **DEPI,** un índice de 7 o 6 tiende a cambiar muy poco en un año de tratamiento, mientras que un índice de 5 sí cambia de acuerdo con los datos de Weiner y Exner (1990). 14. Como fue esperado, el **CDI** no fue estable en este estudio.

Como fue mostrado, la comparación de los grupos apareados como también la correlación Pearson tendieron a confirmar lo que previamente se había registrado en porcentajes.

Résumé

L'objectif de cette étude est d'observer les changements qui ont lieu chez 50 sujets qui ont suivi un traitement psychanalytique. L'auteur s'intéresse plus particulièrement à la stabilité de certaines variables du Rorschach Système Intégré et considéré comme fondamental par Weiner et Exner (1990). Les variables qui sont restées stables à l'étude de Weiner et Exner après un an étaient: EA > 7, ambitant, DEPI > 5, Fr + rF > 0, et 3r + (2)/R.

Les 60 protocoles de cette étude proviennent de patients à revenu économique faible et travaillant dans le social et qui ont suivi un traitement psychanalytique "orthodoxe" d'une année à la clinique Racker de l'association psychanalytique Argentine.

Quatorze variables ont été choisies et mesurées à deux reprises pour être comparées avant et après le traitement.

1. **AP**, 2. **EB** and **EBPer**, 3. **EA**, 4. **Lambda**, 5. **Form-Color Ratio**, 6. **Afr**, 7. **Mp > Ma**, 8. **3r + (2)/R**, 9. **Fr + rF**, 10. **Zd+–**, 11. **X+%**, 12. **SCZI**, 13. **DEPI**, et 14. **CDI**.

Une analyse statistique à été appliquée à ces variables incluant le test de Wilcoxon et Pearson pour comparer les données pré et post traitements.

Discussion: L'approche perceptuelle – **AP** – ne semble pas avoir varié chez les 60 sujets. L'augmentation observée pour le nombre de D (grand détail) suggère une amélioration de la perception de détails concrets, évidents et pratique de la réalité; tandis que la réponse blanc (**S**) semble l'aspect le plus stable du **AP**. L'**EB** semble la variable la moins stable en général et même moins stable que le **EBPer**, toutefois on s'attend à ce que l'**EB** ne soit pas affectée par une seule année de traitement. L'**EA** semble pratiquement inchangée dans 60 % des cas (< 7). Le nombre très restreint de **Lamba** élevé limite les conclusions que l'on pourrait en tirer. Le **ratio forme/couleur** semble stable, toutefois la modulation affective semble s'améliorer. L'Afr semble une variable stable dans cet échantillon (63 %), ce qui ne coïncide pas avec les résultats de Weiner et Exner (1990). On constate que la psychothérapie produit un changement au syndrome de **blanche neige**. Le ratio **3r + (2)/R** semble très variable, ce qui n'est pas le cas dans l'étude mentionnée auparavant. **Fr + rF**: cette variable n'apparaît pas assez fréquemment pour que les différences soient significatives. **Zd+–** semble aussi sujet à des variations, le plus surprenant étant que certains sujets soient devenus "underincorporators" ce qui est une réaction imprévue.

En comparant le **X+%** à l'étude normative de Barcelone (1993) on constate que cette variable reste plutôt constante (50 %), avec quelques améliorations observées après un an de traitement. En ce qui concerne le **SCZI**, en relation au X+% et l'étude de Barcelone (1993), 10 sujets ont un index positif mais ne doivent pas être considérés comme schizophréniques. Les trois sujets dont la variable est devenue positive après le traitement semblent plutôt montrer une phase psychotique que schizophrénique. Un **DEPI** de 6 ou 7 tend à ne pas changer après un an de traitement tandis qu'un indice de 5 change comme indiqué dans l'étude de Weiner et Exner (1990). Comme prévu, le **CDI** n'était pas stable dans cette étude. L'analyse statistique de Wilcoxon et la corrélation de Pearson confirment les changements notés par les pourcentages.

本研究の目的は30名の被験者に1年間の長期精神分析的心理療法のちにどのような変化が生起するかを注目することである。治療の効果や追跡調査、そして特に——基本的には Weiner と Exner（1990）の研究によって示されたような——特定のロールシャッハ変数やスタイルの安定性に対する継続する関心が、ここに示される注目へと導いた。Weiner と Exner の変数において1年後変化していなかったは：EA>7、不定型、DEPI>5、Fr+rF＞0そして3r+(2)/R であった。

方　法

60のロールシャッハ・プロトコルは、1年間の"正統な"精神分析的治療を社会的な職業についており経済的に限度のある被験者に提供するアルゼンチンの精神分析協会の "Enrique Racker 博士クリニック"において施行された。

以下の14の変数が選ばれ、比較のため2回記録された、—比率における検討から始められ—1年の治療の前後での比較。

1．AP、2．EB と EBPer、3．EA、4．Lambda、5．Form-Color Ratio、6．Afr、7．Mp>Ma、8．3r+(2)/R、9．Fr+rF、10．Zd+-、11．X+%、12．SCZI、13．DEPI、そして、14．CDI。

さらに、より統計学的な観点から、対応のあるグループの

比較（Wilcoxon）とピアソンの相関係数と同様に、２つのプ
ロトコル群の 14 の変数の平均と標準偏差が算出された。

考　察

１．予測されたように知覚的接近法—AP—は 30 名の被験者
　　においておおむね変化しなかった。普通部分反応（D）
　　の顕著な増加が、現実の明白で具体的で実用的な側面の
　　より良い統覚への肯定的な変化を示唆している；一方、
　　空白反応（S）は AP において最も安定した側面のよう
　　である。

２．EB は慨してあまり安定していないようであり、EBPer
　　よりも安定していないだけでなく、EB はわずか１年間
　　の治療ではあまり影響を受けないものと想定される。

３．一方で、EA は 60%（＜７）が変化しないままであった。

４．ラムダに関してはハイ・ラムダの被検者が少数のためい
　　かなる結論も限定されてしまう。

５．形態-色彩の比率の方向性はまた安定しているが、明ら
　　かなことは感情の調節が改善していることである。

６．Afr はこのサンプル（63%）においてはかなり安定して
　　いるが、これは Weiner と Exner（1990）において見出さ
　　れたこととは一致していない。

７．白雪姫症候群に関して唯一言えることは、心理療法によ
　　っては変わらないと言うことである。

８．3r+(2)/R は非常に変化しやすいようであるが、これは前
　　述の研究と一致していない。

９．Fr+rF：この変数はなんらかの意味のある言及をするに
　　は少数の被験者にしか示されなかった。

１０．　　　Zd+-はかなり安定しておらず、変化する傾向に
　　あり、最も顕著でわかりづらいのは少数の被験者は、期
　　待されない影響である、アンダーインコーポレイション
　　になったことである。

１１．　　　X+%については、バルセロナの標準化研究から
　　のデータを適用して、１年の治療によりいくらかの改善

は見られるものの、この変数は中程度の安定性（50%）
にとどまっているようである、と指摘できるであろう。

１２．　　　SCZIに関しては、X+%と上で言及したバルセ
ロナの研究と関連させて、X+%が<.50であり、X-%が
>.40である場合の重要性を考慮すると、この指標にヒッ
トした10名が精神病的でなかったことは理解できるよ
うに思える。2回目のロールシャッハにおいてこの指標
にヒットした3人の被験者は精神病状態を示していたが、
彼らのそれぞれの治療においては必ずしも精神病の様相
は示していない。

１３．　　　DEPIに関しては、この指標で7あるいは6で
ある場合は1年間の治療でほとんど変わらないが、5の
場合は変化し、これはWeinerとExnerのデータと一致
している。

１４．　　　予想されたように、CDIは本研究では安定して
いなかった。

　前述したように、ピアソンの相関係数と同様に、対応のあ
るグループの比較は先に比率に関して示したことを裏付けて
いるようであった。

Rorschachiana 30, 129–149
© 2009 Hogrefe Publishing

DOI: 10.1027/1192-5604.30.2.129

Psychodynamic Consultation and the Rorschach with Adolescents

A Small-Scale Comparative Study

Justine McCarthy Woods

Consultant Clinical Psychologist, Tavistock Clinic, London, UK

Abstract. This article presents a comparative pilot study using the Rorschach Test and a four-session psychodynamic consultation for adolescents attending an outpatient clinic. The study used a comparative qualitative approach to look at how both approaches can help in the assessment of young people experiencing psychological and emotional difficulties. Specifically, the study assessed whether the Rorschach might be useful for engaging young people in the assessment process and explored whether it could add anything to this process, above and beyond the standard four-session psychodynamic consultation.

Keywords: Rorschach test, psychodynamic consultation, Tavistock Clinic, pilot study, psychoanalyst

The Adolescent Department

The Tavistock Clinic was established in 1920 as one of the first outpatient clinics in the UK to provide psychoanalytically informed psychotherapy. Initially, the Clinic included the Adult and Children's Department. Then, in 1959, the Adolescent Department was formed to treat the "behaviourally disturbed, acting-out delinquent" (Dicks, 1970), along with the families of disturbed adolescents. Over time the Adolescent Department has developed a wide range of psychotherapeutic approaches for working with young people, their parents, and families from within a psychoanalytic framework. It provides young people the opportunity to undertake psychotherapy up until the age of 21, unlike most other adolescent mental health services in the UK, which only see young people up to the age of 18.

The Adolescent Department sees adolescents from the age of 14 to 21. It accepts referrals from professionals and parents, but young people can also refer themselves directly. In the case of those adolescents who are referred by a professional or their parents, the young person is asked to contact the Department to indicate whether or not they wish to be seen, where they are required to "opt-in." It is thought that this helps the young person to feel that they are starting to take responsibility for their lives as well as for their assessment and subsequent therapy, if relevant. In addition, for those adolescents whose parents are also being seen within the Department, the parents are seen by a different therapist from their adolescent child. This provides the young person with the sense of a separate and private space from their parents, in recognition of their attempts to move away from their parents, both externally and at an intrapsychic level. However, young people will often do things to provoke the enactment of an intrusion from a parent on this separate space, for example, by encouraging or accepting calls/text messages from parents on their mobile phone, or by requesting that their parent be present in the consulting room, etc.

Once the young person opts-in, the referral is taken to a multidisciplinary team meeting, which is attended by qualified and trainee staff representing the disciplines of clinical psychology, psychiatry, child psychotherapy, family therapy, and social work. The decision about which therapist is to see the patient is considered from a number of perspectives. For example, whether it would be beneficial for the young person to be seen by a more experienced member of staff, or whether they might require a psychiatric assessment. In addition, a decision is made about the need for continuity between the consultation and treatment phase. For example, this would be considered important for a patient who had experienced early trauma/loss or difficulties with separation.

Psychodynamic Consultation and the Assessment Process

The psychodynamic consultation, which forms part of the assessment process, typically involves the therapist meeting with the patient for four sessions. In addition to thinking with the young person about the "presenting difficulty," for which the anxiety may be located more with parents or the professional who referred the young person, an important aspect of the psychodynamic consultation is to help the adolescent to develop some interest and curiosity in themselves and their lives. This may lead some adolescents to decide to undertake ongoing psychotherapy. During the psychodynamic consultation the therapist is very much led by the young person, how they present themselves for the first meeting, what they say/do not say, their fantasies about the clinic (Tavistock) they have come to and what goes on there, and what kind of object/therapist they expect to encounter. What the therapist aims to convey is that there is space for the young person to speak about their difficulties, as they see them, to explore this and other aspects of themselves without the therapist imposing a structure. This inevitably means that there will be gaps and periods of silence in the sessions. Both this and the initial lack of structure may prove anxiety-provoking for some adolescents, whereas for other adolescents it may provide a sense of relief to feel that they are not being faced with a series of questions that can often be experienced as an intrusion. The therapist's sensitivity to what is emerging within the transference and countertransference and thinking about this together with the patient is important for helping to contain the young person's anxiety and to increase their understanding of themselves. At some point during the first session, the therapist explains that they will meet for four sessions (though the number of sessions may vary for some adolescents) and also clarifies whether or not they will be available to continue with the young person if the adolescent decides to undertake individual psychotherapy.

As mentioned previously, the content of the assessment sessions is led by what the young person brings to the session. The therapist usually thinks about this material with some consideration of the following:

- The physical appearance, manner, and mode of presentation of the young person, any difference between apparent and actual age, etc.
- How the young person experiences the problem, internally and externally, and where the anxiety is located.
- The nature of the problem/symptom, the time of onset and relationship to life events, and the effect of the problem on family and other relationships, including education/work.
- The young person's view of his or her childhood, school life, including first memories.
- The view of others who are important to them. For example, parents, boyfriend/girlfriend.
- How the young person feels able to use external resources and supports available to them.

131

- The quality of contact with the therapist within the consultation and any shifts that may occur.
- The nature and content of dreams and daydreams.
- Their capacity to take in, think about, and possibly expand upon interpretations or comments made by the therapist within sessions.
- Their capacity to keep in mind the experience of one session until the next.
- Exploration with the young person of the experience of the psychodynamic consultation and what this might indicate in terms of treatment.

The assessment of risk is explored across a variety of dimensions including risk to self (deliberate self-harm, previous suicide attempts and suicidal ideation, risky behavior), risk to others (previous aggressive or violent behavior, along with aggressive feelings, intentions, and alcohol and drug misuse. This is in addition to consideration of psychiatric disorders, such as psychosis, bipolar disorder, etc., where the young person may be asked to see a psychiatrist for a psychiatric assessment.

One of the key considerations at the end of the assessment phase is the capacity and the willingness of the young person to use psychotherapy. Many adolescents make the decision not to continue after the four-session psychodynamic consultation. This pattern is consistent with young people attending other adolescent psychotherapy and mental health services in the UK, but it can also be regarded as being reflective of the adolescent process and the young person's wish to become more autonomous and less dependent. This may also be related to practical issues, such as moving to another part of the country to attend university. Notwithstanding the above, many adolescents find this brief period of exploration beneficial. In addition, an independent evaluation of the pre-/postassessment clinical changes, using the ASEBA (Achenbach, 1997; Achenbach & Rescorla, 2001) indicates that a significant number of adolescents demonstrate a reduction in clinical symptoms over the course of this consultation period. For those adolescents who express a wish for follow-up treatment, there are a range of options to consider – namely, once, twice, or three times weekly psychodynamic psychotherapy, brief therapy (16 sessions), cognitive behavioral therapy (CBT), interpersonal psychotherapy (IPT), group therapy, or family therapy. However, psychodynamic psychotherapy would be the main form of therapy undertaken within the Department.

132

Rorschach Pilot Study

The rationale for utilizing the Rorschach, specifically the Rorschach Comprehensive System (RCS, Exner, 2003), and for undertaking this pilot study was two-fold:

1) Adolescence is a time of development during which the young person experiences confusing and unsettling states of mind, along with intense and painful feelings, which some adolescents attempt to deal with by avoiding thinking and knowing about themselves. For others, there is the tendency to replace thinking (and talking) with action, whereby internal conflicts become enacted or located in others via projection (Waddell, 1998). The adolescent also experiences confusion about themselves and contradictions within themselves regarding their identity, often where the "child" and "adult" aspects of themselves can alternate quite rapidly and in unpredictable ways (Bradley, 1998). It is therefore not unusual for these contradictions and inconsistencies to be conveyed by the young person when talking about themselves. In addition to the interview situation, something similar can be seen to apply with the use of self-report measures, where there is the assumption that the person is willing and able to provide information about themselves. But self-report measures are less useful for adolescents who would rather not disclose information, who do not know themselves very well, and/or who wish to avoid thinking about themselves. For these reasons, it was thought that it might be helpful to be able use other approaches, such as the Rorschach, for engaging young people in the assessment process.

2) A number of senior clinical psychologists within the Adolescent Department had recently completed both the basic and advanced training in the RCS. Therefore, it was considered important to explore whether or not the RCS might contribute to the assessment process within the Department, above and beyond the standard four-session psychodynamic consultation process. Essentially, there was a need to determine whether this would represent a cost-effective use of the psychologists' time.

Initially, the study was intended to include 6 patients. However, because of a change in role for one of the psychologists, she was not available to complete the study. This meant that it was necessary to limit the study to 3 patients.

Subjects

The study involved 3 patients over the age of 16 who were referred to the Adolescent Department during a 6-month period in 2006/2007. They were randomly selected, following the exclusion of patients who were presenting with a psychotic illness, substance misuse, or who were involved with the criminal justice system.

Procedure

The study included three senior-level clinical psychologists, two of whom were psychoanalysts, who were required to undertake the standard four-session psychodynamic consultation and administer the RCS (Exner, 2003). Each patient was invited by the psychologist (A) undertaking the psychodynamic consultation, to participate in a pilot study "to explore how the Rorschach might be of benefit to young people referred to the Adolescent Department." However, it was made clear that the patient was free not to participate, but also to withdraw at any point, if they decided that they did not wish to continue with the study. Each patient signed a consent form that made this explicit. The patient was administered the Rorschach midway through the consultation phase, specifically after Session 2, by one of the other psychologists (B) involved in the study. The patient then completed their consultation with the psychologist (A) undertaking the psychodynamic consultation. Apart from being provided with a brief summary of the reason why the patient was referred, the psychologist who administered the Rorschach was blind to the outcome of the psychodynamic consultation until the postassessment period. This was also the case for psychologist undertaking the psychodynamic consultation, who was not aware of the findings from the RCS until the postassessment phase. At the postassessment phase, the three psychologists met together: The outcome from the psychodynamic consultation was presented by psychologist (A) and compared with the findings from the RCS presented by psychologist (B), with psychologist (C) taking notes. After completing the administration of the RCS, each patient was invited to contact the psychologist for feedback from the RCS, if they wished.

Results

For the purpose of this article the results, illustrated by case studies, focus only on two of the three patients, and they are limited to specific aspects of the findings from the Rorschach and the information derived from the psychodynamic consultation. This is in addition to a brief summary of the overall findings.

Case Study 1

Background Information

Prior to administering the Rorschach, the psychologist knew that the patient was a 20-year-old university student who was grieving the death of her stepfather, who had died suddenly the previous year.

The following information became available to this psychologist only after the interpretation of the Rorschach: The patient's mother had divorced the patient's father when the patient was age 3, and there was very little contact between the patient and her father following the divorce, as he had relocated to a distant country. After divorcing her first husband, the patient's mother met and married the patient's stepfather, who was a successful businessman who had a long-standing dependency on prescription drugs, primarily painkillers. The cause of his death was the result of an overdose, but it was unclear whether this was deliberate (suicide) or accidental.

During her psychodynamic consultation, the patient described having had a close relationship with her stepfather, telling how they had shared similar interests and hobbies. She also mentioned that he had indulged her and allowed her things that her mother would not, so that the therapist got the impression that the patient felt that they had been almost like partners, with her mother perceived more as the outsider and rival. One might conceptualize that, at an unconscious level, the patient felt that she had triumphed over the mother by managing to possess the (step)father in this Oedipal situation.

Approach to the Psychodynamic Consultation

As part of the psychodynamic consultation, the patient arranged her appointments with the therapist so that they were at least 3 weeks apart. The therapist understood this as being the way that the patient attempted to manage the intensity and intimacy evoked by the assessment situation, which appeared to feel threatening to the patient, but also perhaps the patient's way of coping with her ambivalence about becoming too dependent on the therapist. Furthermore, from one session to next, the therapist found it difficult to remember details about the patient from the previous session, which appeared to suggest an internal object that struggled to keep the patient in mind.

Approach to the Rorschach

This young woman's approach to the psychodynamic consultation was largely mirrored during the administration of the Rorschach, where, for each card, there was a significant delay from the point when the patient was presented with the card to when she provided a response. In addition, there were long gaps between the responses this patient provided for each card. With an individual who is resistant to being assessed, one might expect such a person offering a limited number of responses. However, this was not the case with this young woman, the overall number of responses she provided exceeding the average (R = 31). In addition, although she provided a significant number of "space" responses (S = 6; Exner, 2000), these were distributed evenly throughout the protocol and not confined to the first few cards, which one might also expect to see if the patient had been resistant to being assessed (Exner, 2000). This suggests that she managed to engage reasonably well with the Rorschach as an assessment method. Nevertheless, her handling of the inkblots was noteworthy: Although she would hold onto the card for an extended period, at the same time she appeared to wish to restrict her level of involvement with the card, by keeping the manipulation of the card to a minimum, with all responses based on viewing the inkblot in a vertical position (she made no attempt to rotate the card).

Comparison of RCS Findings and Psychodynamic Consultation

From the Rorschach findings, the patient presented as an individual with an "avoidant response style" (λ = 1.58, Exner, 2000), with the wish to avoid and minimize complexity and ambiguity. In addition, she appeared both guarded and mistrusting of her environment, where she was very cautions about taking in new information and investing trust in others (Hypervigilance Index [HVI] = Yes, Exner, 2000). She appeared to be putting considerable effort into carefully scanning her environment, though sometimes taking in more information than she could meaningfully integrate and use, instead putting herself at risk of becoming overwhelmed (Zd = +4.5, Exner, 2000). The patient spoke in the consultation about how she did not feel understood by her mother, and that she was unable to talk to her about significant issues. Indeed, she conveyed the sense of a rather difficult and distant relationship between them. The therapist experienced this in the transference, where the patient often remained silent. With respect to the patient's internal world, one might hypothesize that her first response to Card I relates to whom or what she fantasizes she encounters in the (Rorschach) assessment situation, "I'd say that it looks like a scary creature, with horns and ears and two eyes maybe." Clearly, from the psychodynamic consultation the patient felt uncomfortable and anxious both about the ambiguity and the intimacy evoked by this situation, where the therapist experienced her as attempting to keep control of the contact between them both by extending the period between the sessions and attempting to control her feelings during the sessions, where one might say that the patient was trying to limit what the therapist could "see" of her. The patient's sense of unease and discomfort was also apparent from the Rorschach where it was evident that this young woman was experiencing a significant level of distress and emotional disruption, including possible episodes of depression, moodiness, anxiety, and anger (DEPI = 5; SumY = 4; S = 6, Exner, 2000).

The patient spoke to the therapist about how she had been experiencing difficulties in her relationship with her boyfriend, because of his wish for her to talk more about her feelings, but also about how she felt guilty (SUM V = 1, Exner, 2000) for thinking that she was avoiding her younger brother, who would tend to become very emotional when talking about their deceased stepfather. This was also evident from the Rorschach, the findings suggesting that she had a tendency to avoid emotional confrontations and affect-laden situations (Afr = .35, Exner,

137

2000), and somewhat inhibited in expressing her feelings (Fc: CF + C + 0:0, Exner, 2000).

However, what was not so evident to her therapist during the psychodynamic consultation was the extent of the patient's anger (S = 6, Exner, 2000) and the possible implications of this for the consultation process. Even though the therapist was aware from the transference that the patient appeared to be relating to her at times as if she were her mother, this was not something she felt able to think or talk about with the patient during the consultation. The therapist also wondered whether the patient may have felt that, by establishing a therapeutic relationship, she was in fantasy relinquishing her "exclusive" relationship with her stepfather. But again this was not something which the therapist felt able to explore with this patient.

The therapist was aware of the patient's low mood, depressed feelings, and sense of emotional deprivation, which the patient for the most part attempted to block out of conscious awareness, but which at other times overwhelmed her and left her feeling vulnerable. Some of this was also evident from the Rorschach (DEPI = 5; Adj D = –1; SumY = 4, Exner, 2000). An added concern for the therapist was the extent to which the patient might feel an identification with her dead father and indeed his murderous aspect, which would be represented by his misuse of prescription drugs and possible suicide. However, the findings from the Rorschach (T = 1; Mor = 1) might be what one would anticipate for an individual who is grieving the loss of a very close and significant relationship.

Finally, the therapist believed that the possibility of increased emotional contact with the therapist, along with the possibility of the patient becoming more in touch with painful and uncontrollable feelings and thoughts within herself, felt just too threatening and potentially destabilizing for this young woman at this time. This was evidenced in her breaking off contact with the therapist before the end of the psychodynamic consultation, by deciding not to come for the final session.

Following the administration of the Rorschach, the psychologist provided the opportunity for the patient to ask questions and to meet with her later to obtain feedback on the findings from the Rorschach. However, the patient indicated that she had no questions, and similarly expressed no interest in obtaining feedback from the Rorschach.

Case Study 2

Background

The 16-year-old patient had been referred for individual psychotherapy. At the time of referral, she had been experiencing ongoing eating problems for a number of years, including a period during which she had lost a significant amount of weight.

The following information became available to this psychologist only after the interpretation of the Rorschach: At the time of her assessment, she was living with her mother, a former model, and her father, a surgeon. She described herself as having a difficult relationship with her mother, but she also said that she didn't remember very much about her mother before the age of 10. The patient described her mother as having an eating disorder, where she was very preoccupied with what she ate and how she looked. She appeared to feel close to her father, but experienced him as being quite remote emotionally, as a consequence of his involvement with his work. Prior to her referral to the Tavistock, she had seen a number of therapists and had felt quite affected by the loss of contact with these therapists when the therapy had come to an end.

Comparison of RCS Findings and Psychodynamic Consultation

Overall, the findings from the Rorschach were consistent with the information derived from the psychodynamic consultation.

What was conveyed quite powerfully by the patient during the consultation was a sense of emotional deprivation, which she communicated to the therapist during her consultation sessions and which was evident from her history. This was clearly supported by the Rorschach (SumT = 3, Exner, 2000), with the possibility for this patient that her strong needs for closeness in her relationships remained largely unfulfilled.

It appeared from the Rorschach that this patient was experiencing considerable distress at the time of her assessment, associated with her tendency to engage in painful introspection (SumV = 3; FD = 2, Exner, 2000): She appeared very preoccupied with negative aspects of herself and seemed to be experiencing painful and negative feelings (DEPI = 4, Exner, 2000). Her level of emotional distress was also evident from the consultation, mainly in relation to her social and interpersonal relationships, which was supported by the RCS, suggesting that she was experiencing some difficulties coping, particularly within the interpersonal sphere (CDI = 4, Exner, 2000).

Although the patient had mentioned that she had friends, the therapist did not feel that the patient was able to convey a sense of these individuals with any real depth or substance. This was also indicated on the RCS, where the findings suggested that she appears to struggle to establish relationships, except on a superficial level, which can be explained in part by her lack of social maturity (CDI = 4, Exner, 2000) and perhaps the fact that she has difficulty recognizing the needs of others (Fr + rF = 5, Exner, 2000). Furthermore, the Rorschach findings suggest that this patient generally does not anticipate positive interactions among people (Cop = 0, Exner, 2000), which one might presume only adds to her distress and disappointment concerning her relationships (SumT = 3, Exner, 2000).

Yet it is also possible that, because of her anger (S = 7, Exner, 2000), she has less tolerance or capacity for making the routine compromises usually required in interpersonal relationships. This was consistent with a situation described by her therapist, specifically an impasse between the patient and her mother, where it appeared to the therapist that the patient appeared "just about to tolerate" her mother, but there was no sense that the difficulties in this relationship could be resolved, so as to enable this relationship to feel more satisfying to both patient and her mother.

With respect to her previously described difficulties with anger (S = 7, Exner, 2003), the patient did not mention this during the consultation, nor did the therapist feel this something that could really be thought about with the patient during the consultation phase – even though the therapist did feel that this might be an issue. Nevertheless, neither the scale nor the extent of the patient's anger was apparent to the therapist from the consultation.

Although the patient demonstrated some fixed ideas and some distortions in her thinking with respect to her difficulties concerning eating and food, the RCS identified a greater level of impairment in the patient's thinking and reality testing than was evident from the consultation (X-% = . 33, M- = 1; Wsum6 = 28, Exner, 2000). Her thinking difficulties and occasional disruptions in reality testing appeared to be particularly evident when angry and enraged (S = 7; S- = 3, Exner, 2003).

Another finding from the RCS suggested that the patient has an exaggerated sense of self-worth and importance, which makes her less sensitive to the needs of others (Fr + rF = 5, Exner, 2000). However, if this finding is considered in association with her tendency to focus on negative aspects of herself (SumV = 3; Mor = 1, Exner, 2000) and in conjunction with the "projected material" (such as the minus responses and the human, animal movement, and content responses; Exner, 2000), the Rorschach findings suggest that the patient experiences conflicts regarding her self-image and sexual identity (all of which was borne out in her subsequent therapy). One of the responses she provided for card IX appeared to encapsulate some of her confusion with her self-image, along with her sense of detachment from the world: "The green part looks like a weird image of a woman crouched, and it looks like she is looking through a telescope." It was interesting that, rather than associating the narcissistic qualities suggested by the "reflection" responses with the patient herself, the therapist believed these to be more representative of the patient's internal objects, because she could recognize these qualities in the patient's parents, on the basis of the consultation and from the information provided by the referrer.

The patient attended a follow-up session with the psychologist who administered the Rorschach. She appeared reasonably receptive to the Rorschach findings, mentioning that she found it particularly difficult to establish and maintain close friendships as she generally found that people failed to live up to her expectations, thus providing support for the Rorschach findings.

As a follow-up to the psychodynamic consultation, she was seen by a female child psychotherapist for weekly individual psychodynamic psychotherapy. According to this therapist, the patient appeared to find it difficult to engage in therapy. She would frequently cancel or fail to attend sessions, after an incisive interpretation, where the therapist felt that she had made (meaningful) emotional contact with the patient. Typically, the patient struggled to attend for the full 50 minutes, usually arriving late for her sessions. Overall, her pattern was to stay engaged for brief periods of time, but then she would appear to withdraw when the relationship appeared to have become too intimate, resulting in her disengaging and not attending for some of the subsequent sessions. What also became more evident was the patient's resistance to an exploratory approach as the therapy progressed, her apparent wish being not to think too deeply or to sustain a consistent line of thought. Finally, the patient ended up dropping out of therapy prematurely.

Obviously, with some knowledge of this young woman's history and the material that emerged for the therapist in the transference, this patient's difficulties with engaging with ongoing psychodynamic psychotherapy might have been anticipated. However, the psychologist who had initially undertaken the psychodynamic consultation believed that the findings from the Rorschach helped to provide a particular focus for some of those issues the patient struggled with, along with a clearer sense of how these issues might become manifest over the course of therapy.

Summary of the Overall Findings from the Rorschach Pilot Study

Obviously, considering the very small number of participants, this can only be regarded as a preliminary study, from which it is impossible to draw any definitive conclusions. Nevertheless, the findings from this study had clinical relevance for the Adolescent Department, for the following reasons:

1. The adolescent patients who participated in the study were found to be receptive and responsive to the Rorschach as an assessment tool.
2. For each of the three patients, there were found to be high levels of consistency between the findings from the Rorschach (RCS, Exner, 2000) and the information derived from the standard four-session psychodynamic consultation.
3. Yet it was evident that the Rorschach (RCS, Exner, 2000) findings served to bring some of the young person's underlying conflicts and issues, elicited during the assessment, into sharper relief.
4. The Rorschach findings (RCS, Exner, 2000) served to provide additional information about the patient, which was not always so readily available from the standard four-session psychodynamic consultation. For example, information on the patient's thinking processes, reality testing, levels of anger, available psychological resources, etc.

Conclusion

The main conclusion from this study was that the Rorschach (RCS, Exner, 2003) can serve as a useful adjunct to the standard psychodynamic consultation within the Adolescent Department.

Since the completion of the study, some further work has been undertaken to pilot the use of the Rorschach (RCS) in the Adolescent Department, where it has been found that it is of particular benefit for those adolescents whose difficulties present as part of a complex clinical picture; those who have difficulty engaging with and/or tolerating the psychodynamic consultation approach, which feels too intense and generates too much anxiety for the young person; those who are reluctant/unwilling to talk abut themselves; those who appear motivated to avoid thinking about/knowing themselves; and those for whom it is unclear which intervention might prove most beneficial.

References

Achenbach, T.M. (1997) *Manual for the Young Adult Self Report and Young Adult Behavior Checklist.* Burlington, VT: University of Vermont, Department of Psychiatry.

Achenbach, T.M., & Rescorla, L.A. (2001). *Manual for the ASEBA School Age forms and profiles.* Burlington, VT: University of Vermont, Research Centre for Children, Youth and Families.

Bradley, J. (1998). Confrontation, appeasement or communication. In R. Anderson & A. Dartington (Eds.), *Facing it out: Clinical perspectives on adolescent disturbance* (pp. 53–63). London: Duckworth & Co.

Dicks, H.V. (1970). *Fifty years of the Tavistock Clinic.* London: Routledge & Kegan Paul.

Exner, J.E. (2000). *A primer for Rorschach interpretation.* Asheville, NC: Rorschach Workshops.

Exner, J.E. (2003). *The Rorschach: A comprehensive system. Vol. 1: Basic foundations and principles of interpretation* (4th ed.). Hoboken, NJ: Wiley.

Waddell, M. (1998). *Inside lives: Psychoanalysis and the growth of the personality.* London: Duckworth & Co.

Justine McCarthy Woods
Tavistock Clinic
120 Belsize Lane
London NW3 5BA
UK
Tel. +44 20 7435-7111
Fax +44 20 7435-3733
E-mail JMcCarthyWoods@tavi-port.nhs.uk

Summary

In 1959 the Adolescent Department at the Tavistock Clinic was established to treat the "behaviourally disturbed, acting-out delinquent" (Dicks, 1970), along with the families of disturbed adolescents. Over time the Adolescent Department has developed a wide range of psychotherapeutic approaches for working with young people, their parents, and families from within a psychoanalytic framework. It provides young people the opportunity to self-refer and to undertake psychotherapy up until the age of 21, unlike most other adolescent mental health services in the UK, which only see young people up to the age of 18.

Most young people who are seen within the Adolescent Department are provided with the opportunity to meet with a therapist for a four-session psychodynamic consultation as part of the assessment process. In addition to thinking with the young person about the "presenting difficulty," for which the anxiety may be located more with parents or the professional who referred the young person, an important aspect of the psychodynamic consultation is to help the adolescent to develop some interest and curiosity in themselves and their lives. This may lead some adolescents to decide to undertake ongoing psychotherapy.

In 2006/2007, the Rorschach Pilot Study was undertaken utilizing the Rorschach Comprehensive System (RCS, Exner, 2003), involving three senior-level clinical psychologists (two of whom were psychoanalysts) and three randomly selected patients over the age of 16 who had been referred to the Adolescent Department during this period. The purpose of this study was two-fold: to assess whether the Rorschach might be useful for engaging adolescents in the assessment process, and to explore whether it could add anything to assessment process, above and beyond the standard four-session psychodynamic consultation.

Apart from being provided with a brief summary of the reason why the patient was referred, the psychologist who administered the Rorschach was blind to the outcome of the psychodynamic consultation until the postassessment period. This was also the case for psychologist undertaking the psychodynamic consultation who was not aware of the findings from the RCS until the postassessment phase. At the postassessment phase the three psychologists met together.

Obviously, considering the very small number of participants, it is impossible to draw any definite conclusions. Nevertheless, the findings from this study have clinical relevance for the Adolescent Department, for the following reasons: (1) The adolescent patients who participated in the Project were found to be receptive and responsive to the Rorschach as an assessment tool. (2) For each of the three patients, high levels of consistency were found between the findings from the Rorschach (RCS) and the information derived from the standard four-session psychodynamic consultation. (3) The Rorschach (RCS) findings served to bring some of the young person's underlying conflicts and issues, elicited during the assessment, into sharper relief. (4) The Rorschach (RCS) functioned to provide additional information about the patient, which was not always so readily available from the standard assessment procedure.

The main conclusion from this project was that the Rorschach (RCS) may serve as a useful adjunct to the standard psychodynamic consultation within the Adolescent Department.

Résumé

Le département adolescent de la Tavistock Clinic fut crée en 1959 afin de proposer des traitements aux "délinquants qui passent à l'acte et qui ont des troubles du comportement" (Dicks, 1970) et à leurs familles. Au cours des années, le département adolescent a développé une variété d'approches psychothérapeutiques pour venir en aide aux adolescents, leurs parents et familles. Les jeunes personnes ont la possibilité de prendre rendez-vous eux-mêmes jusqu'à l'âge de 21 ans, ce qui n'est pas le cas dans les autres services adolescents en Grande-Bretagne qui n'offre des services qu'aux jeunes de moins de 18 ans.

La plupart des adolescents qui sont vus dans le département pour une première évaluation, ont la possibilité de rencontrer un thérapeute pour une consultation psychodynamique de quatre séances. La consultation permet à l'adolescent non-seulement de discuter de son "problème immédiat" qui génère l'inquiétude des parents et des professionnels, mais aussi d'aider le jeune patient à développer une curiosité et un intérêt pour sa propre histoire personnelle. Ceci peut déboucher sur une psychothérapie.

En 2006, le Rorschach Système Integré (RSI, Exner, 2003) a été utilisé dans une étude pilote menée par trois psychologues cliniciens de haut niveau (dont deux psychanalystes) et trois participants, âgés de 16 ans et plus, référés au département adolescent et sélectionnés au hasard. Deux objectifs ont motivés cette étude pilote: découvrir si le RSI était un bon instrument pour engager des adolescents dans le processus d'évaluation, et établir si le RSI peut ajouter quelque chose au processus d'évaluation, en plus ou au-delà des 4 séances classiques de consultation psychodynamique.

Le psychologue en charge de la passation du Rorschach n'avait que la raison de la demande de consultation et n'avait accès au résultat des 4 séances d'évaluation qu'en phase de post- évaluation. Cela était de même pour le psychologue en charge de la consultation classique. A la phase de post-évaluation, les trois psychologues été invités à confronter leurs résultats.

La conclusion principale de ce projet est que le RSI est un outil très complémentaire à la consultation classique de 4 séances psychodynamique établit dans le département adolescent de la Tavistock Clinic.

Resumen

En 1959, el Departamento de Adolescentes de la Clínica Tavistock se propuso tratar a menores "con trastornos graves de conducta y actuaciones delincuentes" (Dicks, 1970), junto con las familias. A lo largo del tiempo, este Departamento de Adolescentes ha desarrollado una amplia gama de enfoques terapéuticos para trabajar con jóvenes, padres y familias, desde el marco teórico psicoanalítico. Esta situación proporciona a los adolescentes la oportunidad de contar con una ayuda específica para ellos mismos y ser tratados psicoterapéuticamente hasta la edad de 21 años, lo que significa un lapso de tiempo muy superior al que se ofrece en la mayoría de los servicios de Salud Mental del Reino Unido, que sólo atienden hasta los 18 años.

La mayoría de los jóvenes atendidos en este Departamento de Adolescentes dispone de 4 consultas con un terapeuta, como parte de su proceso de evaluación. Además de reflexionar con cada menor sobre las "dificultades reales" que llevan a los padres u otros profesionales a derivarlos a este servicio, un aspecto esencial de esas consultas evaluativo-terapéuticas ha sido ayudar al adolescente a desarrollar un interés y curiosidad propios acerca de sí mismos y de sus vidas. Esto permite a muchos de ellos decidir comprometerse en una psicoterapia.

En 2006/7, se inició el Estudio Piloto Rorschach, usando el Sistema Comprensivo (CS, Exner, 2003) e incluyendo a 3 Psicólogos Clínicos con experiencia (2 de ellos psicoanalistas) y a 3 pacientes de 16 años seleccionados aleatoriamente, que habían sido derivados al Departamento en ese período. El objetivo de este estudio era doble: valorar si el Test de Rorschach podía ser útil para ayudar a comprometer a los adolescentes en el proceso de evaluación y explorar si esta prueba podía aportar información a la evaluación de cada caso, que complementara la obtenida en las 4 sesiones psicodinámicas estándar.

El psicólogo que administraba el Rorschach sólo contaba con un breve resumen de los motivos por los que cada adolescente había sido derivado y desconocía los resultados de las consultas psicodinámicas hasta la finalización de la evaluación. Asimismo, el psicólogo que realizaba las consultas psicodinámicas, desconocía los resultados del Rorschach. En la fase de post-evaluación, los tres psicólogos se encontraban y contrastaban la información.

Obviamente, considerando el pequeño número de participantes, es imposible extraer conclusiones definitivas. No obstante, los resultados de este estudio tienen gran relevancia clínica para el Departamento de Adolescentes, por las siguientes razones: los pacientes adolescentes que participaron en el Proyecto se mostraron muy receptivos y colaboradores hacia el Rorschach como herramienta de evaluación; en todos los pacientes (aunque sólo fueron 3) aparecieron altos niveles de concordancia entre los resultados del Rorschach y la información derivada de las 4 consultas psicodinámicas estándar; los resultados del Rorschach (CS) sirvieron para que los adolescentes comprendieran mejor algunos de sus conflictos y preocupaciones expresados durante las sesiones; y, aún más relevante, el Rorschach (CS) aportó información adicional sobre cada paciente, que no resulta fácilmente asequible a través del procedimiento estándar de evaluación.

La principal conclusión de este Proyecto ha sido que el Rorschach (CS) servirá como un complemento eficaz a las consultas psicodinámicas estándar en el Departamento de Adolescentes.

　Tavistock Clinic の思春期部門は"行動上混乱しており、行動化している非行少年"（Dicks,1970）を、混乱している思春期の若者の家族と協力して治療するために1959年に設立された。時の経過にともない、思春期部門は青年やその両親、家族と、精神分析の枠組みで協働作業をするために幅広い精神分析のアプローチを発展させた。それは青年に 21 歳まで、自らリファーして、心理療法を開始する機会を提供しており、それは18歳までの若者だけをみるイギリスの思春期のメンタルヘルスサービスの多くとは異なっている。

　思春期部門を訪れるたいていの若者は、4セッションの、アセスメント・プロセスの一部分でもある精神力動的コンサルテーションのために治療者に遭う機会を与えられる。"あらわれている困難"について、不安はより両親に所在するのか、それともこの若者をリファーしてきた専門家に所在するか、若者と共に考えることに加えて、この精神力動的コンサルテーションの重要な側面は思春期にあるものが彼ら自身のことや彼らの人生にいくらかの関心や好奇心を発達させることを助けることにある。

　2006/7 年に、3 人のシニアクラスの臨床心理学者（そのうちの 2 人は精神分析家）と、この期間に思春期部門に紹介されてきた 16 歳以上の患者の中で無作為に選ばれた 3 名の患者を含む、ロールシャッハ包括システム（RCS,Exner,2003）をもちいたパイロット・スタディがおこなわれた。この研究の目的は 2 つであって、ひとつはロールシャッハがアセスメント過程において思春期の若者とかかわるのに有用であるかどうかを査定することと、もうひとつはそれが、標準的な 4 セッションの精神力動的コンサルテーションを超えてアセスメント過程以上に何かを加味する可能性があるかどうかを探求することである。

　その患者がなぜリファーされてきたかの理由の要約を別に
して、ロールシャッハを施行した心理学者はアセスメント終
了後の期間まで精神力動的なコンサルテーションの結果につ
いては"ブラインド"であった。このことはまた精神力動的
コンサルテーションを引き受けた心理学者も、アセスメント
後の期間まではRCSからの発見については知らされること
がなかったので、同様であった。アセスメント後の段階にお
いて3人の心理学者は会っている。

　あきらかに、研究参加者が非常に少数であることを考慮す
ると、明確な結論を導くことは不可能である。しかしながら、
この研究の発見は以下の理由により、思春期部門に臨床的に
重要な観点をもたらした：このプロジェクトに参加した思春
期の患者は、アセスメント・ツールとしてのロールシャッハ
を受け入れ、よく反応したようにみうけられた：3人の患者
それぞれにとって、ロールシャッハ（RCS）から発見された
ことと標準的な4回の精神力動的コンサルテーションから引
き出された情報の間には高いレベルでの一貫性が認められた
こと：ロールシャッハ（RCS）の発見は若者に内在する葛藤
や問題のいくらかを引き寄せ、それはアセスメントの間に顕
在化し、より明確なレリーフに至らせ、ロールシャッハ
（RCS）は標準的なアセスメント手続きからではそれほどい
つも容易には役立てることができない、クライエントに関す
る付加的な情報を提供する機能を果たしていた。

　この研究の主な結論は、ロールシャッハ（RCS）は思春期
部門の標準的な精神力動的コンサルテーションに役に立つ補
助的なものとして機能するということである。

Rorschachiana 30, 150–179
© 2009 Hogrefe Publishing

DOI: 10.1027/1192-5604.30.2.150

Assessing Changes in Psychoanalytic Psychodynamic Therapy with an Early Adolescent

Daniela di Riso[1], Silvia Salcuni[1], Loredana Laghezza[2], Cristina Marogna[3], and Adriana Lis[1]

[1]*Department of Developmental and Socialization Psychology, University of Padova, Italy,*
[2]*Department of Human Science and Pedagogy, University of Perugia, Italy,*
[3]*Department of General Psychology, University of Padova, Italy*

Abstract. This paper describes changes in personality functioning according to Exner's Rorschach Comprehensive System (CS) in an early adolescent boy, Gabriele, referred for anxiety and obsessive compulsive symptoms. The DSM-IV diagnosis was General Anxiety Disorder (GAD). The therapy lasted about 2 years, and sessions were all audio-taped to create a more objective database. A total of 50 sessions were analyzed. The therapist employed a broadly defined, object-relations-focused, psychodynamic framework, with particular emphasis placed on balancing supportive versus insight-oriented modes of therapy (Skean, 2005). After a brief introduction of Gabriele's clinical history and anamnesis, the paper illustrates (a) changes in the symptoms from the beginning to the end of the supportive psychodynamic psychotherapy, which also included some cognitive-behavioral therapy (CBT) interventions; (b) changes in the CS administered at the beginning and at the end of the psychotherapy; and (c) the relevance of therapeutic alliance measured by the Collaborative Interactive Scale (CIS; Colli & Lingiardi, 2007) as a fundamental intervening variable in the psychotherapy process.

Keywords: psychodynamic psychotherapy, process research, outcome research, Rorschach Comprehensive System, therapeutic alliance

Weiner and Exner (1988, 1991) suggested that certain Rorschach variables related to specific personality characteristics might provide a useful measure of progress in dynamic psychotherapy. Accordingly, they examined the interpretative guidelines elaborated in the Comprehensive System (CS; Exner, 1986) to identify some indices of impaired functioning. They proposed that patients would be ready to terminate therapy when they were able to manage stress adequately, display a consistent coping style in problem situations, openly confront their experience, engage in constructive self-examination, and feel comfortable in interpersonal relationships. Weiner and Exner (1991) selected 27 indexes of adjustment difficulty as potentially valid clues of insufficient treatment progress. These variables were used in different psychotherapy outcome research studies (Weiner & Exner, 1978; Exner & Andronikof-Sanglade, 1992). More recently, Bihlar and Carlsson (2000, 2001) proposed a selection of CS Rorschach variables that could be useful in planning therapeutic goals and that could be used to assess therapeutic changes. Recent literature has stressed the importance of process research also in developmental ages (Weersing & Weisz, 2002; Shirk & Karver, 2003). Admittedly, child psychotherapy process research has lagged behind its adult counterpart (Kazdin, Bass, Ayers, & Rodgers, 1990; Russell & Shirk, 1998), but there is growing interest in process predictors of treatment outcomes with children and adolescents (Kazdin & Kendall, 1998; Weisz, Huey, & Weersing, 1998). Single-case studies with CS Rorschach variables have not been carried out very frequently in developmental ages (Murray, 1994). This paper had two aims:

1) to describe planned therapeutic goals according to Bihlar and Carlsson's (2000, 2001) "integrated variables" (i.e., symptoms, rehabilitation, and CS Rorschach variables);

2) to assess actual changes in personality functioning, using the 27 CS Rorschach variables proposed by Weiner and Exner (1991) in an early adolescent boy, Gabriele, referred for anxiety and obsessive compulsive symptoms, stressing the role of therapeutic alliance.

It has been posited that the therapeutic relationship plays a critical role in the treatment of children (Shirk & Saiz, 1992; Goldfried, Raue, & Castonguay, 1998), and it is one of the few process variables that has received attention in child therapy outcome literature (Russell & Shirk, 1998).

The Referral, Sources of Data Available, and Clinical Setting

Gabriele is an early adolescent boy, referred by his parents to a University Service that offered private practice in the community. He presented a very high level of anxiety and obsessive compulsive symptoms. The DSM-IV diagnosis was General Anxiety Disorder (GAD). Some criteria for Obsessive Compulsive Disorder (OCD) were also met. Data were available from Gabriele's referral, assessment phase, and therapy process. His parents were a further source of information.

The Patient: Problems and Symptoms

Gabriele was a 12-year-old Italian boy. He was first-born and had four younger siblings, each born about one year apart. He grew up in a warm intact family of a high socioeconomic level. The main complex of Gabriele's symptoms consisted of pervasive acute anxieties about school achievement and ability to complete schools tasks (without any real basis), anxieties about his parents' physical and socioeconomic well-being, but also some obsessions and compulsions, including maintaining all his books in order. His parents' attempts to cope with Gabriele's requests to be reassured seemed to be completely useless, and they were unable to contain and calm down his states. They showed feelings of impotence, helplessness, and guilt. Before the referral, the parents had tried, in another clinic, a 20-session cognitive-behavioral therapy (CBT) intervention carried out by an experienced CBT therapist.

The Assessment Phase

Gabriele's assessment phase was carried out through clinical interviews, the CS Rorschach, and a variety of quantitative, self-report questionnaires, focusing on anxiety-related symptoms, including the Children's Global Assessment Scale (CGAS; Gould et al., 1983) and the Symptom Checklist-90-R (SCL-90-R; Derogatis & Cleary, 1977).

At the clinical interviews, Gabriele looked immature and young for his age, in spite of his height. He appeared to be a withdrawn, shy, and well-behaved child. He talked clearly, coherently, and his vocabulary was rich and articulated. His discourse, however, was never spontaneous, he talked only if asked. He showed a clear tendency to speak about school topics only, avoiding talk about his family or his affective life. He was worried about not being loved by his parents if he was not good at

152

school. He described how he strictly followed his parents' requests, suggestions and their educational practices.

The therapist hypothesized that:
1) Gabriele showed an idealized representation of his parents' expectations about his school achievement;
2) he had rigidly internalized and followed parental norms in order not to fail parental expectations.

Besides these GAD symptoms, Gabriele had problems in specific areas such as
1) the absence of any emotional involvement in the description of his life events. He talked in a very stiff, intellectual, cold, and detached manner, even in the careful description of his anxieties and worries;
2) problems of isolation and withdrawal with peers: Gabriele had no friends and did not show a great desire for closeness, which made it difficult for him to communicate effectively, not only with the therapist, but with other important figures in his life and peers;
3) a very bossy, cold and detached style of relating to younger brothers and sisters at home.

Treatment Planning

Gabriele was followed for 2 years through once-a-week psychodynamic psychotherapy that also included some CBT interventions. Treatment planning was based on the results of the assessment phase and on therapy guiding conception.

The Results of the Assessment Phase

The Rorschach CS was administered, scored, and interpreted by a therapist reliable in the use of the test. The therapist was in the research team who collected Italian normative data of preadolescent and adolescents. The Rorschach CS interrater range of agreement on coding segments was Iota = .71–.91 (Lis, Salcuni, & Parolin, 2007).

The Bihlar and Carlsson's (2000, 2001) classification of therapeutic goals seemed to help in the planning of therapeutic goals for Gabriele.

The scale included 12 categories: 8 treatment goals, 3 nontreatment goals, and 1 goal about therapeutic tasks. Of the treatment goals, 2 were behavioral goals (Rehabilitation and Symptoms) and the others 6 were formulated according to the psychodynamic tradition (Control, Affects, Self-Perception, Interpersonal Relations, Mediation/Ideation, and Insight). Nontreatment goals included Life Goals, Theoretical Goals, and Not possible to classify. The Therapeutic Tasks category included formulation about therapeutic work. The present study was based on the analysis of Behavioral goals and Psychodynamic goals as in Bihlar and Carlsson (2001). We decided to use Bihlar and Carlsson's goals categories especially because they maintained an "integrated" approach, using clinical information derived from both clinical interview and questionnaires (areas: Symptoms, Rehabilitation, Insight) and Rorschach CS variables (areas: Affect, Mediation-Ideation, Control Capacity, Self- and Interpersonal Perception). This approach could be considered more integrated and powerful in the therapeutic goal description.

Table 1 shows the main findings in the assessment phase of Gabriele's clinical interview and Rorschach CS variables according to the main therapeutic goals suggested by Bihlar and Carlssons (2001, p. 395–396). Gabriele's profile showed many different kind of difficulties, in control capacities, interpersonal and self-perception areas. Key variables at the first Rorschach CS administration were CDI > 3 and EA low. This outlined a state of intense or chronic crisis with potentially disorganizing elements.

In the Rehabilitation and Symptoms area, Gabriele reported a great number of anticipatory anxieties about school subjects or possible family well-being problems. He was totally involved in school and study, and, in particular, he reported having few hobbies (reading and personal computer) and showed no form of pleasure when talking about them. According to SCL-90 scores, Obsessive-Compulsive and Hostility subdimensions were in the clinical range. The specific therapeutic goal in Rehabilitation and Symptoms areas was to eliminate, reduce, or deal with anxiety and obsessive behavior in a more adaptive way, to shift his high cognitive capacity and resources toward more pleasant and adaptive activities, such as friends, play, sports, to make his daily life more various and enjoyable.

In the Affect area, Gabriele showed psychological distress including diffuse anxiety and excessive internalization of feelings (C'), with a marked tendency to avoid emotional stimulation (Afr). His deliberated emotional discharges and interchanges were also totally blocked (FC:CF + C); he seemed unable to adequately manage any kind of deliberately

Table 1. Bihlar and Carlssons's (2001, p. 395–396) planned therapeutic goal categories in Gabriele's assessment phase

Goal categories: definitions according to Bihlar and Carlsson (2001, p. 395)	Assessment phase findings
Rehabilitation: Better functioning in everyday life.	
Symptoms: Elimination or reduction of symptoms.	
Affects: Improving capacity to contain, handle, and express affects.	
Shd-Shd > 0 or Col-Shd > 0	Shd-Shd = 0 & Col-Shd = 0
CF + C > FC + 1	FC: CF + C = 0: 0
FC > 1.5 × CF + C and C = 0	
S > 3	S = 3
SumC' > 2 and Afr < .46	SumC' = 2 and Afr = .27
Meditation-Ideation: A grater capacity to evaluate own thoughts and conclusions more critically and capacity to interpret reality more realistically.	
X-% > .29 or M- > 1	X-% = 0.21 and M- = 1
Sum6 > 6 and WSum6 > 17	Sum6 = 9 and WSum6 = 12
Intell > 4	Intell. = 1
Control Capacity: A greater capacity to maintain psychological control in demanding or stressful situations. Also goals referring to reducing exaggerate control and greater accessibility to more effective and flexible psychological defences.	EA = 3
EA < 7	AdjD = -1
AdjD > 0	Lambda = .40 and Blends = 3
Lambda > .99 or Blends < 4	EB style = introversive with EB = 3: 0.0
EB style = ambitent	FM + m: Sum-Shd = 3:5 end es = 8 >
Sumshd > FM + m or es > EA	EA = 3
Interpersonal Relationships: Improving capacity for interpersonal relations.	
COP + AG < 3	COP + AG = 1
AG > 3	AG = 1
Isol/R .24 and T = 0	Isol/R = .36 and T = 0
Fd > 0 or T > 1	Fd = 0 and T = 0
H < 2 or SumH < 5	H = 1 and SumH = 6
HIV positive	HVI negative
Self-Perception: Improving changes and realistic evaluation of self-definition.	
Fr + rF > 0 or Ego > .44	Fr + rF = 2 and Ego = .79
Ego < .33 and MOR > 2	MOR = 0
SumV + FD > 2	SumV = 1 and FD = 0
FD = 0	
Insight: Improving consciousness and knowledge about oneself.	

initiated emotions. The therapeutic goals in managing affective problems were to help Gabriele to (a) be in contact with his affections, (b) to acknowledge his painful emotions, (c) limit his depressive-like mood, and (d) indirectly overcome his difficulties in social adjustment.

From a ideational-meditative point of view, Gabriele usually interpreted reality in an appropriate way but sometimes inaccurately (X-%). He showed concrete and immature reasoning for his age, and his preoccupations could interfere with clarity and fluidity of thought (M- and Sum6). Following Bihlar and Carlson's, therapeutic goals were to increase Gabriele's capacity to evaluate in an adaptive way his thoughts and the conclusions he arrived at, and also to better manage fantasies and to use a less concrete and more realistic thought, in particular when having to deal with intense emotions and primitive rage.

In the Coping area, Gabriele was in a state of chronic stimulus overload (AdjD). His control ability for dealing with stress was effectively lower than might be expected, and he displayed a moderate functioning impairment in social skills due to his obsessive rituals and anxiety. Gabriele showed a significant immaturity in both his personality organization and adjustment to interpersonal environment, which caused vulnerability in managing situational and chronic life requests (AdjD and es). He showed a very low amount of resources (EA), and this pattern displayed a massive inhibition in affect (affective side EB), that runs contrary to the adolescent condition. He was in a state that could rarely be maintained over lengthy periods of time, and the perceived stress could sometimes make him to be impulsive (EB). Therapeutic goals in this area were to support Gabriele in this highly critical situation, to overcome this peculiar state of crisis in relation to control abilities and inhibited emotional expression, increasing his capacity to manage internal and external demands, and learning to keep control in stressful situations, when he usually reacts with anguish and immature behaviors.

Self- and interpersonal perception appeared to be very complicated in Gabriele's profile. On one hand, Gabriele showed exaggerated self-involvement, an inflated sense of personal worth, a need for reaffirmation or reinforcement of his exaggerated sense of personal pride (Ego and Fr + rF), but with an absent objective introspective process (FD). On the other hand, even if he seemed to be interested in other people, he displayed some difficulties seeing them in an objective way, and he frequently tended to misinterpret social gestures (H and Sum H). He tended to be quite isolated (Isol/R), and he did not consider relationships as one of the meaningful parts of his experience (COP and AG). In particular, Gabriele showed immaturity in dealing with social situations and difficulties in establishing or maintaining deep and intimate relationships with others. Specific therapeutic goals in these areas were to help Gabriele to become more prone to introspective behavior to get to know himself and the reasons for his sufferance, with the aim of reaching a more realistic idea of the self and building a strong and consistent identity, through the acceptation of his limitations and aspects of fragility. These modulations in self-image could be useful consequently to attaining and increasing his social abilities, becoming less socially maladjusted, and to enjoying interaction with others.

Besides these specific goals, the therapist was asked to work primarily to establish a good working alliance, in order to give Gabriele space and a relationship to invest trust in. The treatment had to help Gabriele go beyond words, to discover the emotional meaning hidden beneath words; the therapeutic space could become one in which Gabriele might experience an adaptive modality to express and modulate anxiety and anger that are tightly blocked inside him. Theoretically, Gabriele was facing a very delicate period of his development, approaching adolescence and the specific phase of separation-individuation process to becoming emotionally separate in an adaptive from the family. The severe maladjustment he was living through could be modulated through the therapeutic meaningful relationships and to the encouragement by improving enjoyable activities in everyday life.

Therapy Guiding Conception

Although, as already reported, Gabriele had already undergone a CBT intervention that had helped reduce symptoms, anxieties still persisted at referral. Two important contextual conditions, the meaningful role of the therapeutic alliance and Bihlar and Carlsson's goal categories profile (Bihlar & Carlsson, 2001) suggested that psychodynamic concepts and strategies could be usefully employed. The therapist chose to employ a broadly defined, psychoanalytic psychodynamic framework, with a particular emphasis on balancing supportive versus insight-oriented modes of therapy (Skean, 2005). This balance turned out to be a key factor in developing an effective therapeutic relationship with Gabriele. The major concepts and strategies employed in his psychoanalytic psychodynamic therapy included the following:

1. *The use of therapeutic relationship and alliance.* Gabriele and his therapist established an excellent working relationship, and he was motivated to work with her within a model that integrated psychodynamic concepts into some "supportive techniques" drawn from other psychotherapy models. The therapeutic encounter became a vehicle for observing and understanding the client's interpersonal behavior (Spence, 1982; Binder, Henry, & Strupp, 1987). Through this relationship, the patient brought his interpersonal world into the treatment room and allowed the therapist to experience aspects of the client's structuring of reality (Skean, 2005, p. 3).

2. *Psychodynamic intervention takes numerous factors into account.* Among these, relationships with the self and others (internal and external), inferred defensive/adaptive processes ("personality structure"), and "internal conflict formulation" versus an "ego deficit formulation" (Shirk & Russell, 1996) were identified. By examining client transference and therapist countertransference – characteristic defence mechanisms – and by having an interpersonal experience in the therapy that differs from others he or she may have known, the patient is encouraged to expand his or her understanding of the self in a way that provides more options and choices (Vaillant, 1977; McWilliams, 1999, 2004; Skean, 2005). From a psychodynamic point of view, it seemed coherent to link Gabriele's great sense of his inability to control external events and his consequent fears and rancorous emotions with not being "good enough" for his parents. Consequently, Gabriele's attitude for an ideational and performance-based approach to experience, also encouraged by his parents, instead of an affective and emotional one, could be seen as a defence against his inner emotional affective world, full of negative, aggressive, and fearful emotions. His affect isolation and inability to express emotions, in particular the negative ones, could be interpreted along this theoretical defensive line.

Psychodynamic Diagnosis and "Supportive" Strategies

Particularly at the beginning, Gabriele's therapy process was concerned with "here-and-now" processes going on in the session. Few references were made to connect his ways of living with the past (Shirk & Russell, 1996; Misch, 2000). Moreover, especially at the beginning of the therapy,

Gabriele was not ready for transference and countertransference inter-pretation. Instead, "supportive" strategies were used to help him deal with his emotional-affective world. The therapist worked as a "good par-ent" (Winnicott, 1965; Misch, 2000) who made suggestions for dealing with anxieties, for helping behave in a more adaptive way, and thinking about alternative ways to deal with the symptoms and social deficits (CBT). All this was done within a secure and affectionate environment. Corrective parenting (Shirk & Russell, 1996), which allowed for new positive parental relationships, was proposed. This allowed Gabriele to identify with the therapist, as a less strict and more flexible parental representation (Misch, 2000). This process also made it possible for him to internalize the therapist's function of monitoring, approval and dis-approval, structuring in more flexible and adaptive Ego and Super-ego deficits. Greenberg and Safran (1987) underlined the importance of "emotion experiencing" in the therapy process to help identification, recognition, modulated expression, and verbalization of emotions and feelings. Gabriele needed to open his "box of affection," which was com-pletely closed and needed to be modulated and integrated, with the therapist's support, without feeling overwhelmed. In the central part of the therapy process entirely nonmodulated aggressive fantasies and feel-ings appeared. The causes and consequences of these feelings at the cognitive level (CBT strategies) also needed to be recognized. Support-ive strategies were used to increase Gabriele's self-esteem and to encour-age him to think in different ways about himself and others (Misch, 2000; Shirk & Russell, 1996).

Gabriele's therapy process was also facilitated by using play therapy, whereby children communicate their thoughts and feelings through play more naturally than they do through verbal communication. When the child is playing, the therapist recognizes themes and patterns or ways of using the materials that are important to the child. Play therapy was introduced by the therapist during the first period of the therapeutic relationship as an important step to learn to be in tune with affective activation, by means of inflated balloons. Initially, Gabriele was very shy and fearful in flying the balloons. After several sessions, however, he started to play harder, hitting the balloons more strongly, making them bounce against the walls. In a free but organized way, he kicked them, running around the room, laughing about his strength and starting to have fun at it. Over time, the clinician helped Gabriele to begin to make meaning out of the play and to express worries and fears through play. Gabriele became more and more trusting in his ability to play and express emotions (and to remain with the therapist in the therapy), and he was finally able to explore emotions toward play in the secure and stable context of the therapy.

A Measure of the Psychodynamic Process

Therapeutic alliance is one of the most important aspecific process factors correlated with a positive psychotherapy outcome (Shirk & Karver, 2003). The Collaborative Interaction Scale (CIS; Colli & Lingiardi, 2007) is a measure of therapeutic alliance in terms of collaborative processes, scoring ruptures, and reparations of the alliance assessed from transcripts of therapy sessions. The scale comprises two subscales: The first measures the patient therapeutic alliance identifying rupture markers (direct marker, DM, and indirect marker IM) and reparative collaborative interventions (Collaborative Process, CP); the second measures clinician therapeutic alliance, taking into account positive collaborative and reparative (PI) and negative oppositional and disruptive (NI) interventions. These measures led to three global indexes: the average Therapist's Collaboration Level (TCL), the average Patient's Collaboration Level (PCL), and the average Collaboration Level between Therapist and Patient (CL). The CIS was scored by two blind judges for 50 audio-recorded sessions of therapy (Cohen's κ = .87).

The CIS trends showed a very important change in Gabriele's therapeutic alliance along the therapy process: He became more and more collaborative. The therapist maintained a good and stable level of collaboration. The global therapeutic alliance index increased. The patient – fearful, untrusting and anxious at the beginning of the therapy – involved the therapist with his own rupture style. However, the therapist's empathic, coherent, and collaborative answers allowed Gabriele to develop a new way to manage and cope with anxiety, needs, and fear. The therapist made it possible for him to change from his shy, routine-like, and nontalking approach to a more free and warm one. The therapist provided him with a "secure stable base" from which learn new ways to construct a relationship, explaining and sharing emotions, instead of only cognitions and ideas.

Treatment Achievements

A follow-up was carried out 4 months after the end of therapy. The follow-up included the administration of a clinical interview, the SCL-90-R, C-GAS, and Rorschach CS. Table 2 shows actual goals described by the comparison between Gabriele's assessment phase and retest phase according to CS Rorschach, SCL-90, and GAS. CS Rorschach was examined according to the 27 Rorschach CS indices of impaired functioning proposed by Weiner and Exner (1991) in order to assess achievements in Gabriele's treatment. Rorschach CS Key variables in the follow-up were D < AdjD and CDI > 3. Gabriele was still in a state of potential disorganization as well as intense or chronic crisis and still showed immaturity in dealing with social and daily situations.

With respect to the CS Rorschach, in the Managing stress area, at the end of the intervention, Gabriele still maintained some aspect of social immaturity (CDI). Chronic stress decreased, but situational stress increased, showing a higher level of stable control in life situations, though some problems have occurred when something new took place (D and AdjD). Psychological resources have increased (EA). In the Dealing with experience area, he showed an avoidant-ambient style; this lack of a well-defined coping style could be related to an attempt to avoid the new emotional complexity and new nuances of his experiences he was starting to deal with (Lambda and Zd). At the end of treatment he still showed an inability to perceive events as most people would do (X-%), but he showed a more accurate perception of situation and an increased capacity to anticipate consequences of actions (X+%). In the Modulating affect area, at the end of treatment, Gabriele did not show emotional distress related to his painful emotions; he seemed to pay more attention to his inner and unmet needs, and he seemed to have few constricted feelings (FM + m:SumShading). However, he still showed episodes of confusion and emotional difficulties, experiencing disappointment, tension, anxiety, and avoiding situations that imply emotional stimulation (DEPI). Gabriele seemed to be particularly uncomfortable when he had to deal with emotions (Afr). The most striking achievement was related to the capacity to process affective discharges and interchanges: At the end of the treatment Gabriele was able to recognized emotions, totally blocked before the intervention (FC:CF + C). In the Using ideation area, Gabriele improved in his thinking procedures, becoming less prone to conceptual failure to discriminate and use concrete reasoning, although

D. di Riso et al.

Table 2. Comparison between Gabriele's assessment and retest phase according to Weiner and Exner indices (1991), SCL-90 and GAS

Weiner and Exner variables (1991)	Assessment phase	Retest phase
Managing Stress		
D < 0	D = -1	D = -3
AdjD < 0	AdjD = -1	AdjD = 0
EA < 7	EA = 3.0	EA = 6.0
CDI > 3	CDI = 5	CDI = 4
Dealing with Experience		
Zd < -3.0	Zd = +5.5	Zd = -4.0
Lambda > .99	Lambda = .40	Lambda = 1.00
X+% < .70	X+% = .36	X+% = .20
X-% > .20	X-% = .21	X-% = .15
Modulating Affect		
SumShading > FM + m	FM+ m:SumShading = 3:5	FM + m:SumShading = 12:4
DEPI = 5	DEPI = 5	DEPI = 5
DEPI > 5		
Afr < .50	Afr = .27	Afr = .44
CF+ C > FC + 1	FC:CF + C = 0:0	FC:CF + C = 2:2
Using Ideation		
Sum6SpSc > 6	Sum6SpSc = 9	Sum6SpSc = 8
M- > 0	M- = 1	M- = 0
Mp > Ma	Ma:Mp = 1:2	Ma:Mp = 0:3
Intellec > 5	Intellect = 1	Intellect = 1
Examining Oneself		
Fr + rF > 0	Fr + rF = 2	Fr + rF = 0
Ego > .43	Ego = .79	
Ego < .33		Ego = .26
FD > 2	FD = 0	FD = 3
Feeling Comfortable in Interpersonal Relationships		
p > a + 1	a:p = 3:3	a:p = 6:10
T = 0	T = 0	T = 0
T > 1		
PureH < 2	PureH = 1	PureH = 1
H < (H) + Hd + (Hd)	H:(H) + Hd + (Hd) = 1:5	H:(H) + Hd + (Hd) = 1:6
SCL-90 subscales (clinical cutoff > 1)		
Somatization	Som = .38	Som = .00
Obsessive-Compulsive	O-C = 1.60	O-C = .40
Interpersonal Sensitivity	Int = .44	Int = .00
Depression	Dep = .80	Dep = .18
Anxiety	Anx = .90	Anx = .20
Hostility	Hos = 1.20	Hos = .00
Phobic Anxiety	Phob = .00	Phob = .00
Paranoid Ideation	Par = .38	Par = .00
Psychoticism	Psy = .00	Psy = .00
Global Severity Index	GSI = .58	GSI = .10
C- GAS	Clinician evaluation: 49	Clinician evaluation:70

162

he still maintained some aspect of arbitrary thinking (Sum6). Moreover, preoccupation no longer interferes with his reasoning (M-). At the end of treatment he still tended to show an orientation in which flights into fantasy become a routine for dealing with unpleasant situations in order not to take responsibility (Ma:Mp). In the Examining oneself area, Gabriele's self-involvement has decreased strongly, and he has begun to underestimate his personal worth (Ego and Fr + rF). Gabriele started to pay attention also to the feedback external world, so that he seemed to be more aware of his fragility, becoming more ruminative about himself (FD). In the Feeling Comfortable in interpersonal relationships area, Gabriele still seemed to be overly concerned with personal space, and much more cautious about intimate relationships than what is usual for adolescents (T = 0). At the end of treatment he still displayed difficulties in understanding people (H), leading to unrealistic expectations concerning relationship (H:(H) + Hd + (Hd)), and he showed a more passive role in interpersonal relations (a:p).

With respect to SCL-90, Gabriele showed very different profiles, comparing the assessment phase and the re-test phase. Overall psychological distress has decreased, as shown by the decrease of all SCL-90 dimensions. The most important ones were O-C (Obsessive-Compulsive) and HOS (Hostility), which in the assessment phase were clinically meaningful. At the end of treatment, Gabriele reported few thoughts, impulses, and actions experienced as irresistible and reported few negative affect states of anger, irritability, rage, and resentment.

With respect to GAS, the clinician in the assessment phase said that Gabriele's functioning was impaired by Serious symptoms, in different areas such as social and school domain. At the end of the treatment, the clinician noticed a meaningful improvement: Gabriele showed mild symptoms and some difficulties in social and school functioning, but generally his functioning was pretty consistent with some meaningful interpersonal relationships.

Concluding Evaluation of the Therapy Process and Outcome

For many years, the therapeutic relationship has been viewed, especially in psychodynamic and experiential traditions (Axline, 1947; Shirk & Russell, 2003), as a basic change mechanism in child psychotherapy.

More recently, the therapeutic relationship has taken on a more prominent role in behavioral and cognitive-behavioral therapy (CBT) with
children (Kendall, 1991). From a developmental perspective, it has in
fact been suggested that the therapeutic relationship may be more critical in child than adult therapy (Shirk & Saiz, 1992). Therapeutic alliance
in Gabriele's therapeutic process became more and more consistent,
indicating that he learned to be more in contact with meaningful others.
Therapeutic alliance appeared to represent a very important positive
baseline in his treatment. The qualitative information reported by Gabriele in the last part of the therapy and in the follow-up sessions supported the findings from the CS Rorschach, SCL-90, and GAS (see Table 2).
At the end of the treatment, Gabriele reported no longer having anxiety
about school tests, homework, or family well-being problems. He was
still very tidy with his comics and schoolbooks, but this aspect did not
interfere with his everyday functioning. Gabriele has started new hobbies, playing the guitar and meeting new friends. He still enjoys these
new activities very much. He has started to play with pleasure with his
younger brothers, spending time with family and friends. He also interpreted his experience in a more consistent way. He has now accepted
that his 3-year-old brother can mess up his comics, without thinking he
has bad intentions. In therapy, he has used fantasy, identifying himself
with imaginary powerful heroes, so he has felt himself to be stronger in
dealing with difficulties. On the other hand, he has just started to face
concrete difficulties, and is still unable to fully take responsibilities and
personal decision-makings. Gabriele made new friends with persons he
met at guitar lessons, and he has started to become engaged in social
interaction, though he is still cautious. He can invite friends home now,
but is still careful that they do not use his things without permission. He
reported being more at ease with some peers, but does not like enlarged
groups. Sometimes he went with friends to the movies or to MacDon-
ald's, although he did not like these places very much. At the end of the
treatments he was able to recognize his difficulties in being totally at
ease with his school mates. He no longer felt like an "immortal hero."
He admitted his difficulties in being the best at school, and that his
schoolmates consider him a grind or a bore. Gabriele has become able
to reflect on his fragility, and he has also started to be in contact with
his main difficulties with peers or little brothers.

This paper, however, has some limitations. First, because children
develop both adaptive and maladaptive behavior in the context of the
family (Sameroff, 1994), child treatment often directly involves other

family members (Russ & Ollendick, 1999). It would be interesting to analyze Gabriele's changes also according to his parents' evaluations. Second, this paper has all the limitations typical of single-case studies. Issues of internal validity remain one of the greatest challenges to single-case research. Even when the validity of clinical data derived from controlled or formal single-case research is conceded, critics of single-case methodology are frequent (Jones, 1993). Although single-case research might be useful in testing particular clinical hypotheses concerning individual patients, this is still a long way from testing more general explanatory hypotheses. Finally, single-case studies in a developmental age have specific implications. For example, it is hard to say whether changes are due to natural growth and development taking place during the same period of the intervention or to the treatment itself.

As Murray (1994) pointed out, single cases of early adolescents or adolescents using Rorschach CS variables are not very frequent. He suggested using a detailed analysis of changes based on two protocols, integrated with themes deriving from the clinical interviews. He concluded that the Rorschach CS is very important to highlight changes and underlined the importance of reading its findings in a general view of personality dynamics. In this paper, different tools, in outcome and process evaluation, were used together to monitor therapeutic change. The use of a multilevel perspective in the single-case study prevented the known tendency of the therapist overestimating symptoms and allowed for monitoring and better definition of different dimensions of outcome. This should enhance complexity of thinking about clinical cases (Messer & Wolitzky 2007).

References

Axline, V.M. (1947). *Play therapy; The inner dynamics of childhood.* Oxford, England: Houghton Mifflin.

Bihlar, B., & Carlsson, A.M. (2000). An exploratory study of agreement between therapists' goals and patients' problems revealed by the Rorschach. *Psychotherapy Research, 10,* 196–214.

Bihlar, B., & Carlsson, A.M. (2001). Planned and actual goals in psychodynamic psychotherapies: Do patients' personality characteristics relate to agreement? *Psychotherapy Research, 11,* 383–400.

Binder, J.L., Henry, W.P., & Strupp, H.H. (1987). An appraisal of selection criteria for dynamic psychotherapies and implications for setting time limits. *Psychiatry, 50*, 154–66.

Colli, A., & Lingiardi, V. (2007). Valutare l'alleanza terapeutica attraverso trascritti di sedute: L'attendibilita dell'IVAT-R nello studio di quattro psicoterapie [Evaluating the therapeutic alliance by session transcripts: The IVAT-R reliability in the study of four psychotherapies]. *Ricerca in Psicoterapia, 10*, 75–97.

Derogatis, L., & Cleary, P.A. (1977). Confirmation of the dimensional structure of the SCL-90-R: A study in construct validation. *Journal of Clinical Psychology, 33*, 981–989.

Exner, J.E. (1986). Structural data IV. Special indices. In J.E. Exner (Ed.), *The Rorschach: A comprehensive system. Vol. 1. Basic foundation* (2nd ed., pp. 411–428). New York: Wiley.

Exner, J.E. (1988). Scoring issues. *Alumni Newsletter*, pp. 4–8.

Exner, J.E. (1991). *The Rorschach: A comprehensive system: Vol. 2. Interpretation* (2nd ed.). New York: Wiley.

Exner, J.E., & Andronikof-Sanglade, A. (1992). Rorschach changes following brief and short-term therapy. *Journal of Personality Assessment, 59*, 59–71.

Goldfried, M.R., Raue, P.J., & Castonguay, L.G. (1998). The therapeutic focus in significant sessions of master therapists: A comparison of cognitive-behavioral and psychodynamic-interpersonal interventions. *Journal of Consulting and Clinical-Psychology, 66*, 803–810.

Gould, M.S., Brasic, J., Ambrosini, P., Fisher, P., Bird, H., & Aluwahlia, S. (1983). A children's global assessment scale (CGAS). *Archives of General Psychiatry, 40*(1), 1228–1231.

Greenberg, L.S., & Safran, J.D. (1987). *Emotion in psychotherapy: Affect, cognition, and the process of change.* New York: Guilford.

Jones, E.E. (1993). How will psychoanalysis study itself?. *Journal of American Psychoanalytic Association, 41*, 91–108.

Kazdin, A.E., Bass, D., Ayers, W.A., & Rodger, A. (1990). Empirical and clinical focus of child and adolescent psychotherapy research. *Journal of Consulting and Clinical Psychology, 58*, 729–740.

Kazdin, A.E., & Kendall, P.C. (1998). Current progress and future plans for developing effective treatments: Comments and perspectives. *Journal of Clinical Child Psychology, 27*, 217–226.

Kendall, P.C. (1991). Guiding theory for treating children and adolescents. In P.C. Kendall (Ed.), *Child and adolescent therapy: Cognitive-behavioral procedures* (pp. 3–24). New York: Guilford.

Lis, A., Salcuni, S., & Parolin, L. (2007). Rorschach comprehensive system data for a sample of 116 preadolescent and 117 adolescent nonpatients from Italy. *Journal of Personality Assessment, 89*, 91–96.

McWilliams, N. (1999). *Psychoanalytic case formulation.* New York: Guilford.

McWilliams, N. (2004). *Psychoanalytic Psychotherapy – A practitioner's guide.* New York: Guilford.

Messer, S.B., & Wolitzky, D.L. (2007). The psychoanalytic approach to case formulation. In T.D. Eells (Ed.), *Handbook of psychotherapy case formulation* (2nd ed.) New York: Guilford.

Misch, D. (2000). Basic strategies of dynamic supportive therapy. *Journal of Psychotherapy Practice and Research, 9*, 173–189.

Murray, J.F. (1994). The Rorschach and diagnosis of neurotic conditions in children and adolescents: A case study. *Journal of Personality-Assessment, 63*, 39–58.

Russ, S., & Ollendick, T.H. (1999). *Handbook of psychotherapies with children and families*. Dordrecht, The Netherlands: Kluwer.

Russell, R.L., & Shirk, S.R. (1998). Child psychotherapy process research. *Advances in Clinical-Child Psychology, 20*, 93–124.

Sameroff, A. (1994). Ecological perspectives on longitudinal follow-up studies. In S.L. Friedman & H.C. Haywood (Eds.), *Developmental follow-up: Concepts, domains, and methods* (pp. 45–64). San Diego: Academic Press.

Shirk, S.R., & Karver, M. (2003). Prediction of treatment outcome from relationship variables in child and adolescent therapy: A meta-analytic review. *Journal of Consulting and Clinical Psychology, 71*, 452–464.

Shirk, S.R., & Russel, R.L. (1996). *Change processes in child psychotherapy: Revitalizing treatment and research*. New York: Guilford.

Shirk, S.R., & Saiz, C.C. (1992). Clinical, empirical, and developmental perspectives on the therapeutic relationship in child psychotherapy. *Development and Psychopathology, 4*, 713–728.

Skean, K.R. (2005). The case of "CG": Balancing supportive and insight-oriented, psychodynamic therapy with a client undergoing intense life stresses. *Pragmatic Case Studies in Psychotherapy, 1*(3), 1–18.

Spence, D.P. (1982). *Narrative truth and historical truth*. New York: Norton.

Vaillant, G.E. (1977). *Adaptation to life*. Boston: Little Brown.

Weersing, V.R., & Weisz, J.R. (2002). Mechanisms of action in youth psychotherapy. *Journal of Child Psychology and Psychiatry, 43*, 3–29.

Weiner, I.B., & Exner, J. E (1978). Rorschach indices of disordered thinking in patient and nonpatient adolescents and adults. *Journal of Personality Assessment, 42*, 339–343.

Weiner, I.B., & Exner, J.E. (1988, October). *Assessing readiness for termination with the Rorschach*. Paper presented at the Austen Riggs Conference on Psychological Testing and the Psychotherapy Process, Stockbridge, MA.

Weiner, I.B., & Exner, J.E. (1991). Rorschach changes in long-term and short-term psychotherapy. *Journal of Personality Assessment, 56*, 453–465.

Weisz, J.R., Huey, S.J., & Weersing, V.R. (1998). Psychotherapy outcome research with children and adolescents: The state of the art. *Advances in Clinical Child Psychology, 20*, 49–91.

Winnicott, D.W. (1965). *The maturation processes and the facilitating environment*. London: Hogarth Press.

D. di Riso et al.

Adriana Lis
Professoressa di Psicologia Clinica
Dipartimento di Psicologia dello Sviluppo e della Socializzazione
Università di Padova, L.I.RI.P.A.C.
via Belzoni 80
35131 Padova
Italy
Tel. +39 049 8278460
Fax +39 049 8278451
E-mail adriana.lis@unipd.it

Summary

This paper assesses changes in psychoanalytic psychodynamic therapy in a early adolescent boy according to personality functioning (as assessed by the Rorschach Comprehensive System) and therapeutic alliance. Weiner and Exner (1988, 1991) suggested that certain Rorschach variables related to specific personality characteristics might provide a useful measure of progress in dynamic psychotherapy. More recently, Bihlar and Carlsson (2000, 2001) proposed a selection of CS variables that may be useful in planning assessment of therapeutic goals and that could be used to assess therapeutic change. Although single-case studies with CS variables have not been carried out frequently in a developmental age (Murray, 1994), recent literature has stressed the importance of process and outcome research also in youth. There is a growing interest in process predictors of treatment outcome, such as therapeutic alliance, with children and adolescents (Kazdin & Kendall, 1998; Weisz et al., 1998).

An early adolescent, Gabriele, was referred for anxiety about school achievement and the ability to complete schools tasks as well as obsessive compulsive symptoms, including maintaining all his books in order. His parents' attempts to cope with his requests to be reassured seemed to be fruitless. The DSM-IV diagnosis was General Anxiety Disorder (GAD). Gabriele's assessment phase was carried out through Clinical Interviews, the CS, and a variety of quantitative, self-report questionnaires, focusing on anxiety-related symptoms, such as C-GAS and SCL-90-R. He showed problems in specific areas such as: (a) absence of any emotional involvement in the description of his life events; (b) problems of isolation and withdrawal with peers; (c) a very bossy, cold, and detached style of relating with younger brothers and sisters at home. Therapeutic goals were defined according to the Weiner and Exner's (1988, 1991) 27 variables included in the Bihlar and Carlsson (2001) categories. The main therapeutic goals, based on the construction of a consistent working alliance, were to eliminate, reduce, or deal with anxiety and obsessive behavior in a more adaptive way; to help Gabriele be in contact with his affections, acknowledging his painful emotions and limiting his depressive-like mood; to support him in this highly critical situation; to overcome this peculiar state of crisis in relation to his control abilities; to increase his social abilities so that he could enjoy interaction with others; to help him reach a more realistic idea of the self. The therapy lasted about 2 years, and the 50 sessions were all audio-taped and analyzed. The therapist employed a broadly defined object-relations-focused psychodynamic framework, with particular emphasis on balancing supportive versus insight-oriented modes of therapy (Skean, 2005). Gabriele and his therapist established an excellent working relationship, and he was motivated to working with her within a model that integrated psychodynamic concepts into some "supportive techniques" drawn from other psychotherapy models. The therapist maintained a good and stable level of collaboration. The global therapeutic alliance index increased. The therapy allowed Gabriele to change from a shy, routine-like, and noncommunicative approach to a freer and warm one. A follow-up was carried out 4 months after the end of the therapy, which highlighted that although he still displayed anxiety and obsessive compulsive symptoms, they were in a more regulated and less severe way. He started to process affective dimensions and experienced some meaningful relationships; his self-involvement strongly decreased, and he seemed to be more aware of his fragilities; his reality testing improved and obsessive thoughts no longer interfered with his reasoning. Overall, Gabriele attained a better quality of life, had new hobbies and had made new friends.

This paper, however, has some limitations, typical of single-case studies, such as the issues of internal validity and generalizability of results. It also has some strengths, such as the use of a multilevel perspective, which prevents the tendency of the therapist to overestimate symptoms and to allow for monitoring and better definition of different dimensions of outcome.

Riassunto

Scopo di questo lavoro è valutare il cambiamento nel processo della psicoterapia psicodinamica di un adolescente, in relazione al funzionamento della sua personalità valutato tramite il Rorschach secondo Sistema Comprensivo di Exner e l'alleanza terapeutica. Weiner e Exner (1988, 1991) suggeriscono come alcune variabili del Rorschach, connesse a specifiche caratteristiche di personalità, possano essere molto utili per valutare l'andamento della psicoterapia. Bihlar e Carlsson (2000, 2001) hanno proposto una selezione di specifiche variabili del CS utili per pianificare gli obiettivi del trattamento e valutare, a fine terapia, il loro raggiungimento. Sebbene gli studi di ricerca in psicoterapia che usano il Rorschach CS su single case in età evolutiva non siano così frequenti (Murray, 1994), di recente da più parti ne è stata evidenziata l'importanza e la necessità e si assiste a un interesse crescente rispetto allo studio dei predittori del outcome, come ad esempio l'alleanza terapeutica, sia per i bambini che per gli adolescenti (Kazdin & Kendall, 1998; Weisz et al., 1998). Gabriele è un preadolescente segnalato per ansia, legata al rendimento scolastico, e alcuni sintomi di tipo ossessivo compulsivo, come tenere tutti i libri in un preciso ordine. I genitori di Gabriele non riescono in nessun modo a contenerlo e rassicurarlo quando viene preso dall'ansia. Viene diagnosticato, secondo i criteri del DSM-IV, un Disturbo di Ansia Generalizzata (GAD). Nella fase di assessment iniziale vengono somministrate un'intervista clinica, il CS e una serie di questionari self-report, focali sul disturbo d'ansia e i sintomi, come la C-GAS e la SCL-90-R. gabriele presentava problemi in diverse aree del suo funzionamento, come: (a) assenza di qualsiasi coinvolgimento emotivo nelle questioni della vita, (b) problemi di isolamento e ritiro dal gruppo dei pari, (c) un comportamento molto provocatorio, freddo e distaccato nel rapporto con il fratello e la sorella più piccoli. I goal terapeutici sono stati definiti secondo le 27 variabili indicate da Weiner e Exner (1988, 1991), che includono anche le categorie di Bihlar e Carlsson (2001). I principali goal terapeutici, successivi alla costruzione di una stabile alleanza terapeutica, sono stati: eliminare o ridurre l'ansia e i sintomi ossessivi, imparando a gestirli in modo più adattivo; aiutare Gabriele a entrare in contatto con le sue emozioni e gli affetti, a conoscere le sue paure e contenere lì'umore depresso, supportandolo nel momento critico iniziale; inoltre, aiutarlo a aumentarle sue capacità sociali e a provare maggiore piacere nel contatto e nella condivisione con gli altri, portandolo ad avere un'idea più realistica di se stesso. La terapia è durata all'incirca due anni ed è stata interamente audio registrata per tutte le 50 sedute, oggetto di questo lavoro. Il terapeuta, di orientamento psicodinamico e relazionale, si è focalizzato in particolare un su un lavoro che bilanciasse interventi di tipo supportivo e interpretativo, orientato all'insight (Skean, 2005). L'alleanza di lavoro stabilitasi tra Gabriele e il suo terapeuta è stata eccellente, e il paziente è risultato motivato a lavorare all'interno di un modello integrato, tra approccio psicodinamico e tecniche supportive, ricavate anche da altri modelli. Il terapeuta ha mantenuto un livello buono e stabile di collaboratività e l'indice globale di alleanza terapeutica è aumentato durante la psicoterapia, portando Gabriele a cambiare da un atteggiamento timido, routinario e abbastanza mutacico, a una modalità più libera e calda. Il follow-up, effettuato circa 4 mesi dopo la fine della terapia, ha evidenziato ancora la presenza di ansia e sintomi ossessivi le paziente, ma molto più modulati. Gabriene ha iniziato a avere un maggiore contatto con le dimensione affettiva delle esperienze relazionali, stando maggiormante a contatto con le sue fragiilità e attuando un esame di realtà più adeguato, che non metteva più in scacco la sua capacità di pensare. In generale, la sua qualità della vita è migliorare e è stato capace di incontrare nuovi amici e appassionarsi ad alcuni hobbies.

Il presente lavoro mostra alcuni limiti, tipici degli studi single case, come ad esempio quelli relativi alla validità interna e alla generalizzabilità dei risultati, e alcuni punti di forza, come l'uso di un approccio multi livello al caso, che previene la tendenza comune nei terapeuti di sovrastimare i sintomi, per monitorare e definire in modo più specifico le dimensioni dell'outcome.

Résumé

L'objectif de cet article consiste à évaluer les changements, au moyen du Rorschach System Intégré (RSI), dans le fonctionnement de la personnalité d'un adolescent suivi en psychothérapie psychanalytique et dans la qualité de l'alliance thérapeutique. Weiner et Exner (1988, 1991) suggèrent que certaines variables du RSI mettent en évidence des traits de personnalité et rendent compte des progrès d'un patient en psychothérapie analytique. Récemment, Bihlar et Carlsson (2000, 2001) ont proposé une sélection de variables du RSI qui peuvent être utiles pour la planification et l'évaluation des changements thérapeutiques. Bien que le RSI n'est généralement pas utilisé pour des études de cas d'enfants ou d'adolescents, de nombreux chercheurs portent un intérêt grandissant aux variables prédictrices de bons résultats thérapeutiques et à la mesure de l'alliance thérapeutique dans les traitements d'enfant et d'adolescents (Kazdin & Kendall, 1998; Weisz, et al., 1998).

Jeune adolescent, Gabriel vient consulter pour des troubles de l'anxiété, des problèmes scolaires, et des symptômes obsessifs compulsifs, incluant une incapacité à mettre de l'ordre dans ses cahiers. La capacité de ses parents à le rassurer semble sans effet. Le diagnostique DSM-IV est celui de troubles généralisés de l'anxiété. L'évaluation psychologique de Gabriel inclut des entretiens cliniques, le Rorschach, des questionnaires, le C-GAS et le SCL-90-R. Des troubles spécifiques se sont révélés: a) une absence émotionnelle lorsqu'il décrit sa vie, b) des problèmes d'isolation et de retrait social vis-à-vis de ses camarades c) un garçon têtu, froid et détaché de sa fratrie à la maison. Des objectifs thérapeutiques ont été définis en référence aux 27 variables Wiener et Exner (1988, 1991) incluses dans les catégories proposé par Bihlar et Carlsson (2001).

Les objectifs thérapeutiques, basés sur une bonne alliance thérapeutique, étaient de réduire et de gérer l'anxiété et les troubles obsessif-compulsifs pour les rendre plus adaptatifs, d'aider Gabriel à être plus en contact avec ses affects, à reconnaitre sa douleur émotionnelle, à réduire son humeur légèrement dépressive, à dépasser son état de crise en relation à sa capacité de contrôle, à augmenter ses compétences sociales pour qu'il puisse s'enrichir de ses interactions avec les autres, et enfin de lui permettre d'avoir une idée plus réaliste de lui-même. La thérapie a duré 2 ans et les 50 séances on été enregistrées et analysées.

La thérapeute a utilisé une approche psychodynamique basée sur la théorie de la relation d'objet avec un accent porté sur l'équilibre entre le soutien et le développement introspectif (Skean, 2005). Gabriel et son thérapeute ont établi une excellente relation de travail et étaient motivés pour travailler avec elle dans un cadre de soutien intégrant des principes thérapeutiques mais utilisant des techniques inspirées d'autres modalités. La thérapeute a maintenu relation stable et un bon niveau de collaboration. L'index global de l'alliance thérapeutique a augmenté durant la thérapie. La thérapie a progressivement permis à Gabriel d'évoluer, d'un garçon timide et discret, il est devenu un adolescent plus libre et chaleureux.

Un suivi, 4 mois après la fin de la thérapie, a montré que, malgré la persistance des symptômes d'anxiété et obsessif-compulsifs, ceux-ci avaient diminué en intensité et étaient mieux régulés. Gabriel était capable de mieux comprendre ses émotions et pouvait faire l'expérience de relations plus satisfaisantes. Son auto-préoccupation a diminué, il était plus conscient de sa fragilité, son REALITY TESTING s'est amélioré et ses pensées obsessives ont cessé d'interférer avec son raisonnement. Dans l'ensemble, la qualité de vie de Gabriel s'est améliorée et il a adopter de nouveaux passe-temps et s'est fait des amis.

Cet article comporte toutefois certaines limites, classiques aux études de cas, incluant la validité interne et la généralisation des résultats. L'utilisation de perspectives multiples, à différents niveaux, permet par contre au thérapeute d'éviter de surestimer les symptômes et de mieux suivre l'évolution des objectifs thérapeutiques.

Resumen

El objetivo de este trabajo es evaluar los cambios, gracias a una terapia psicodinámica psicoanalítica, de un adolescente temprano siguiendo el funcionamiento de la personalidad (evaluada con el Sistema Comprehensivo de Rorschach) y la alianza terapéutica. Weiner y Exner (1988, 1991) sugirieron algunas variables de Rorschach relacionadas con características específicas que podían proveer medidas útiles para medir el progreso en psicoterapia dinámica. Más recientemente, Bihlar y Carlsson (2000, 2001) propusieron una selección de variables del SC que resultaban útiles en la planificación de la evaluación de los objetivos terapéuticos y que podían ser usadas para evaluar el cambio terapéutico. Aunque no existen muchos estudios de casos individuales con variables del SC en sujetos menores (Murray, 1994), la literatura reciente ha subrayado la importancia de la investigación del proceso terapéutico y sus resultados también en jóvenes y hay un interés creciente en los predictores y resultados del tratamiento, como es el caso de la alianza terapéutica, con niños y adolescentes (Kazdin & Kendall, 1998; Weisz et al. 1998).

Gabriele, un joven adolescente, fue derivado por ansiedad respecto de sus logros escolares y su habilidad para completar las tareas escolares y síntomas obsesivo-compulsivos que incluían el mantener todos sus libros en orden. Los intentos de sus padres para hacer frente a sus demandas de reaseguramiento parecían ser completamente inútiles. El diagnóstico del DSM-IV era Trastorno de Ansiedad Generalizada (GAD). La fase de evaluación de Gabriele se llevó a cabo a través de entrevistas clínicas, el test de Rorschach (SC) y una variedad de cuestionarios cuantitativos autoadministrados, focalizados sobre los síntomas relacionados con la ansiedad., como los C-GAS y el SCL-90-R. Mostraba problemas en áreas específicas como (a) ausencia de cualquier compromiso emocional en la descripción de eventos vitales, (b) problemas de aislamiento y de apartarse de sus pares, (c) un estilo muy frío, distante y de dar órdenes al relacionarse en el hogar con sus hermanos menores. Los objetivos terapéuticos se definieron de acuerdo con las 27 variables de Weiner y Exner (1988, 1991) incluidas en las categorías de Bihlar y Carlsson (2001). Los principales objetivos, basados en la construcción de una alianza terapéutica consistente, fueron: eliminar, reducir o hacer frente a la ansiedad y a las conductas obsesivas de una manera más adaptada; ayudar a Gabriele a estar en contacto con sus afectos; facilitar el reconocimiento de sus emociones dolorosas; disminuir su humor de tipo depresivo; apoyarlo en esta situación altamente crítica para él; mejorar su peculiar estado de crisis en relación con sus habilidades de control; aumentar sus habilidades sociales de tal modo que pudiera disfrutar de la interacción con los otros, y ayudarlo a alcanzar una idea mas realista del *self*. La terapia duró alrededor de dos años y las cincuenta sesiones fueron todas grabadas en audio y analizadas. El terapeuta empleó un marco psicodinámico definido ampliamente como focalizado sobre las relaciones objetales, con un énfasis particular en equilibrar el apoyo versus los modos de terapia orientados al insight (Skean, 2005). Gabriele y su terapeuta establecieron una excelente relación de trabajo y él estaba motivado para trabajar con ella dentro de un modelo que integraba conceptos psicodinámicos y algunas "técnicas se apoyo" sacadas de otros modelos psicoterapéuticos. La terapia mantuvo un nivel de colaboración bueno y estable. El índice global de alianza terapéutica se incrementó. La terapia permitió a Gabriele cambiar desde una actitud tímida, una conducta de tipo rutinario y callada, a una modalidad de relación más abierta y cálida.

Al finalizar la terapia, se realizó un seguimiento a lo largo de cuatro meses, lo que puso en evidencia que, a pesar de que mantenía la ansiedad y síntomas obsesivo-compulsivos, éstos eran menos severos y más (adaptados) que antes. Comenzó a procesar dimensiones afectivas y tuvo la experiencia de algunas relaciones importantes; su autocentramiento disminuyó significativamente y pareció ser más conciente de sus fragilidades; su registro de la prueba de realidad mejoró y los pensamientos obsesivos no interfirieron con su razonamiento. En conjunto, Gabriele alcanzó una mejor calidad de vida, comenzó a tener nuevas aficiones e hizo nuevos amigos.

Este artículo posee, sin embargo, algunas limitaciones típicas de los estudios sobre un sólo caso, como las cuestiones referidas a la validez interna y a la posibilidad de generalización de los datos. Posee también algunas fortalezas como el uso de una perspectiva de múltiples niveles, que previene la tendencia del terapeuta a sobreestimar síntomas a la vez que permite seguimientos y una mejor definición de diferentes dimensiones de los resultados.

Resumen en Castellano

El objetivo de este trabajo es evaluar los cambios gracias a la terapia psicodinámica psicoanalítica de un joven adolescente temprano siguiendo el funcionamiento de la personalidad (evaluada con el Sistema Comprehensivo de Rorschach) y la alianza terapéutica. Weiner y Exner (1988, 1991) sugirieron algunas variables de Rorschach relacionadas con características específicas que podían proveer medidas útiles para medir el progreso en psicoterapia dinámica. Más recientemente, Bihlar y Carlsson (2000, 2001) propusieron una selección de variables del SC que podían ser útiles en la planificación de la evaluación de los objetivos terapéuticos y que podían ser usadas para evaluar el cambio terapéutico. Aunque los estudios de casos individuales con variables del SC no han sido llevados adelante con frecuencia con sujetos en edades en desarrollo (Murray, 1994), literatura reciente ha subrayado la importancia de la investigación del proceso y el resultado también en jóvenes y hay un interés creciente en los predictores del proceso del resultado del tratamiento, como es el caso de la alianza terapéutica, con niños y adolescentes (Kazdin & Kendall, 1998; Weisz et al. 1998).

Gabriele, un joven adolescente fue derivado por ansiedad respecto de sus logros escolares y su habilidad para completar las tareas escolares y síntomas obsesivo-compulsivos que incluían el mantener todos sus libros en orden. Los intentos de sus padres para hacer frente a sus solicitudes para ser reasegurado parecían ser completamente inútiles. El diagnóstico del DSM-IV era Desorden de Ansiedad General (GAD). La fase de evaluación de Gabriele fue llevada adelante a través de entrevistas clínicas, el SC y una variedad de cuestionarios cuantitativos autoadministrados, focalizados sobre los síntomas relacionados con la ansiedad., como los C-GAS y el SCL-90-R. Mostraba problemas en áreas específicas como (a) ausencia de cualquier compromiso emocional en la descripción de eventos vitales, (b) problemas de aislamiento y de apartarse de sus pares, (c) un estilo muy frío, distante y de dar órdenes al relacionarse en el hogar con sus hermanos y hermanas menores. Las metas terapéuticas se definieron de acuerdo con las 27 variables de Weiner y Exner (1988, 1991) incluidas en las categorías de Bihlar y Carlsson (2001). Las metas terapéuticas principales, basadas en la construcción de una consistente alianza terapéutica, fueron de eliminar, reducir o hacer frente a la ansiedad y a las conductas obsesivas de una manera más adaptada; ayudar a Gabriele a estar en contacto con sus afectos; el reconocimiento de sus emociones dolorosas, y disminuir su humor de tipo depresivo; apoyarlo en esta situación altamente crítica para él; mejorar su peculiar estado de crisis en relación con sus habilidades de control; aumentar sus habilidades sociales de tal modo que pudiera disfrutar la interacción con los otros; ayudarlo a alcanzar una idea mas realista del self. La terapia duró alrededor de dos años y las cincuenta sesiones fueron todas grabadas en audio y analizadas. El terapeuta empleó un marco psicodinámico definido ampliamente como focalizado sobre las relaciones objetales con un énfasis particular en equilibrar el apoyo versus los modos de terapia orientados al insight (Skean, 2005). Gabriele y su terapeuta establecieron una excelente relación de trabajo y él estaba motivado por trabajar con ella dentro de un modelo que integraba conceptos psicodinámicos a algunas "técnicas se apoyo" sacadas de otros modelos psicoterapéuticos. La terapia mantuvo un nivel de colaboración bueno y estable. El índice global de alianza terapéutica se incrementó. La terapia permitió a Gabriele cambiar desde una actitud tímida, una conducta de tipo rutinario, y callado a una modalidad de relación más abierta y cálida.

Luego del fin de la terapia, un seguimiento fue realizado a lo largo de cuatro meses, lo que puso en evidencia que a pesar de que mantenía la ansiedad y síntomas obsesivo-compulsivos, éstos eran menos severos y más (adaptados) que antes. Comenzó a procesar dimensiones afectivas y tuvo la experiencia de algunas relaciones importantes; su autocentramiento disminuyó significativamente, y pareció estar más conciente de sus fragilidades; su registro de la prueba de realidad mejoró y los pensamientos obsesivos no interfirieron con su razonamiento. En conjunto, Gabriele alcanzó una mejor calidad de vida, comenzó a tener nuevos hobbies e hizo nuevos amigos.

Este artículo posee sin embargo algunas limitaciones típicas de los estudios sobre un solo caso, como las cuestiones referidas a la validez interna y a la posibilidad de generalización de los datos. Posee también algunas fortalezas como el uso de una perspectiva de múltiples niveles que previene la tendencia del terapeuta de sobreestimar síntomas y de permitir seguimientos y una mejor definición de diferentes dimensiones de los resultados.

本論文の目的はある思春期前期の少年の精神分析的力動心理療法における変化を、人格の機能（ロールシャッハ包括システムにより査定）と治療同盟によって査定することである。Weiner と Exner（1988,1991）は特定の人格の特徴と関連しているロールシャッハ変数が力動的心理療法における進展の役に立つ測度を提供する可能性を示唆している。さらに、近年、Bihlar と Carlsson（2000,2001）は治療目標の査定を立案するのに役立ち、治療による変化を査定するのに利用することができる CS（包括システム）の変数の選択を提案している。CS の変数をもちいた発達年齢にともなうシングル・ケース・スタディは多くはおこなわれていないが（Murray,1994）、最近の文献はまた、青年期における過程と結果の研究の重要性を強調しており、子どもや思春期における治療同盟といったような、治療の結果の進行を予測する変数への関心が増している（Kazdin と Kendall,1998;Weisz ら,1998）。

　思春期前期の Gabriele は学業成績と学校での課題を遂行する能力についての不安、自分の本をすべて順番どおりに並べるといったことを含む強迫症状により紹介されてきた。彼の両親の彼の要求に応えて安心させようという試みはまったく役に立っていないように見えた。DSM-IV の診断は全般的不安障害（GAD）であった。Gabriele の査定段階は、臨床面接と CS、不安に関する症状に焦点を当てた、C-GAS や SCL-90といった自己報告の質問紙によって遂行された。彼は以下のような特定の領域の問題を示した：(a)彼のライフ・イベントを説明する際に情緒的なかかわりが欠如していること、(b)孤立していて、仲間からひきこもっていること、(c)家庭おいて弟や妹にかかわるのにとても横柄で冷たく、切り離されたスタイル。治療目の標は Bihlar と Carlsson（2000,2001）のカテゴリーにも含まれている Weiner と Exner（1988,1991）の 27の変数により定められた。主な治療の目標は、安定した治療同盟の構築にもとづいて、以下のようにされた。不安と強迫行動をなくしたり、減らしたり、より適応的な方法で処理することができること；Gabriele が彼の感情と接触することを助け、苦痛な感情に気がつき、彼の抑うつ的な気分を限定すること；この高度に危機的な状況にある彼をサポートすること；彼のコントロールする能力に関連するこの特殊な危機状況を克服すること；彼の社会的能力を増し、彼が他者との交流を楽しむことができるようにすること；彼がより現実的な自己の観念にたどり着けるように助けること。治療は 2 年以上継続され、50 セッションがテープに録音され、分析された。治療者は、特に支持的対洞察志向の治療のモードのバランスをとること（Skean,2005）を強調する、広義の対象関係の焦点をあてた精神力動的枠組みを採用した。Gabriele と彼の治療者はすばらしい治療関係を確立し、Gabriele は、精神力動概念が他の心理療法モデルから引き出された "支持的技法" に統合されたひとつモデルの中で彼女と作業をすることに動機付けられた。治療者はよい安定したレベルの協働を維

持した。全般的な治療同盟の指標は上昇していた。治療により、Gabriele は内気で、決まりきっていてあまり話さないアプローチから、自発的で暖かいアプローチに変わった。治療の終結から 4 ヶ月後に追跡調査がおこなわれ、彼はなお不安や強迫症状は示していたが、それらはより調整されており、あまり深刻なものではなくなっていたことがはっきりとしていた。彼は感情の強さを処理し始めており、いくらかの意味のある関係性を経験していた；彼の自己へのとらわれはかなり少なくなり、自らの脆さについてより気がついているようであった；彼の現実検討は改善し、強迫観念的思考はもはや彼の推論には干渉していなかった。全体的に Gabriele はよりよい生活の質を達成しており、新しい趣味をもち、新しい友人を有していた。

　しかしながら、本研究は典型的なシングル・ケース・スタディであり、内的妥当性や結果の一般化の問題といった、限界を有している。また、多次元的な観点を用いることにより、治療者が症状を過大評価することを防ぎ、多様な結果のモニタリングとより良い定義をもたらす、というような強みを本研究は有している。

Rorschachiana 30, 180–218
© 2009 Hogrefe Publishing

DOI: 10.1027/1192-5604.30.2.180

Evaluation of an EMDR Treatment Outcome Using the Rorschach, the TAT, and the IES-R

A Case Study of a Human-Caused Trauma Survivor

Naomi Inoue

Ochanomizu University, Tokyo, Japan

Abstract. In order to better understand treatment outcome through eye movement desensitization and reprocessing (EMDR) trauma therapy, the author conducted comprehensive pre- and posttreatment assessments using the Impact of Event Scale-Revised (IES-R), the Rorschach Comprehensive System (CS), and the Thematic Apperception Test (TAT) on a survivor of human-caused trauma. The results of the Rorschach CS and the TAT showed significant improvements in terms of interpersonal relationships after the treatment. On the other hand, the posttreatment Rorschach scores indicated that the EMDR therapy promoted self-insight in much the same way as a traditional uncovering therapy. In this case study, the findings gained through the two performance-based methods shed light on what a successful EMDR trauma therapy can yield aside from symptom reduction.

Keywords: Rorschach, TAT, treatment outcome, EMDR, trauma

Although the study of trauma has advanced considerably over the last three decades, its origins go back to the 19th century. Prior to the current advancements, it had been periodically taken up as a subject for psychiatric research (Herman, 1992; van der Kolk, 2002). Recent study has shown that the central concept of posttraumatic stress disorder or PTSD (American Psychiatric Association, 1994) is today not very different from what Freud called "psychological trauma" nearly 100 years ago (Wilson, 1994). Yet Freud never succeeded in his attempts to process trauma by having his patients verbally express facts and feelings associated with the intense experiences (van der Kolk, 2002).

After the emergence of the diagnosis of PTSD, trauma research has focused on commonalities in the resulting symptoms rather than on differences in the original traumatic stimuli. Many epidemiological studies have shown that the major symptom axes of this diagnosis, which were originally based on psychiatric symptoms observed in combat veterans (van der Kolk, 1996), also appear in the victims of a single traumatic event, including natural disasters or traffic accidents, as well as in survivors of prolonged and repeated victimization such as child abuse and domestic violence.

This generalization of the concept of PTSD can be considered to be the first stage of the current revitalization in trauma research. The second stage, still ongoing, is related to the treatment of PTSD. Increased understanding of how the brain processes traumatic memories has accelerated the refinement of psychological treatment for PTSD including eye movement desensitization and reprocessing (EMDR; Shapiro, 1995) and prolonged exposure (Foa et al., 1999). Outcome research of trauma therapies has increased, and guidelines concerning the treatment of PTSD have been proposed by organizations such as the International Society for Traumatic Stress Studies (Foa, Keane, & Freidman, 2000), the American Psychiatric Association (2004), and the National Institute for Health and Clinical Excellence (NICE; 2005) of the United Kingdom. According to NICE, only trauma-focused cognitive behavior therapy and EMDR are recommended as evidence-based psychological treatments for PTSD.

Trauma research has now reached its next transitional stage, where researchers and clinicians explore the diversity of traumatic expressions, rather than focusing solely on the study of PTSD symptoms. In other words, researchers should recognize individual differences in trauma impact and resiliency as well as in treatment responses and within-person differences in treatment outcomes during different treatment phases. To plan appropriate person-oriented clinical interventions, it is vital to accumulate research data of diverse traumatic expressions and treatment outcomes at both individual and group levels.

For the purpose of individual trauma treatment and outcome evaluation, the benefits of performance-based methods such as the Rorschach test and the Thematic Apperception Test (TAT; Murray, 1943) have been numerously stressed in the literature (Parson, 1998a,b; Ephraim, 2002). Nevertheless, most trauma treatment outcome research has been limited to verifying treatment effectiveness only by the reduction of PTSD and other trauma-related symptoms, as assessed by self-report measures and diagnostic clinical interviews. Therefore, it is still unclear how different the treatment process and outcome would be for those who do not meet the full criteria of PTSD diagnosis, and how different the recovery process would be depending on each person's initial psychological state, pretraumatic personality, and the nature of the traumatizing stimuli.

As a first step toward developing more sophisticated trauma treatment and planning in the future, this case study evaluated the trauma treatment outcome through EMDR in a survivor of domestic violence by conducting pre- and posttreatment assessments with a test battery composed of the Impact of Event Scale-Revised (IES-R; Weiss & Marmar, 1997), the Rorschach Comprehensive System (CS), and the TAT. Using this test battery was assumed to be appropriate for the following reasons:

– First, the EMDR treatment itself is said not to address specific symptoms, but rather "the emotions, thoughts, physical sensations, attitudes, behaviors, and more" (Shapiro, 1997, p. xx). Therefore, measures such as the Rorschach, which can assess a "relatively broad range of psychological operations and experiences" (Exner, 2003, p. 4), are required for the thorough evaluation of treatment outcomes.

– Second, subjective units of disturbance scales (SUDS), indicating the level of distress associated with the traumatic memory, is the measure used to evaluate treatment progress in EMDR, and the process of traumatic memories is considered complete when the client reports satisfactory SUDS. Therefore, measures including performance-based tests, which provide implicit experiences and underlying psychodynamics (Weiner, 2004), are necessary.

– Third, trauma caused by a human mostly influences interpersonal relationships (Herman, 1992), so that methods such as the TAT, which "provide considerable access to cognitive and affective-motivational patterns related to interpersonal functioning" (Westen, 1991, p. 56), are indispensable.

Concerning trauma assessment using the TAT, there are numerous studies on the object relations of abused children (Kernhof, Kaufhold, & Grabhorn, 2008; Ornduff, 1997; Ornduff, Freedenfeld, Kelsey, & Critelli, 1994; Ornduff & Kelsey, 1996) measured by the Social Cognition and Object Relations Scale (SCORS; Westen, 1985, 1990). Since trauma impact is dependent on age, developmental stages, intelligence, cognition, and coping skills (Harvey, 1996), different assessment criteria from scales such as the Understanding of Social Causality scale in the SCORS is needed for the assessment of adult survivors. The author has developed an original assessment framework for adult human-caused trauma survivors using the TAT (Inoue, 2007). One can detect the defense capacities of a traumatized person in TAT responses, which are considered a kind of imaginary exposure to emotionally laden interpersonal situations. Research has also shown that particular cards induce particular trauma defense-patterns.

To date, there have been no studies of EMDR treatment assessing changes not only in symptoms but also in psychodynamics. Only Levin, Lazrove, and van der Kolk (1999) have examined the EMDR treatment outcome in a PTSD patient using the Rorschach CS in addition to some self-report tests and neuroimaging. However, they reported changes solely in some Rorschach variables, which limited their interpretation. Since this study was investigatory, I examined changes in various Rorschach variables as well as in the self-report test and the TAT in order to explore the wide range of treatment outcomes that are expected to result from successful EMDR trauma treatment, including changes in symptoms, cognition, emotions, self-image, interpersonal relationships, behavior, and coping style.

Methods

Participant

The participant of this study, Ms. S, was a 44-year-old female who answered a recruitment advertisement to participate. The inclusion criteria were survivors of human-caused trauma in adulthood, the reception of EMDR treatment, and the completion of the pre- and posttreatment assessment. When Ms. S applied to participate in the study, she had been approved by an EMDR therapist to receive EMDR treatment, and the author conducted an intake interview with her.

Ms. S was born into a middle-class Japanese family, the eldest of five children. Her father owned and managed a small company, while her mother was a devoted stay-at-home parent. When she was 20 and an undergraduate student, she began a relationship with a classmate. Violence began soon thereafter: She was abused physically, psychologically, sexually, and financially. After 4½ years, when a graduate student, she successfully left the relationship with the help of acquaintances. Although she had to take a temporary leave of absence from graduate school, she returned a few months later to continue her studies. She underwent supportive counseling for almost 2 years. She struggled with her recovery, but was able to continue her day-to-day life without significant setbacks. Still, she often experienced flashbacks and nightmares.

After receiving a master's degree as well as a doctorate degree, she took up employment in social work, specializing in domestic-violence-related issues. Her work began to be well recognized, and soon her workload began to increase. Despite such achievements, she could not rid herself of her nightmares, which occurred on average once every 2 or 3 months. In her nightmares, she would find herself in an enclosed setting, always together with her ex-partner, which caused her extreme fears and anxiety. One day she had yet another terrible nightmare, in which she was stabbed by the ex-partner. After this particular nightmare, she was unable to function for 4 days. This incident became the catalyst for her seeking new ways to manage her trauma from the past. She made the decision to seek EMDR therapy, about which she was somewhat apprehensive for quite some time.

Procedures

The study was conducted in accordance with the regulations of Research Ethics Committee, Ochanomizu University, Japan. Ms. S signed a written informed consent.

The EMDR treatment was administered by a qualified therapist, following the standard protocol for trauma (Shapiro, 1995). Duration of the therapy was determined according to her needs, and the process was repeated until her trauma-associated distress was reduced to a minimum. A total of 20 sessions were conducted concerning her main traumatic memories over the course of approximately 10 months. By this time, the frequency of her nightmares had decreased dramatically, and she had not had one for the preceding 5 months. Ms. S completed the assessment battery within 2 weeks before beginning of her first EMDR session and within 2 weeks after accomplishing the series of treatments. All tests were conducted by the author.

Measures

The IES-R is a standardized and widely used self-report questionnaire for symptom severity related to the traumatic experiences. The questionnaire comprises 22 items in three subscales of intrusions, avoidance, and hyperarousal. The validated Japanese version (Asukai et al., 2002) was used, and a cutoff point of 24/25 was applied, as recommended by the Japanese version.

Administration and scoring of the Rorschach protocols followed Exner's CS procedures and guidelines (2003, 2005). All protocols were reviewed by three clinical psychologists with proper training in the CS including the author to ensure the coding accuracy. Disagreements were resolved through group discussions. The interpretative strategy is based on key variables, as recommended by Exner (2003, 2005).

Administration of the TAT followed the procedures and guidelines articulated by Murray (1943). A total of ten TAT cards were conducted and the following seven cards were selected for analyses based on the author's research (Inoue, 2007): 2, 3BM, 5, 8GF, 9GF, 14, and 20. The TAT responses were analyzed according to the Trauma Assessment Framework (TAF; Inoue, 2007) and included categories such as emotional engagement, defense style or PTSD-like symptoms, image of others and the self, self-esteem, and prospect for the future. Scoring of the protocols were completed independently by the author and another clinical psychologist, who were randomly shown the pre- and posttreatment protocols and were unaware of all other test data and the author's scoring. Percentage of absolute agreement and Cohen's κ were calculated. We discussed any disagreements on the coding and decided on the final records.

Results

Changes in the IES-R Scores

Table 1 displays the changes in the IES-R scores before and after the treatment. The total score fell from just above the cutoff point to below the cutoff point.

Table 1. Changes in the IES-R scores

	Pretreatment	Posttreatment
IES-R total score	25	21
Intrusions	10	10
Avoidance	5	3
Hyperarousal	10	8

Note. IES-R = Impact of Event Scale-Revised.

Changes in Rorschach CS

The Rorschach protocols, sequences of scores, and structural summaries of pre- and posttreatment are presented in the Appendices A, B, and C, respectively. The recommended interpretative search strategy based on key variables did not change before and after the treatment indicating her Introversive Erlebnistypus (EB) as the first positive key variable. Under the special indices, the Hypervigilance index (HVI) shifted from positive to negative after the treatment. Therefore, I made the decision to begin with HVI.

HVI

The most remarkable change in Rorschach scores was indicated by HVI, which altered from positive to negative after the treatment, because the Sum of Texture scores (SumT) increased from zero to one. One texture response appeared, meaning that willingness for interpersonal contact had developed. This posttreatment texture response was the two "laughing sheep" which were "helping the raccoons play tricks" on Card VIII. During the pretreatment testing, she had also seen a "sheep's face" on Card VIII, and had remarked that "facial angle pointing upward toward its target." Thus, the change from a tension-filled animal face (Ad) response of minus Form Quality (FQ–) to enjoying two sheep (A) involving cooperative human movement (M, COP) suggests her transition from persisting threat for others to growing willingness to cooperate with others.

Cognition

With respect to her ideational functioning, Weighted Sum Special Scores (WSum6) decreased, because of a disappearance of a Level 2 Fabulized Combination (FAB2) response after the treatment. Since FAB2 signifies that extremely implausible relationship is posited to exist between two or more objects, this change also means her improvement in trauma-distorted thought of relationships.

On the other hand, the active:passive ratio (a:p) remained passive after the treatment (5:11), signifying her unwavering passivity in her thinking style. Moreover, her fewer W than M responses prior to treatment did

186

not change after the treatment (W:M = 6:12), indicating that her goal setting remained far below what her abilities allow her to achieve.

As for her cognitive mediation, Ms. S showed a significant improvement after treatment, with XA% increasing from 0.43 to 0.78 and WDA% increasing from 0.71 to 0.86. This is based on a considerable decrease in human face responses (Hd) of minus Form Quality (FQ-) in unusual detail areas (Dd). The large number of [Dd, Hd, FQ-] responses prior to the treatment was an indication of her distorted representations of others based on human-caused trauma. Therefore, these substantial decreases in number after treatment indicate the decline in her distorted human-related preoccupations and improvement in reality testing.

Controls

Her Experience Actual (EA) increased more from the average range of 9.0 to 14.5 after treatment, due to an increase from 8 to 12 for M and from 1.0 to 2.5 for WSumC. This shows that her available resources in dealing with experience increased not only in the ideational manner (M), but also in an emotional manner (WSumC). Since her WSumC of 1.0 prior to treatment indicate very limited ability to cope with the emotional experience, the increased WSumC of 2.5 after treatment means that Ms. S had acquired "minimally adequate capacities to process affect" (Weiner, 1998, p. 139).

On the other hand, whereas her L was 0.35 and within the normal range prior to treatment, it fell to 0.13 after the treatment, suggesting that Ms. S had become excessively open to internal and external stimuli (Weiner, 1998). Furthermore, her intrusive ideation rose after the treatment (m = 3), while her awareness of her needs and wants remained at insufficient level (FM = 0).

Affect

In accordance with the increase in WSumC, her Color Projection (CP) response, which indicates the defensive effort to deny unpleasant affect, disappeared after the treatment. Her test behavior also revealed an increased tolerance for emotional stimuli. She showed her rejection to Card IX prior to treatment by stating that she "cannot see anything" and then reluctantly adding "if anything, a pattern, maybe." Because this

response occurred just after she had given many human content responses to Card VII and Card VIII, it is apparent that the rejection response
to Card IX occurred in order to avoid experiencing emotions caused by
intrusive recollections of traumatic memories. In her posttreatment administration, she did not demonstrate any such rejection to color cards
and in fact tried to seek responses slowly and carefully.

The proportion of blends responses increased after treatment (44%),
and her affective world became more complex. These blend responses
consist of m, C', FD, or V, suggesting that her affective stress increased
due to the recollection of the past through the treatment process. Meanwhile, the intellectualization index was 0 prior to treatment and increased to 5 after treatment. The increased usage of intellectualizing
defense can be seen as a result of coping with the arousing unpleasant
affect.

Self-Perception and Interpersonal Relations

The egocentricity index was above average before treatment (0.48),
while it fell to within average limits after treatment (0.39). This implies
that her self-evaluation before treatment was not very low, and that, after
therapy, her negative preoccupation with herself decreased.

As for interpersonal relations, corporative movement (COP) revealed
a great increase from 0 to 3. Furthermore, the posttreatment value of
good human representations became greater than that of poor human
representations (GHR:PHR = 7:6), while the pretreatment value of PHR
was more than twice that of GHR (GHR:PHR = 4:9). Thus, a substantial
improvement in interpersonal relations was observed after the treatment.

Changes in the TAT

The pre- and posttreatment TAT protocols are presented in Appendix
D. Interrater reliability statistics are provided in Table 2, and TAT data
analysis is presented in Table 3 and Table 4.

Table 2. Interrater reliability statistics for Inoue's (2007) TAF variables

	% Agreement	Cohen's κ
Emotion	100	1.00
Defense/PTSD	98	.96
Negative image	96	.94
Self-esteem	100	1.00
Future	93	.85

Note. Data from 14 protocols. TAF = Trauma Assessment Framework; Emotion = Emotional engagement; Defense/PTSD = Defense style or PTSD-like symptoms; Negative image = negative image of others and self; Future = prospect for the future.

Table 3. Analysis of TAT protocols with Inoue's (2007) TAF: pretreatment

Categories of analysis	Sub categories	Card No.						
		2	3BM	5	8GF	9GF	14	20
Emotion	Not engaged[1]	+	−		−	+	+	+
Defense style or PTSD-like symptoms	Avoidance[2]	+	−	+	−	+	+	+
	Numbing[3]							
	Intrusions[4]		+					
	Hyperarousal[5]				+		+	
Negative image of	Others[6]	+	+	+				+
	Self[7]	+	+	+	−			
Self-esteem	Low[8]		−		−			
Future	Negative[9]		+					+

Note. TAF = Trauma Assessment Framework. + = if tendencies of the category are positive; − = if tendencies of the category are negative; no sign = not available from the narratives, or neither positive nor negative. 1 = no references are made to what the character(s) is feeling or thinking; 2 = evasive attitude toward associating with others; 3 = markedly diminished interest in people, or narrowing of the perceived field in response to card stimuli; 4 = associating card stimuli with traumatic experiences of the subject; 5 = being restless or irritable, or being overly alert to the outside world; 6 = attaching negative attributes to the character(s), or making reference to unwillingness in association with others; 7 = attaching negative attributes to the character, to whom the subject is likely to project him- or herself; 8 = underestimation of the self, or illogical self-blaming attitude; 9 = description of the future as continuation of negative situation, or anticipation of unfavorable future events.

Table 4. Analysis of TAT protocols with Inoue's (2007) TAF: posttreatment

Categories of analysis	Subcategories	Card no.						
		2	3BM	5	8GF	9GF	14	20
Emotion	Not engaged	–	–	–	–	–	–	–
Defense style or PTSD-like symptoms	Avoidance	–	–	–	–	–	–	–
	Numbing							
	Intrusions							
	Hyperarousal							
Negative image of	Others	–		–		–		–
	Self				–			
Self-esteem	Low				–			
Future	Negative		–	–		–		

Interpersonal Relationships and Emotional Engagement

Her pretreatment protocol revealed that she did not have an emotional engagement related to the figures on the cards, indicating her apparent tendencies not to prefer interpersonal situations that accompany emotional interaction. She showed defensive and evasive attitudes toward interpersonal relationships, saying "She looks to be just passing through. It's a bit strange to have her standing here" (Card 2), and "I don't really understand the connection between the two" (Card 9GF). Moreover, for Card 9GF, she said, "She keeps her distance and watches people," having probably identified herself with the woman depicted above the tree. For Card 14 of a man breathing in fresh air, she said "He's come to this place, where there is no one else," a response reflecting Ms. S's withdrawal from social situations.

After the treatment, that characteristic tendency disappeared, and an adequate level of emotional engagement developed for all of the cards. For instance, for Card 5 she described the picture as "This is about a couple," and narrated an emotional exchange between the two, as a wife is looking after her husband. In addition, she even described a cooperative relationship between the two, saying that "(the husband) follows her to the bedroom, where they'll both go to bed." Furthermore, for Card 20, she commented that "He probably won't go home immediately, because that would be too lonely, I think. So, he'll head to a bar, maybe, as there'll be people there." Her manifestation indicates that she no longer avoids relationships with others, and that she has even begun to feel a need for interpersonal connectedness.

Image of Others and the Self

Prior to treatment, Ms. S's comments on unhappy images seemed to be projections of herself onto the women depicted on the cards: "The pregnant woman – she doesn't look very happy, does she?" (Card 2), "This woman is totally devastated" (Card 3BM), and "This woman doesn't look too happy; maybe she's feeling totally stressed out" (Card 5). Moreover, aggression toward "her partner" was expressed for Card 3BM. After treatment, the aggression to men and the unhappy image of women disappeared, and the image of others and the self improved.

On the other hand, her self-esteem does not seem to be low even prior to treatment, as she commented that "She is a very capable person" for Card 8GF. This can be attributed to her effort to overcome her difficult past, and her various successes in study and work.

PTSD-Like Symptoms

Many characteristics resembling PTSD-like symptoms were observed in the pretreatment protocol. For example, even though she told stories with the theme of taking a break at one's work for Card 8GF, there were tendencies of restlessness: "She's not really sitting back in a comfortable position," "She won't be sitting for too long," and "If someone were to call for her, she'll probably tell that person that she'll be coming soon and will go right back to work." Furthermore, a similar theme of resting during work appeared with Card 14, and Ms. S replied that "It's not a long break, so he'll have to go back to work in a few minutes." These responses are likely due to the effects of violence from her past, where Ms. S was severely abused for being even only slightly late.

After treatment, all of these features disappeared, as she began to take control back into her life. This change in her mind frame can be seen in her responses: "When she is done taking her break, she'll get up and go back to work" (Card 8GF) and "It might take some time before it all gets done to his liking" (Card 14).

191

Prospects for the Future

There were many statements in the pretreatment protocol concerning the continuation of life without change such as "(The future) will continue as is" (Card 2), and "She's going to keep crying" (Card 3BM). Moreover, descriptions of negative outlook were predominant, as in "I don't think that the meeting is going to be a fun one, and so he isn't really looking forward to it" (Card 20).

After treatment, she began to make comments such as "Whether or not she'll achieve her dreams will all depend on her. But, at the rate she's going, I think that she'll make it happen" (Card 8GF), offering a positive outlook for the future. Perhaps Ms. S's statements such as "(They) will move on to the next place" (Card 9GF) and "He's opened the window for air and is thinking about how to go about making the changes" (Card 14) are indicative of her current status in life, as she is about to make a transition onto next phase.

Discussion

This study comprehensively investigated various changes in a female human-caused trauma survivor who underwent EMDR therapy by conducting pre- and postassessments with the IES-R, the Rorschach, and the TAT.

Generally, following treatment, the results of the Rorschach and the TAT indicated apparent improvements in many variables examined, whereas there were no significant changes in the IES-R scores between pre- and posttreatment, due to the fairly low pretreatment IES-R scores. These differences are ascribed to the nature of the assessment technique and to Ms. S's traumatic condition. The IES-R inquires about the subjective difficulties (i.e., impact) regarding the originating traumatic event during the past 7 days. As can be seen from the interview with her, before the treatment her flashbacks and nightmares had occurred once every 2 or 3 months. The total IES-R pretreatment scores would have been much higher, had she been assessed soon after experiencing a strong symptom such as a nightmare related to the original traumatic events. Because this was not the case, the subjective impact of the original traumatic events on her may have been weakened or rather assuaged. Since performance-based measures are better suited for detecting underlying concerns, they were instrumental in detecting the implicit influences of the trauma on Ms. S before the treatment. In the following section, I elaborate on Ms. S's treatment changes, focusing upon the correlations and augmentation of the findings from the Rorschach and the TAT.

The most remarkable improvement in Ms. S was that she became much less avoidant of the emotionally laden interpersonal relationships and developed willingness for interpersonal connectedness, best indicated by the TAT. Whereas the IES-R Avoidance subscale provides no distinction between emotional avoidance and emotional numbing, the analysis of TAT responses makes it possible to set apart these two defense styles, which have been shown to have different psychological mechanisms (Foa, Riggs, & Gershuny, 1995; van der Kolk & McFarlane, 1996). A notable feature in the TAT protocol of subjects using emotional avoidance strategies is the large number of descriptions of facial expressions and situations of people in the pictures, while there are few descriptions of their feelings and the emotional exchanges between the people. In emotional numbing, the protocols lack descriptions about feelings as well as detailed descriptions about the people in the pictures (Inoue, 2007).

Prior to treatment, Ms. S's TAT responses clearly revealed tendencies of emotional avoidance. Ms. S described many facial expressions or postures about the figures, but the description lacked emotional engagement. Such close examination into a person or a person's facial expression at the TAT corresponds with the high frequency of seeing human (H) or human faces (Hd) in unusual detail areas (Dd) on the Rorschach in the pretreatment. As the high frequency of [H + (H) + Hd + (Hd)] responses is one of subconditions composing the HVI, Ms. S's close inspections into human faces and postures on the TAT cards are interpreted as signs of her persisting fear for others. Although there were still many descriptions about human expressions in the posttreatment TAT protocols, Ms. S began to narrate stories that contained an emotional exchange between people, cooperative behavior, and willingness for human connectedness as well.

These changes in TAT narratives also correspond to improvements in Rorschach variables under the interpersonal cluster. In addition to increases in COP and GHR, the HVI, an indication for extreme threat for others and mistrust of people, turned from positive to negative because of the development of one T, an indication of interpersonal connectedness. Thus, one of the major destructive influences on victims of human-caused trauma is that they are deprived of feeling secure in interpersonal relationships, and their recovery from trauma begins with regaining trust in close relationships.

In their case report of EMDR treatment outcomes, Levin et al. (1999) indicate that a male with PTSD resulting from abusive experiences in childhood developed one texture response following three sessions of EMDR. They emphasize the significance of the change by referring to the results of Exner's outcome research (1993). According to Exner (1993, 2003), it generally takes an average of 9 to 15 months of psychotherapy for T-less patients to develop a T regardless of the type of therapeutic intervention. Thus, the growth of T from 0 to 1 after three sessions of EMDR treatment may be considered quite rapid. Meanwhile, given that the participant in their research was a typical PTSD patient (unlike Ms. S), and that the trauma experience targeted by the treatment was quite different from that of Ms. S, a simple comparison is impossible. Further research is necessary to examine how the required treatment sessions vary among T-less human-caused trauma survivors to develop a T, or how the recovery process varies among survivors depending on their initial traumatic conditions.

That Ms. S became less avoidant of experiencing her emotions is also reflected in increased WSumC, disappearance of CP, and change in her test behavior in the Rorschach after treatment. Van der Kolk (2002) states that "awareness, as opposed to avoidance, of one's internal states allows feelings to become known and to be used as guides for action." By being aware of and tolerating their sensations, "people have new options for solving problems" (p. 71). Thus, Ms. S became more capable of controlling her own emotions associated with traumatic memories, and she also gained the ability to think more rationally. This increased coping capacity (EA) seemed to lead to adequate reality testing, as indicated by substantial improvement in variables under the cognitive clusters (FAB2, XA+%, WDA%).

The remarkable treatment results described above occurred while Ms. S was still in the process of recovery. Although she had learned to better cope with her inner feelings, this improvement was achieved mainly through the high usage of intellectualization. She still displayed passivity in her thinking style and attitudes (a:p, Ma:Mp, W:M), and her awareness for her inner desires (FM) remained at an insufficient level. Nevertheless, such treatment results may be considered as normal in most recovery process for survivors like Ms. S, who had experienced powerlessness concerning her own thoughts, intentions, and basic desires. It might not be appropriate to ascribe her steadfast passivity solely to her introversive dispositions.

On the other hand, her ideational stressors of intrusive thinking (m) increased after the treatment, and Ms. S was able to feel pain (V). It is said that the presence of vista answers can be viewed positively, only "when a person has been in some form of uncovering or developmental intervention for several months" (Exner, 2003, p. 255). This suggests that EMDR trauma therapy promoted self-inspection and confrontation with the past experiences and triggered irritable and painful feelings, in just the same way as an insight-oriented uncovering therapy. While symptom reduction or changes at the behavioral level occurred early, changes in long-term dispositions and underlying conflicts may occur much later, as is shown in normal psychological intervention (Weiner, 2004). As she narrated in the TAT, she may actually be in the uncovering phase of her recovery process, in which she has just "opened the window" and "is thinking about how to go about making the changes." However, her outlook on future possibilities is favorable, as she expressed in her statement that "at the rate she's going, she'll make it happen," and her relative high self-esteem would continue to help her further recovery.

The various changes that Ms. S experienced as a result of EMDR treatment would not have been identified if the Rorschach and the TAT had not been used. Since Ms. S was not a typical PTSD participant, but rather "asymptomatic" except for the recollections occurring several times a year, the mere employment of a self-report test about PTSD symptoms would not have properly revealed her implicit traumatic conditions at pre- and posttreatment. Nor would it have been possible for a self-report test to depict the various changes, which a successful EMDR trauma treatment can yield aside from symptom reduction. Because there are not many diagnosable full-PTSD patients in natural clinical settings, this study also suggests the usefulness of the Rorschach CS and the TAT in daily clinical settings for the evaluation of initial traumatic condition and the treatment outcome, which are critical for appropriate treatment planning.

Furthermore, the usage of these performance-based personality measures provided a deeper understanding about the recovery mechanism through EMDR trauma treatment. Levin et al. (1999) suggest that a newer therapy such as EMDR may yield benefits in terms of processing traumatic memories which other traditional insight-oriented verbal therapies cannot achieve. From this case study, it can be concluded that an EMDR therapy can promote insight through its process, in much the same way as traditional verbal therapies do. At the same time, an EMDR therapy can achieve this result of processing traumatic memories, without necessarily having traumatized people "talk through the problem" (Shapiro, 1997, p. xiv) and re-experiencing them.

Van der Kolk (2002) states in *Beyond the Talking Cure* that, in contrast to traditional top-down psychotherapy, which is based on cognition and focuses on inhibiting unpleasant sensations and emotions, the EMDR information processing is based on bottom-up processing, which helps people fully experience their inner feelings and accept trauma-related emotions even if reminders of the past. As the recovery process of Ms. S shows, the process began with an increased tolerance of emotions related to past traumatic experiences and a growing willingness for interpersonal relationships. These results seem to support the theory that EMDR trauma treatment is based on bottom-up processing.

Closing Remarks

This study showed that a successful EMDR trauma treatment yields improvements in emotional tolerance, willingness to engage in interpersonal relationships, coping capacities, cognition, and perspectives for the future above and beyond symptom reduction. Moreover, this study also shed light on the painful and stressful feelings EMDR trauma treatment can cause through its process of symptom reduction. Though this case study relied on EMDR trauma treatment, these resulting effects may not be attributed solely to this therapy, as similar successes may also occur as a result of other types of trauma therapies. However, what is certain is the need to employ assessment methods beyond self-rating scales for an appropriate evaluation of clients' remarkable resilience and their painful endeavor to overcome trauma.

Acknowledgments

Part of this article was presented at the XIXth International Congress of Rorschach and Projective Methods in Leuven, July 2008. My very special thanks go to Dr. Namiko Nihashi, whose guidance and suggestions were invaluable in writing this paper. I am also grateful to Professor Munekazu Fujita for his advice on the TAT, and to Keiko Shimazaki for her help in the interrater agreement scoring.

References

American Psychiatric Association. (1994). *Diagnostic and statistical manual of mental disorders* (4th ed.). Washington, DC: Author.

American Psychiatric Association. (2004). *Practice guideline fro the treatment of patients with acute stress disorder and posttraumatic stress disorder.* Retrieved December 28, 2008, from http://www.psychiatryonline.com/pracGuide/pracGuideChap-Toc_11.aspx

Asukai, N., Kato, H., Kawamura, N., Kim, Y., Yamamoto, K., Kishimoto, J. et al. (2002). Reliability and validity of the Japanese-language version of the impact of event scale-revised (IES-R-J): Four studies of different traumatic events. *Journal of Nervous and Mental Disease, 190,* 175–182.

Ephraim, D. (2002). Rorschach trauma assessment of survivors of torture and state violence. *Rorschachiana, 25,* 58–76.

Exner, J.E. (1993). *The Rorschach: A comprehensive system: Vol. 1. Basic foundations* (3rd ed.). New York: Wiley.

Exner, J.E. (2003). *The Rorschach: A comprehensive system: Vol. 1. Basic foundations and principles of interpretation* (4th ed.). Hoboken, NJ: Wiley.

Exner, J.E., & Erdberg, P. (2005). *The Rorschach: A comprehensive system: Vol. 2. Advanced interpretation* (3rd ed.). Hoboken, NJ: Wiley.

Foa, E.B., Dancu, C.V., Hembree, E.A., Jaycox, L.H., Meadows, E.A., & Street, G.P. (1999). A comparison of exposure therapy, stress inoculation training, and their combination for reducing posttraumatic stress disorder in female assault victims. *Journal of Consulting and Clinical Psychology, 67,* 194–200.

Foa, E.B., Keane, T.M., & Freidman, M.J. (Eds.). (2000). *Effective treatment of PTSD: Practice guidelines from the international society for traumatic stress studies.* New York: Guilford.

Foa, E.B., Riggs, D.S., & Gershuny, B.S. (1995). Arousal, numbing, and intrusion: Symptom structure of PTSD following assault. *American Journal of Psychiatry, 152,* 116–120.

Harvey, M.R. (1996). An ecological view of psychological trauma and trauma recovery. *Journal of Traumatic Stress, 9,* 3–23.

Herman, J.L. (1992). *Trauma and recovery.* New York: Basic Books.

Inoue, N. (2007). DV 被害者に対するトラウマのアセスメント：TAT を用いたトラウマの影響に関する多次元的アプローチ　[Trauma assessment of domestic violence victims: A multi-dimensional approach for the assessment of trauma impact using the TAT]. *Bulletin of Centre of Clinical Psychology and Counseling at Ochanomizu University, 9,* 40–53.

Kernhof, K., Kaufhold, J., & Grabhorn, R. (2008). Object relations and interpersonal problems in sexually abused female patients: An empirical study with the SCORS and the IIP. *Journal of Personality Assessment, 90,* 44–51.

Levin, P., Lazrove, S., & van der Kolk, B. (1999). What psychological testing and neuroimaging tell us about the treatment of posttraumatic stress disorder by eye movement desensitization and reprocessing. *Journal of Anxiety Disorders, 13*(1–2), 159–172.

Murray, H.A. (1943). *Thematic Apperception Test: Manual.* Cambridge, MA: Harvard University Press.

National Institute for Health and Clinical Excellence. (2005). *Posttraumatic stress disorder (PTSD): The management of posttraumatic stress disorder in adults in primary, secondary and community care.* Retrieved December 28, 2008, from http://www.nice.org.uk/guidance/CG26

Ornduff, S.R. (1997). TAT assessment of object relations: Implications for child abuse. *Bulletin of the Menninger Clinic, 61*(1), 1–15.

Ornduff, S.R., Freedenfeld, R.N., Kelsey, R.M., & Critelli, J.W. (1994). Object relations of sexually abused female subjects: A TAT analysis. *Journal of Personality Assessment, 63,* 223–238.

Ornduff, S.R., & Kelsey, R.M. (1996). Object relations of sexually and physically abused female children: A TAT analysis. *Journal of Personality Assessment, 66,* 91–105.

Parson, E.R. (1998a). Traumatic stress personality disorder (TrSPD), part II: Trauma assessment using the Rorschach and self-report tests. *Journal of Contemporary Psychotherapy, 28,* 45–68.

Parson, E.R. (1998b). Traumatic stress personality disorder (TrSPD), part III: Mental/physical trauma representations-from focus on PSTD symptoms to inquiry into who the victim has now become. *Journal of Contemporary Psychotherapy, 28,* 141–171.

Shapiro, F. (1995). *Eye movement desensitization and reprocessing: Basic principles, protocols, and procedures.* New York: Guilford.

Shapiro, F., & Magot S.F. (1997). *EMDR: The breakthrough therapy for overcoming anxiety, stress, and trauma.* New York: Basic Books.

van der Kolk, B.A. (1996). The complexity of adaptation to trauma: Self-regulation, stimulus discrimination, and characterological development. In B.A. van der Kolk, A.C. McFarlane, & L. Weisaeth (Eds.), *Traumatic stress: The effects of overwhelming experience on mind, body and society* (pp. 182–213). New York: Guilford.

van der Kolk, B.A. (2002). Beyond the talking cure: Somatic experience and subcortical imprints in the treatment of trauma. In F. Shapiro (Ed.), *EMDR as an integrative psychotherapy approach: Experts of diverse orientations explore the paradigm prism* (pp. 57–83). Washington, DC: American Psychological Association.

van der Kolk, B.A., & McFarlane, A.C. (1996). The blackhole of trauma. In B.A. van der Kolk, A.C. McFarlane, & L. Weisaeth (Eds.), *Traumatic stress: The effects of overwhelming experience on mind, body and society* (pp. 3–23). New York: Guilford.

Weiner, I.B. (1998). *Principles of Rorschach interpretation.* Mahwah, NJ: Erlbaum.

Weiner, I.B. (2004). Monitoring psychotherapy with performance-based measures of personality functioning. *Journal of Personality Assessment, 83,* 323–331.

Weiss, D.S., & Marmar, C.R. (1997). The impact of the Event Scale-Revised. In J.P. Wilson & T.M. Keane (Eds.), *Assessing psychological trauma and PTSD: A practitioner's handbook* (pp. 399–411). New York: Guilford.

Westen, D. (1985). *Social Cognition and Object Relations Scale (SCORS): Manual for scoring TAT data.* Unpublished manuscript, Ann Arbor, University of Michigan.

Westen, D. (1990). Psychoanalytic approaches to personality. In L.A. Pervin (Ed.), *Handbook of personality theory and research* (pp. 21–65). New York: Guilford.

Westen, D. (1991). Clinical assessment of object relations using the TAT. *Journal of Personality Assessment, 56,* 56–74.

Wilson, J.P. (1994). The historical evolution of PTSD diagnostic criteria: From Freud to DSM-IV. *Journal of Traumatic Stress, 7,* 681–698.

Naomi Inoue
Clinical Psychologist and Student in Doctoral
Program of Human Developmental Sciences
Ochanomizu University
2-1-1 Otsuka, Bunkyo-ku
122-8610 Tokyo
Japan
Tel./Fax +81 3 5978 5777
E-mail NSA33963@nifty.com

Appendix A1:
Ms. S's Rorschach protocol of pretreatment

		Response	Inquiry
I	1	It's an insect that looks like a butterfly, maybe a moth. (Take your time and look more, I think you will find something else.) Nothing else.	E: (Repeats S's response.) S: Here are the wings, this is the body, and here's the tail. These are the eyes, feelers and patterns on the wings.
II	2	People with their hands together, wearing traditional costumes.	E: (Repeats S's response.) S: The head is the red part and, I don't know why, but they're sharp. They are with their hands together.
	3	There are two animals standing on their hind legs and they look like bears. But, they look hurt and bleeding because you see red around their faces.	E: (Repeats S's response.) S: These are the front legs, here's the face. Back legs are here and the back is bent like this. There's blood running from his head.
	4	Just looking at the black parts, it looks like bears with their noses touching.	E: (Repeats S's response.) S: This is the nose and these are the ears.
III	5	Looks like two black African women facing each other.	E: (Repeats S's response.) S: This is the head and the breast. Her bottom is sticking out and she is wearing high heels.
	6	Just looking at the middle part, it looks like a skull with glasses.	E: (Repeats S's response.) S: This big black part looks like sunglasses. Skull wearing sunglasses is what it looks like. E: You said a skull? S: The back part is gray, so . . .

		Response	Inquiry
IV	7	A big man like a monster walking toward this way. Can't see anything else.	E: (Repeats S's response.) S: You can see the bottoms of his feet, as he's walking this way. I don't know what that is . . . maybe a tree or something in the background.
V	8	Something that's a mix between a butterfly and a moth. But maybe a moth. It's facing the other way and is stuck onto something, that's the only thing I can see.	E: (Repeats S's response.) S: I've seen butterfly wings like these, but with this thick, I think it's a moth. These are two big wings. It's looking the other way and is stuck on something.
VI	9	Shamisen or some type of stringed instrument using pelt that's spread out on top of the instrument. The only thing I can see is fur or an animal's skin that's spread out.	E: (Repeats S's response.) S: This is like a stringed instrument, like shamisen and here's a pelt spread out on top. From here down is the fur. E: What makes it look like a fur? S: Because there are 4 legs and it looks spread out.
VII	10	It looks like two women face to face.	E: (Repeats S's response.) S: Here's the face with the head this way.
	11	Evil . . . person, or rather two monsters looking outward are what I see.	E: (Repeats S's response.) S: They've got bulging eyes and piggy noses. But the one on the left is scarier because his eyes are darker. The eye color of the one on the right is lighter and a little bit faded. They're yelling because they have their mouths open.
	12	Here too you see two women, though small.	E: (Repeats S's response.) S: This part. Background is black and here's the face, nose, and mouth. This part is her brownish thick hair.
	13	Here, two people are walking away from the place.	E: (Repeats S's response.) S: These are the two people. They're facing the other way. Here's the head and below is the body.
	14	A man with the beard on the left.	E: (Repeats S's response.) S: This black part is the beard. Above that is his nose. There seems to be someone on the right but you can't see him clearly.
	15	On the right, the face of a monkey, turned upside down.	E: (Repeats S's response.) S: The white part is the monkey's face. The black part is the back of its head. It's facing the other way and it's upside down, but the eyes are a little bit sunken. The eyes aren't all that clear, though. The blurry side face of a monkey is upside down.

		Response	Inquiry
	16	Two people are here. You can only see half of their faces.	E: (Repeats S's response.) S: Here and here. The one on the left has his eyes wide open and the one on the right has his eyes pulled up.
VIII	17	There are two animals that look like chameleons.	E: (Repeats S's response.) S: The red part. You can see 3 legs each and here's the tail.
	18	A sheep's face on the right.	E: (Repeats S's response.) S: A sheep's face, facial angle pointing upward toward its target.
	19	Here it looks like a Chinese person.	E: (Repeats S's response.) S: Here are the eyes, narrow and droopy. His beard is really long. He's looking out from behind something.
	20	Two shrimps, facing each other and they're on the other side of the rock.	E: (Repeats S's response.) S: This is the shrimp or rather a lobster. This is the rock. There's something here, so you can't see their faces.
	21	There are two legs by the rock.	E: (Repeats S's response.) S: Here, you can see two legs. They look like cartoon. Maybe it's the shadow of a fat person, but he's behind something and you can't really see the shape. You can only see the legs.
IX	22	Cannot see anything, if anything, a pattern, maybe.	E: (Repeats S's response.) S: I can't even tell what it is. That is, if I had to see something in there.
X	23	If I had to see something, I see two women standing, dressed in art deco design clothes and hats. The thing in the background may look like the tower in Paris, but I can't see anything else.	E: (Repeats S's response.) S: These are the women, the hat, and the tower. E: Art deco design? S: Because it's kind of thin and long.

Appendix A2:
Ms. S's Rorschach protocol of posttreatment

		Response	Inquiry
I	1	There's a person in the middle, talking real loud. There are two other people standing by listening to him preach. You can't see the head of the person in the middle. The two people are women and they look alike, as if they were twins. (Take your time and look more, I think you will find something else.) That's all I can see.	E: (Repeats S's response.) S: All three are wearing coats, because they all look rather bulky. You can see his legs through his coat. It's some kind of see-through, so . . . E: Talking real loud? S: From how his hands are. E: Two women? S: Their hair's tied and how they're tilting their heads to listen. This one (Dd34) ignore it.

		Response	Inquiry
II	2	Two people are crouched down and they have their hands together, wearing red hats, coats and shoes. They are talking.	E: (Repeats S's response.) S: There are two people facing the center, wearing red hats and with what looks like gloves. The coats have hoods. E: You said they are talking? S: Their mouths are open and you can see their spit flying.
III	3	Two people again. Both with their palms out. It looks like high heels, so they're probably women. Both of them have their hands out toward the center, where there is something that looks like a hibachi (brazier).	E: (Repeats S's response.) S: Yes, this here is the hibachi. This is the black rim and there're ashes and it's warm. They're talking, putting their hands over the hibachi.
	4	The red in the middle looks like a butterfly, or more like a ribbon.	E: (Repeats S's response.) S: It's the shape of the ribbon and because it's red.
	5	That red thing in the corner, it's not an angel, but some creature that whispers to you. Not as cute as Tinker Bell in Peter Pan, but similar to that, and it's floating.	E: (Repeats S's response.) S: Not angels, but they're floating and whispering. Their mouths are open and they look like they're pointing a magic wand or something. You can see their mouths and a part of their noses, too. A bit like in cartoons.
IV	6	Looking up from below at somebody huge. Maybe not even a human being, but more like a monster. Monster that looks like fallen leaves ... or not fallen leaves exactly, but maybe a dead branch covering this monster and it's walking toward me. That's why its feet look big and its head so small. I'm looking at it from below. It was walking toward me but it has just stopped. Standing motionless, or rather, just standing there. And you can see this tree growing behind the monster. Around the root of the tree, you can see weeds. It's so big that it's a bit scary, but it doesn't look like it's about to do any harm.	E: (Repeats S's response.) S: What would you call it ... fallen leaves or dead leaves. Everywhere, basically, they're in layers (by gesture). E: Where are you seeing weeds? S: Here (to the right of D1), there are flowers blooming.
V	7	This looks like a specimen of a moth. And it's on display. Maybe it's a butterfly, but because its antennas are thick, it's probably a moth. It has very sturdy looking big wings. You can tell that they're sturdy because of their dark gray color.	E: (Repeats S's response.) S: When you display them as specimens, you spread their wings nicely and this one is facing the other way and I think its wings are spread out for display.

		Response	Inquiry
VI	8	It looks like a fur rug. You know the kind you see sometimes being sold, with fluffy animal fur and shaped like this. Other than that, nothing.	E: (Repeats S's response.) S: You see how the legs are spread out? You often see them like this for bears. This here is not fluffy. Fur is pretty short and flattened.
VII	9	This one is the one that looks like it has lots of human faces. At the top, the one on the left is a man and the one on the right is a woman. But they look young, maybe teenagers.	E: (Repeats S's response.) S: The one on the left, his hair is short and you can see his hat. The one on the right, her hair is long and curly. The boy is miffed and the girl is trying to coax him into better mood.
VII	10	It looks like two women looking at each other.	E: (Repeats S's response.) S: There are two women in the middle and they are looking toward the center. This woman is also miffed, but the other woman seems to be coaxing her too.
	11	Here too, there are two monsters. They look like a mixture of a pig and a human. They have horns. You can see their brows scrunched, which means they're angry.	E: (Repeats S's response.) S: These two are especially angry. This one has got wrinkles between his brows. This white part. The other one is surprised and his eyes are wide open.
	12	There are two men with beards. The one on the left, you can see his eyes. You can't see the eyes of the man on the right.	E: (Repeats S's response.) S: The black part is his beard. The one on the left looks scary. The one on the right looks friendlier.
	13	There are two people walking between these two mountains. You can see the sunset between the two mountains. They are holding hands, and the one on the right is taller. They've just reached a beach or a river bank.	E: (Repeats S's response.) S: There are two mountains and here's the valley in between. The gray parts are the sunset clouds. People walking toward me can be seen as white silhouettes. They are coming in from the mountains toward this side and it looks like they finally reached the shore.
VIII	14	There's a chandelier hanging from the ceiling and there are raccoons playing with it, trying to hang down from it. There are two sheep at the bottom, helping the raccoons play tricks. The two raccoons are placing their feet on the sheep around their chest and they're trying to climb onto the chandelier. The sheep look like they are laughing, so they must be enjoying it. The chandelier is swaying a bit, so it's a little lopsided. The raccoons are trying to figure out where to place their feet next.	E: (Repeats S's response.) S: The chandelier is where it's gray and blue. I would think that lighting this fancy would have to be a chandelier. It looks like it's hanging from above. E: Two sheep? S: This here is the face and this other shape toward the bottom and here (touching the card), this part has a fuzzy feel, just like this (touching the subject's own sweater). Eyes are narrow, so he's laughing.

203

		Response	Inquiry
IX	15	It looks like a modern art type of poster. The orange part, there are two men doing shooting practice. The people here, wearing flamenco dresses, are dancing, lifting one of their arms and striking a pose. There are also some people in the middle. One of them is facing the other way and looks like he's directing someone. In the bottom red part, there's someone rowing a boat. It almost looks like a photo taken from below, looking up at him. On both sides, there are his knees and legs, and there are two oars in the middle. So, all in all, there are 1, 2, 3, 4, 5, 6 people in the picture. You have shooting, dancing, and rowing being coached, so it's probably some type of promotional poster for some kind of sports. Everyone's working really hard.	E: (Repeats S's response.) S: A person here, he's holding a gun and pointing it toward the other direction, ready to shoot. The green parts, you can't see their faces, but they are holding up the hems of their dresses and dancing. So the skirts are lopsided (by gesture), their legs are high up and it's this moment where everything stopped all at once. E: Directing someone? S: This is the head and is facing away and this here is the hand. E: Looking up at him? S: This (D4) is the knee, and here (Dd35) is the chest. Around here, to the front, there's a camera placed inside of the boat, so.
X	16	There are two people, about to do a "ready, get set, go," and begin their run in the other direction. You can see a bridge far away, and they're all ready to start running toward it. On both sides, there are animals that look like boars, waving leaves to cheer for the women. These women are wearing long black hats like those worn by the guardsmen in London, and they are holding a watering can. So they will have to run in tandem. The orange one in the middle is pointing the direction that these people are heading to.	E: (Repeats S's response.) S: When you look at the bridge, there are thin strings, like in a suspended bridge. It looks like a marathon course, but there's a bridge at the furthest point. Here is the pig-like nose of the boar, its tail, and a leaf. They're waving leaves to root for the women. The women are holding a watering can and so they have to be aware of each other's pace and to run together. I don't know about the orange one, but it's pointing a direction.
	17	A pair of green pincers toward the center at the bottom.	E: (Repeats S's response.) S: This here is the handle and this is the metal part.
	18	There are yellow flowers, brown roots and they are in two places. They look like butterbur sprouts. There's a dead leaf by the roots, so maybe they're branches and not roots. The one in the middle is a flower shaped like a trumpet. The center part is orange.	E: (Repeats S's response.) S: This one (D2) is blooming and this (D15) is the bud. It's blooming, so you can see the orange part. This (D13) is brown, so it's a dead leaf.

Appendix B1:
Ms. S's sequence of scores of pretreatment

Card	Resp. no.	Location and DQ	Loc. no.	Determi- nant(s) and form quality	(2)	Con- tent(s)	Pop	Z score	Special scores
I	1	WSo	1	Fo		A		3.5	
II	2	W+	1	Mpo	2	H,Cg		4.5	GHR
	3	D+	1	Ma.mp.CF-	2	A,Bl		3.0	FAB, MOR, PHR
	4	D+	1	FMpo	2	A	P	3.0	
III	5	D +	9	FC'o	2	H,Cg	P	3.0	GHR
	6	D+	7	FC'-		An,Cg		3.0	FAB2
IV	7	W +	1	Ma.FDo		(H),Bt	P	4.0	GHR
V	8	Wo	1	FMpo		A		1.0	
VI	9	W+	1	FDo		Sc,Ad	P	2.5	
VII	10	Do	1	Fo	2	Hd	P		GHR
	11	Do	3	Ma.FYu		Hd			AG, PHR
	12	Ddo	99	C'F-	2	Hd			CP, PHR
	13	Ddo	99	Ma-	2	H			PHR
	14	Ddo	99	F-		Hd			PHR
	15	Ddo	99	FY-		Ad			
	16	Ddo	99	Mp-		Hd			PHR
VIII	17	Do	1	Fu	2	A			
	18	Ddo	99	F-		Ad			
	19	Dd+	99	Mp.FD-		Hd,Id		3.0	PHR
	20	D+	4	FD-	2	Ad,Ls		3.0	DV
	21	Dd+	99	FD-	2	Hd,Ls		3.0	PHR
IX	22	Wv	1	F-		Id			
X	23	Dd+	21	Mp-	2	H,Cg,Sc		4.0	PHR

Appendix B2: Ms. S's sequence of scores of posttreatment

Card	Resp. no	Location and DQ	Loc. no.	Determinant(s) and form quality	(2)	Content(s)	Pop	Z score	Special scores
I	1	Dd +	99	Map.FVo	2	H,Hd,Cg		4.0	GHR
II	2	W +	1	Mp.mp.FCo	2	H,Cg		4.5	GHR
III	3	D+	1	Mp.FC'o	2	H,Hh,Cg	P	3.0	GHR
	4	Do	3	FCo		Cg			
	5	D+	2	Mpo		(H),Id		4.0	GHR
IV	6	W+	1	Mp.FDo		(H),Bt	P	4.0	MOR, PHR
V	7	Wo	1	FC'o		A,Art		1.0	
VI	8	Wo	1	Fo		Ad	P	2.5	
VII	9	Dd +	99	Mp-		Hd,Cg		3.0	PHR
	10	D+	9	Mpo		Hd	P	3.0	GHR
	11	Do	3	Mau		(Hd)			AG, PHR
	12	Ddo	99	F-		Hd			PHR
	13	Dd+	28	Ma.FD.FC'u		Ls,Cl,H		1.0	GHR
VIII	14	W +	1	Ma.mp.FTo	2	A,Hh,Art	P	4.5	COP, FAB, GHR
IX	15	W +	1	Mp.mp.FD-	2	H,Hd,Sc, Cg,Art	P	5.5	COP, PHR
X	16	D+	1	Ma.FD.FC'-	2	H,Sc,A,Bt, Cg,Hh		4.5	FAB, AB, COP, PHR
	17	Do	10	FCu		Sc			
	18	Do	15	CFo	2	Bt			MOR

Appendix C1:
Ms. S's RIAP™ structural summary of pretreatment

Location Features		
Zf	=	13
ZSum	=	40.5
ZEst	=	41.5
W	=	6
(Wv	=	1)
D	=	8
W+D	=	14
Dd	=	9
S	=	1

DQ			
			(FQ-)
+	=	11	(6)
o	=	11	(6)
v/+	=	0	(0)
v	=	1	(1)

Form Quality			
	FQx	MQual	W+D
+	= 0	0	0
o	= 8	2	8
u	= 2	1	2
-	= 13	5	4
none	= 0	0	0

Determinants		
Blends	**Single**	
M.m.CF	M	= 3
M.FD	FM	= 2
M.FY	m	= 0
M.FD	FC	= 0
	CF	= 0
	C	= 0
	Cn	= 0
	FC'	= 2
	C'F	= 1
	C'	= 0
	FT	= 0
	TF	= 0
	T	= 0
	FV	= 0
	VF	= 0
	V	= 0
	FY	= 1
	YF	= 0
	Y	= 0
	Fr	= 0
	rF	= 0
	FD	= 3
	F	= 6
	(2)	= 11

Contents	
H	= 4
(H)	= 1
Hd	= 7
(Hd)	= 0
Hx	= 0
A	= 5
(A)	= 0
Ad	= 4
(Ad)	= 0
An	= 1
Art	= 0
Ay	= 0
Bl	= 1
Bt	= 1
Cg	= 4
Cl	= 0
Ex	= 0
Fd	= 0
Fi	= 0
Ge	= 0
Hh	= 0
Ls	= 2
Na	= 0
Sc	= 2
Sx	= 0
Xy	= 0
Idio	= 2

S-Constellation		
☑	FV+VF+V+FD > 2	
☐	Col-Shd Blends > 0	
☑	Ego < .31 or > .44	
☐	MOR > 3	
☐	Zd > ±3.5	
☐	es > EA	
☑	CF + C > FC	
☑	X+% < .70	
☐	S > 3	
☐	P < 3 or > 8	
☐	Pure H < 2	
☐	R < 17	
4	Total	

Special Scores			
		Lvl-1	Lvl-2
DV	=	1 x1	0 x2
INC	=	0 x2	0 x4
DR	=	0 x3	0 x6
FAB	=	1 x4	1 x7
ALOG	=	0 x5	
CON	=	0 x7	
	Raw Sum6 =	3	
	Wgtd Sum6 =	12	
AB = 0		GHR = 4	
AG = 1		PHR = 9	
COP = 0		MOR = 1	
CP = 1		PER = 0	
		PSV = 0	

RATIOS, PERCENTAGES, AND DERIVATIONS

AFFECT

R = 23	L = 0.35	

EB	= 8 : 1.0	EA	= 9.0	EBPer = 8.0
eb	= 3 : 5	es	= 8	D = 0
		Adj es	= 7	Adj D = 0

FM	= 2	SumC'	= 3	SumT	= 0
m	= 1	SumV	= 0	SumY	= 2

AFFECT	
FC:CF+C	= 0 : 1
Pure C	= 0
SumC' : WSumC	= 3 : 1.0
Afr	= 0.44
S	= 1
Blends:R	= 4 : 23
CP	= 1

INTERPERSONAL		
COP = 0		AG = 1
GHR:PHR		= 4 : 9
a:p		= 4 : 7
Food		= 0
SumT		= 0
Human Content		= 12
Pure H		= 4
PER		= 0
Isolation Index		= 0.13

IDEATION

a:p	= 4 : 7	Sum6	= 3
Ma:Mp	= 4 : 4	Lvl-2	= 1
2AB+(Art+Ay)	= 0	WSum6	= 12
MOR	= 1	M-	= 5
		M none	= 0

MEDIATION

XA%	= 0.43
WDA%	= 0.71
X-%	= 0.57
S-	= 0
P	= 5
X+%	= 0.35
Xu%	= 0.09

PROCESSING

Zf	= 13
W:D:Dd	= 6:8:9
W : M	= 6 : 8
Zd	= -1.0
PSV	= 0
DQ+	= 11
DQv	= 1

SELF-PERCEPTION

3r+(2)/R	= 0.48
Fr+rF	= 0
SumV	= 0
FD	= 6
An+Xy	= 1
MOR	= 1
H:(H)+Hd+(Hd)	= 4 : 8

PTI = 3	☑ DEPI = 5	☐ CDI = 3	☐ S-CON = 4	☑ HVI = Yes	☐ OBS = No

Appendix C2:
Ms. S's RIAP™ structural summary of posttreatment

Location Features		
Zf	=	13
ZSum	=	43.5
ZEst	=	41.5
W	=	6
(Wv	=	0)
D	=	8
W+D	=	14
Dd	=	4
S	=	0

DQ			
			(FQ-)
+	=	11	(3)
o	=	7	(1)
v/+	=	0	(0)
v	=	0	(0)

Form Quality			
	FQx	MQual	W+D
+	= 0	0	0
o	= 11	7	10
u	= 3	2	2
-	= 4	3	2
none	= 0	0	0

Determinants		Contents	
Blends	Single	H = 6	
M.FV	M = 4	(H) = 2	
M.m.FC	FM = 0	Hd = 5	
M.FC'	m = 0	(Hd) = 1	
M.FD	FC = 2	Hx = 0	
M.FD.FC'	CF = 1	A = 3	
M.m.FT	C = 0	(A) = 0	
M.m.FD	Cn = 0	Ad = 1	
M.FD.FC'	FC' = 1	(Ad) = 0	
	C'F = 0	An = 0	
	C' = 0	Art = 3	
	FT = 0	Ay = 0	
	TF = 0	Bl = 0	
	T = 0	Bt = 3	
	FV = 0	Cg = 7	
	VF = 0	Cl = 1	
	V = 0	Ex = 0	
	FY = 0	Fd = 0	
	YF = 0	Fi = 0	
	Y = 0	Ge = 0	
	Fr = 0	Hh = 3	
	rF = 0	Ls = 1	
	FD = 0	Na = 0	
	F = 2	Sc = 3	
		Sx = 0	
	(2) = 7	Xy = 0	
		Idio = 1	

S-Constellation	
☑	FV+VF+V+FD > 2
☐	Col-Shd Blends > 0
☐	Ego < .31 or > .44
☐	MOR > 3
☐	Zd > ±3.5
☐	es > EA
☐	CF + C > FC
☑	X+% < .70
☐	S > 3
☐	P < 3 or > 8
☐	Pure H < 2
☐	R < 17
2	Total

Special Scores			
		Lvl-1	Lvl-2
DV	=	0 x1	0 x2
INC	=	0 x2	0 x4
DR	=	0 x3	0 x6
FAB	=	2 x4	0 x7
ALOG	=	0 x5	
CON	=	0 x7	
	Raw Sum6	=	2
	Wgtd Sum6	=	8
AB	= 1	GHR	= 7
AG	= 1	PHR	= 6
COP	= 3	MOR	= 2
CP	= 0	PER	= 0
		PSV	= 0

RATIOS, PERCENTAGES, AND DERIVATIONS

R = 18		L = 0.13
EB = 12 : 2.5	EA = 14.5	EBPer = 4.8
eb = 3 : 6	es = 9	D = +2
	Adj es = 7	Adj D = +2
FM = 0	SumC' = 4	SumT = 1
m = 3	SumV = 1	SumY = 0

AFFECT

FC:CF+C	= 3 : 1
Pure C	= 0
SumC' : WSumC	= 4 : 2.5
Afr	= 0.38
S	= 0
Blends:R	= 8 : 18
CP	= 0

INTERPERSONAL

COP = 3	AG = 1
GHR:PHR	= 7 : 6
a:p	= 5 : 11
Food	= 0
SumT	= 1
Human Content	= 14
Pure H	= 6
PER	= 0
Isolation Index	= 0.33

IDEATION

a:p	= 5 : 11	Sum6	= 2
Ma:Mp	= 5 : 8	Lvl-2	= 0
2AB+(Art+Ay)	= 5	WSum6	= 8
MOR	= 2	M-	= 3
		M none	= 0

MEDIATION

XA%	= 0.78
WDA%	= 0.86
X-%	= 0.22
S-	= 0
P	= 6
X+%	= 0.61
Xu%	= 0.17

PROCESSING

Zf	= 13
W:D:Dd	= 6:8:4
W : M	= 6 : 12
Zd	= +2.0
PSV	= 0
DQ+	= 11
DQv	= 0

SELF-PERCEPTION

3r+(2)/R	= 0.39
Fr+rF	= 0
SumV	= 1
FD	= 4
An+Xy	= 0
MOR	= 2
H:(H)+Hd+(Hd)	= 6 : 8

PTI = 1	☑ DEPI = 5	☐ CDI = 3	☐ S-CON = 2	☐ HVI = No	☐ OBS = No

Appendix D1: Ms. S's TAT protocol of pretreatment

2. Hmm . . . this is difficult. About the past . . . the man turning his back toward me and the woman standing against the tree are husband and wife. They have been working in the field together. The wife, she is pregnant, so right now, she's resting a bit and the husband is doing all the work for now. As for the future . . . for these two . . . maybe for three, after a birth of a child, will continue as is, I guess. About the girl that's standing in front . . . She looks to be just passing through. It's a bit strange to have her standing here . . . The pregnant woman, she doesn't look very happy, does she? I guess that's it.

3BM. This woman is totally devastated. She probably had something happen between her and her partner. Maybe the partner didn't listen to what she had to say. Maybe he yelled at her and then took off. So, now, she's totally exhausted and can't get up. There is something that looks like a key at her feet, but she has no energy to get up and go out. As for her future . . . she'll probably get up eventually, but until then, she's going to keep crying.

5. She is a mother, who had just come to tell whoever that is in the room that there is a phone call. That someone will get up and will go to get the phone. This woman doesn't look too happy, I don't think. Maybe her life is not a happy one or maybe she's feeling totally stressed out.

8GF. She is thinking about something fun. That's why she has a smile on her face. This woman, she is a very capable person. Something good must have happened, and so she is thinking about it and wondering how things are going to turn out. She's taking a break right now. She's not really sitting back in a comfortable position, so I guess she won't be sitting down for too long. If someone were to call for her, she will probably tell that person that she'll be coming soon and will go right back to work.

9GF. I don't really get this picture . . . maybe something is happening to the left of this scene and the woman below is running toward that direction. The woman above the tree is watching what is happening below her. I don't really understand the connection between the two, and I don't know what's happening either, but the woman above the tree is staying put and thinking about what she'll do next. This girl, she's like that. She keeps her distance and watches people, like the girl below. They're really different. And, let's see . . . the girl below, she hasn't noticed the girl above, but the girl above is watching the other one, so that's another difference.

14. A man is taking a break at his work. He wants to get some fresh air, he's come to this place, where there is no one else, and is looking out the window. It's not a long break, so he'll have to go back to work in a few minutes.

20. This man is waiting for someone. He is standing under the lamp so that the people he will be meeting with will find him easily. But these people, they will be coming from the darker side, so he can't really see from where he's at. I don't think that the meeting is going to be a fun one, and so he isn't really looking forward to it. When they come, he'll be joining them and will go off to a different place to talk.

209

Appendix D2: Ms. S's TAT protocol of posttreatment

2.   This is a family of three. They're farmers and you have the parents and the daughter here. The daughter is about to go to school. The mother is taking a break, since she's been up and working since early morning. The father is plowing the field. Sun's come out, so the father has taken off his shirt. The daughter looks a bit stressed because she has lots of homework to do, and she feels bad that she's not helping her parents with their work. [E: Turns out?] She'll head to school.

3BM.   This person, she has fallen asleep. She is exhausted from all the crying she'd done and she has fallen asleep in the same position. Something very sad had happened to her and that's why she had been crying. There is something that looks like a key and a key chain, so maybe she heard the bad news as she stepped into her house. She must have been devastated and broke down crying on the spot. She cried so hard that she had fallen asleep crying. But, she will be waking up soon and coming to her senses. She'll then go to the phone to make calls to people.

5.   This is about a couple. The wife is getting ready to go to bed and she notices the light still on in the living room. So she says "Are you going to be up for a while?," to which her husband says "Oh, I didn't realize it was so late" and follows her to the bedroom, where they'll both go to bed.

8GF.   This woman is really built. She's always worked at a job that's physically intensive. She is working hard toward making her dream come true. Right now, she is taking a break and she is dreaming of her future. She is planning on saving her money for that. When she is done taking her break, she'll get up and go back to work. Whether or not she'll achieve her dreams will all depend on her. But, at the rate she's going, I think that she'll make it happen.

9GF.   It is a scene from summer vacation of maybe about 50 years ago. Maybe it's a school trip and the girls are on the beach. Because it's a school event and there's some learning to do. The girl at the front has a notebook in her hand to write down her observations about nature. Somebody's calling the girls, and so the girl on the beach is running toward the gathering place. The girl above is also about to run after her. They will join each other later and move on to the next place. It's a fun trip, maybe an excursion? At any rate, they're having fun.

14.   This is a picture of an attic. A man is standing by the window. It's very dark there even during the day, because there is no electricity. So, it's bright only by the window. The man wants to renovate the room and make it into a usable room. So he'd just come up, and he'd noticed that the air is really stale. So, he's opened the window for air and is thinking about how to go about making the changes. It might take some time before it all gets done to his liking, as he'll only work on it whenever he has some time to spare.

20.   A man is standing under a lamp. It's night time. Maybe it's Christmas? Because I see some lights in the trees in the background. He doesn't look too happy, does he? Maybe he just had something bad happen to him . . . like separating from his partner . . . So, he's feeling lonely at Christmas time. He probably won't go home immediately, because that would be too lonely, I think. So he'll head to a bar maybe, as there'll be people there. After spending some time at the bar, he'll probably go home.

Summary

Trauma research has advanced considerably during the last 30 years, and it has reached its next transitional phase, where researchers must explore individual differences in traumatic expressions and treatment outcomes for an appropriate person-oriented clinical interventions. For the purpose of individual trauma treatment and outcome evaluation, the benefits of employing the Rorschach Comprehensive System (CS) and the Thematic Apperception Test (TAT) have often been stressed in the literature. However, to date, most trauma treatment outcome research has been limited to verifying treatment effectiveness only by the reduction of posttraumatic stress disorder (PTSD) and other trauma-related symptoms, as assessed by self-report measures and diagnostic clinical interviews. Therefore, it is still unclear how different the treatment process and outcome would be for those who do not meet the full criteria of PTSD diagnosis, and how different the recovery process would be depending on the initial psychological state, pretraumatic personality, and the nature of the traumatizing stimuli.

For the purpose of developing more sophisticated trauma treatment and planning for the future, this case study evaluated the trauma treatment outcome through Eye Movement Desensitization and Reprocessing (EMDR) in a survivor of human-caused trauma, Ms. S, by conducting comprehensive pre- and posttreatment assessments with a test battery composed of the Impact of Event Scale-Revised (IES-R), the Rorschach CS, and the TAT. Ms. S underwent 20 sessions of EMDR treatment over approximately 10 months, until her subjective distress about the traumatic experiences had been reduced to a minimum.

Because Ms. S was a survivor with partial PTSD, the total score of the IES-R before treatment was just above the cut-off point, whereas the other two measures clearly revealed her implicit trauma-related conditions. Her pretreatment Rorschach scores were marked by a high number of [Dd, Hd, FQ-] responses, indicating her trauma-distorted human representations and impairments in reality testing. Her TAT responses showed apparent feature of avoidance in emotion-laden interpersonal situations. However, after treatment, these trauma-related characteristics were significantly reduced. Her posttreatment TAT responses showed great improvements in terms of emotional engagement in interpersonal relationships. Furthermore, the Hypervigilance Index (HVI) on the Rorschach shifted from positive to negative after the treatment, because of the appearance of one Texture response (T), which indicated her growing willingness for interpersonal connectedness. Aside from these improvements, her ideational stressors of intrusive thinking (m) increased after treatment, and a painful feeling (V) also occurred to Ms. S. This suggested that EMDR trauma therapy had in fact promoted self-inspection and caused irritable and painful feelings, in much the same way as an insight-oriented uncovering therapy.

In this case study, the findings gained through the CS and the TAT augmented the result from the IES-R, and through their correlations provided a deeper understanding about the recovery mechanism and treatment outcome as seen in Ms. S, thus proving the clear usefulness of these two measures in trauma treatment outcome studies.

要約

　トラウマ研究は過去 30 年の間に飛躍的な進歩を遂げ，新たな局面を迎えよう
としている。今後はトラウマ反応や治療効果の個人差に関する研究を深め，個々
人に適した臨床的介入を追求すべきであるといえよう。このような個別的な治
療計画と治療効果の評価のために，包括システムによるロールシャッハ・テス
トや主題統覚検査（TAT）が有用であることは先行研究でも充分に指摘されてき
た。しかしながら，今日までのトラウマ治療の効果研究においては，自記式質
問紙や構造化面接を用いて，外傷後ストレス障害（PTSD）をはじめとするトラ
ウマ関連症状の軽減のみを評価することに主眼があった。そのため，PTSD 診断
基準の全てを満たさないクライエントの治癒過程や治療効果がどのように異な
るのか，また，個々人の治療前の心理的状態やパーソナリティ，トラウマの原
因となった刺激によって，どのように治癒過程が異なるのかということについ
ては未だ明らかにされていない。

　本ケース研究は，より洗練されたトラウマ治療と治療計画への第一歩として，
眼球運動による脱感作と再処理法（EMDR）による治療を受けた人為的トラウマ
のサバイバー女性である S さんに対し，治療前後に PTSD 症状を測る自記式質
問紙の改定出来事インパクト尺度（IES-R）とロールシャッハ・テストと TAT か
ら成るテスト・バッテリーを用いた包括的なアセスメントを行い，その治療効
果を測定したものである。S さんは，トラウマ体験にまつわる主観的苦痛が最小
限に軽減するまで，約 10 ヶ月間に渡り 20 回の EMDR 治療を受けた。

　S さんは，再体験症状が年に数回という部分 PTSD を抱えたサバイバーであっ

たため，PTSD 症状についての自記式質問紙である IES-R では，治療前の合計得点はカット・オフ値の辛うじて上でしかなかった。しかしながら，治療前のロールシャッハ・テストや TAT の結果には，自記式質問紙ではとらえきれない潜在的なトラウマの影響が示されていた。ロールシャッハ・テストにおいては，Dd 領域に形態水準がマイナスの人間表象反応が多数出現するなど，S さんのトラウマの影響によって歪められた対人表象と現実検討の低さが現れていた。TAT 反応では，感情の負荷がかかる対人場面への明らかな回避傾向が示された。治療後には，これらのトラウマに関連した特徴は大幅に減少した。TAT の物語には対人関係における感情の関与についての著しい改善が示された。さらに，ロールシャッハ・テストでは，一個の濃淡材質反応（T）の出現によって警戒心過剰指標（HVI）がネガティブになったことから，S さんに対人接触感情が生まれたという大きな変化が示された。これらの改善の一方で，ロールシャッハ・テスト結果からは，思考への侵入的なストレス（m）や苦痛な感情（V）も治療によってもたらされたことが明らかにされた。このことより，EMDR による治療が防衛を取り除き内省を促すセラピーと同様に，その過程においては自己検閲を促し，苦痛な感情体験や苛立ちを生じさせているという作用機序に関する示唆も得られた。

　本ケース・スタディでは，ロールシャッハ・テストと TAT の結果が　IES-R の結果を補足し，相互の関連性をもって S さんの治癒プロセスと治療効果に関する詳細な理解を提供した。これらにより，ロールシャッハ・テストと TAT がトラウマの治療効果の評価研究において有用であるということが示された。

Résumé

La recherche sur le traumatisme a beaucoup avancé au cours des 30 dernières années et est prête a entrer dans une nouvelle phase, où les chercheurs devraient explorer les différences individuelles de la manifestation traumatique et rechercher des résultats de traitements pour des interventions cliniques individualisées appropriées. Dans le but d'un traitement traumatique individuel et d'une évaluation des résultats, les bénéfices de l'utilization des tests de Rorschach Système Intégré (SI) et du Thematic Apperception Test (TAT) ont souvent été mis en avant dans la littérature. Cependant, jusqu'à présent, la plupart des recherches de résultats de traitements se sont limitées à la seule vérification de l'efficacité du traitement par la réduction du Stress posttraumatique (PTSD) et autres symptômes liés au traumatisme, évaluée par des mesures d'autoévaluation et des diagnostics d'entretiens cliniques. Par conséquent il est encore difficile de juger quelles seraient la différence du processus de traitement et du résultat pour ceux qui ne remplissent pas complètement les critères du diagnostic PTSD, et quelle serait la différence dans le processus de guérison selon leur état psychologique initial, leur personnalité pré traumatique, et la nature du stimuli traumatique.

Dans le but de développer un traitement du traumatisme plus sophistiqué et se préparer pour le futur, cette étude de cas a évalué le résultat d'un traitement de traumatisme via Eye Movement Desensitization and Reprocessing (EMDR) sur une survivante d'un traumatisme causé par l'Homme, Mme S, en mettant en place une évaluation d'un pré et post traitement avec une batterie de tests composée du Impact of Event Scale-Revised (IES-R), du Rorschach SI, et du TAT. Mme S a subi 20 sessions de traitement EMDR pendant approximativement dix mois jusqu'à ce que sa détresse subjective liée aux expériences traumatiques soit réduite à un minimum.

Parce que Mme S était une survivante avec un PTSD partiel, le score total du IES-R avant traitement était juste au dessus de la limite, considérant que les deux autres mesures révélaient clairement ses conditions implicites d'état traumatique.

Les scores de son précédent Rorschach montraient un nombre élevé de réponses Dd, Hd, FQ-, ce qui indiquait des représentations humaines altérées par son traumatisme ainsi que des altérations dans des tests en situations réelles. Ses réponses au TAT montraient un trait apparent d'évasion dans des situations interpersonnelles émotionnellement chargées. Cependant, après traitement, ces caractéristiques liées au traumatisme étaient significativement réduites. Ses dernières réponses au TAT ont montré une grande amélioration d'un point de vue de son engagement émotionnel dans des relations interpersonnelles, et de plus son précédent score positif au Rorschach Hypervigilance Index (HVI) est devenu négatif, dû à l'apparition d'une réponse Texture (T), ce qui indiquait sa volonté grandissante d'avoir des contacts interpersonnels. Mis à part ces améliorations, ses causes de stress conceptuelles de pensées intrusives (m) ont augmenté après traitement, et une sensation douloureuse (V) est apparue chez Mme S. A partir de cela, il a été suggéré que la thérapie de traumatisme EMDR favorisait une auto inspection et provoquait des expériences de souffrances et d'irritations, de la même façon qu'une thérapie de découverte par introspection.

Dans cette étude de cas, les découvertes apportées par le Rorschach SI et le TAT ont augmenté le résultat du IES-R, et à travers leurs corrélations, ont apporté une plus profonde compréhension du processus de guérison et du résultat du traitement chez Mme S, et a ainsi prouvé la grande utilité de ces deux mesures dans l'étude de résultat de traitement de traumatisme.

Resumen

La investigación sobre el trauma ha avanzado considerablemente en los últimos 30 años y ha alcanzado un punto que permite hacer una transición hacia un próximo paso desde el cual los investigadores deberían ir más allá del Trastorno de Stress Postraumático (DSP) y explorar la diversidad de las expresiones del trauma y de los resultados de los tratamientos para una intervención clínica adecuada y orientada hacia cada persona. Con el propósito de evaluar los tratamientos individualizados del trauma y de sus resultados, se han destacado con frecuencia los beneficios del Test de Rorschach (Sistema Comprehensivo) y del Test de Apercepción Temática. Sin embargo, hasta la fecha, muchas de las investigaciones sobre resultados de tratamientos de traumas se han limitado a verificar la eficacia del tratamiento sólo a través de los criterios del Trastorno de Stress Postraumático (DSPT) y de otros síntomas relacionados con el trauma, evaluados a través de autoinformes (datos aportados por el propio sujeto) y de entrevistas clínicas diagnósticas. En consecuencia, aún están poco claras las diferencias en el proceso del tratamiento y sus resultados en aquellos casos que no se ajustan completamente a los criterios del diagnóstico de DSPT, y qué diferencias habría en el proceso de recuperación con respecto al estado psicológico inicial, la personalidad pre-traumática y la naturaleza del estímulo traumatizante.

Con el objetivo de desarrollar tratamientos del trauma más sofisticados y realizar mejores planificaciones en el futuro, este estudio de caso evalúa el resultado del tratamiento del trauma a través de la terapia EMDR (Desensibilización y Reprocesamiento por el Movimiento Ocular) en la señorita S., sobreviviente a un trauma causado por otras personas, a través de una amplia evaluación anterior y posterior al tratamiento con una batería de tests compuesta por el Impact of Event Scale-Revised (IES-R), el Rorschach (Sistema Comprehensivo) y el TAT. La señorita S. tuvo veinte sesiones del tratamiento EMDR durante unos diez meses, hasta que su angustia subjetiva respecto de las experiencias traumáticas vividas se redujo al mínimo.

Como la Srta. S. presentaba sólo parcialmente los criterios de DSPT, las puntuaciones totales en el IES-R antes del tratamiento eran sólo algo por encima de la línea de corte, mientras que las otras dos medidas revelaban claramente las condiciones traumáticas implícitas. Las puntuaciones de su primer Rorschach estaban marcadas por un elevado número de respuestas Dd, Hd, FQ-, que indicaban distorsiones en las representaciones humanas debido al trauma y dificultades en la percepción de la realidad. Sus respuestas en el TAT mostraban una tendencia a la evitación en situaciones interpersonales emocionalmente cargadas. Sin embargo, después del tratamiento, estas características relacionadas con el trauma se redujeron significativamente. Las respuestas de su último TAT señalaban una gran mejoría en términos de compromiso emocional en las relaciones interpersonales y su Índice de Hipervigilancia (HVI) positivo del primer Rorschach se transformó en negativo en el segundo, debido a la aparición de una respuesta de Textura (T), lo que indicaba su creciente bienestar en el contacto interpersonal. Junto a estas mejorías, los indicadores ideacionales de pensamientos intrusivos (m) se incrementaron después del tratamiento y los sentimientos dolorosos relacionados con el autoexamen (V) también se hicieron presentes en la Srta. S. De esto se puede deducir que la terapia del trauma EMDR promovió la autoobservación y generó experiencias de dolor e irritación, del mismo modo que lo hacen las terapias orientadas al insight, por el autodescubrimiento y el uso de la introspección.

En este estudio de caso, los hallazgos obtenidos a través del Rorschach y el TAT confirmaron el resultado surgido del IES-R y, a través de su mutua complementareidad, aportaron una comprensión más profunda sobre del proceso de recuperación y de los resultados del tratamiento en la Srta. S. De este modo, se muestra la gran utilidad de estas medidas en los estudios sobre resultados de los tratamientos del trauma.

Rorschachiana 30, 219–222
© 2009 Hogrefe Publishing

DOI: 10.1027/1192-5604.30.2.219

Advice for Authors

The Editor-in-Chief will screen manuscripts in order to ensure that they fall within the aims and scope of *Rorschachiana*. Those that fit will be reviewed by two independent reviewers. All papers will be subject to peer review under the auspices of the Editor-in-Chief and the Editorial Board in terms of their merits, readability, and interest. Unsolicited manuscripts will not be returned to the author(s).

Authors are advised to review the *Rorschachiana* Submission Checklist before submission, in addition to the advice below. For more information please visit www.hogrefe.com/journals/rorschach.

Submission of Manuscripts

Manuscripts should be first submitted by e-mail to the Editor-in-Chief for initial screening:

Sadegh Nashat
Editor – *Rorschachiana*
Child and Family Department
Tavistock Clinic
120 Belsize Lane
London NW3 5BA
UK
E-mail rorschach.submission@gmail.com

Alternatively or upon request, manuscripts should be submitted in duplicate on paper and as an e-mail attachment, preferably in rtf format.

Format of Manuscripts

Manuscripts must be written in English and printed on one side only of good quality plain white paper with margins of at least 2.5 cm all around (typescript). Every line of the manuscript, without exception, should be typed double-spaced. The right margin of the text should be ragged: do not justify the right margin. The first line of each paragraph should be indented. Without exception, the entire manuscript should be typed in upper case and lower case Roman letters. Please do not type anything (e.g., the names of the authors) in capital letters. For emphasis, words or numbers may be set in italics; please do not use bold typeface or underlining. The entire text should be typed in regular paragraphs. Computer techniques for highlighting text and other embellishments should be avoided. All pages should be numbered beginning with 1 on the title page and continuing with the text, then the references, then any tables or figures, and finally the Summaries. Footnotes should be avoided if at all possible; if they are unavoidable, then they should be placed at the end of the text, after the references. Place the page number and a short version of the title at the top right of each page.

The first page of the manuscript should list the title, the author(s), the affiliation of the author(s), the address for correspondence (including e-mail address and telephone and fax numbers, if available), a short version of the title for the column title, as well as a short English abstract (max. 200 words) with up to five keywords.

The second page should begin with the title and then continue with the text (do not repeat the name(s) of the author(s)).

The positioning of tables or figures should be indicated with the following statement placed in the text at the appropriate place: "Enter Table x about here."

At the end of the text, the reference list should begin on a new page with the heading "References." Reference citations in the text and in the reference list proper should follow the conventions listed in the Publication Manual of the American Psychological Association (5th edition). Non-English titles should be translated into English in brackets following the original title. The name and volume number of journals and the title of books should be set in italics. All references listed must be mentioned in the text and all references mentioned in the text must be listed in the "References" section.

Following the references, each table or figure should be placed on a separate page. Tables and figures should be numbered using Arabic numerals. Figures must be accompanied by a legend; tables should have a brief descriptive title. All tables and figures must be referred to in the text. *Rorschachiana* is printed in black and white only, so that figures should be supplied as greyscale images rather than in color, as either vector graphics (EPS) or high-resolution (300 dpi) bitmap (TIF) images.

Summaries

The final part of the manuscript is the "Summary," 1–2 pages long, which should be submitted both in English and in the native tongue of the first author. If French, Spanish, and Japanese versions of the summary cannot be provided, then please inform the Editor immediately as the Editorial Board will need time to prepare these. The Editor retains the right to modify the presentation and/or wording of the text whenever necessary.

Style

Please use a clear and readable style, avoiding jargon. Technical terms should be defined when first used. It is recommended to use plurals instead of he/she whenever possible: "if a patient is depressed, he or she ..." is better expressed as "When patients are depressed, they ..." American spelling is preferred.

Cover Letter

Please attach a letter confirming that all authors have agreed to the submission of the article, and that the article is not currently under consideration for publication elsewhere.

Assignment of Copyright

By submitting an article, the author confirms and guarantees on behalf of him- or herself and any coauthors that he or she holds all copyright in and titles to the submitted contribution, including any figures, photographs, line drawings, plans, maps, sketches, and tables, and that the article and its contents do not infringe in any way on the rights of third parties. The author agrees, upon acceptance of the article for publication, to transfer to the publisher the exclusive right to reproduce and distribute the article and its contents, both physically and in nonphysical, electronic, or other form, in the volume to which it has been submitted and in other independent publications, with no limitations on the number of copies or on the form or the extent of distribution. These rights are transferred for the duration of copyright as defined by international law. Authors will be asked to complete, sign and return a Copyright Agreement form upon acceptance of their article.

Online Rights for Journal Articles

Authors of articles in journals published by the Hogrefe Group may post a copy of the final accepted manuscript for non-commercial purposes, as a word-processor, PDF, or other type of file, on their personal web page or on their employer's website after it has been accepted for publication. The following conditions apply:

1. Only the final draft manuscript post-refereeing shall be used for this purpose, not the published version, and this final draft manuscript may only be posted 12 months after the article has been published.
2. The posted version of the article must carry the publisher's copyright notice in the form "[Journal Title], [Volume No.], [Issue No.], © [Year] by [Publisher's name]," (as it appears in the published journal/article) and a link to the publisher's journal home page must be included.
3. Further, the posted article must include the following statement: "This article does not exactly replicate the final version published in the journal "[Add title of Journal]". It is not a copy of the original published article and is not suitable for citation." The publisher does not permit archiving in any repositories other than the publisher's own. The publisher cannot provide electronic copies of the published version of the article for posting. Creation of an electronic or digital copy of the published version of the article for the purposes of posting or distributing it is not permitted.